A Memoir

Breaking the Cycle of Family Trauma

FELICIA P. ROCHE

Unravel is a work of nonfiction. Some names and identifying details have been changed.

Copyright © 2020 by Felicia P. Roche

All Rights Reserved

This book or any portion thereof may not be reproduced or used in any manner without the express written permission of the publisher except for the use of brief quotations and professional book review.

Printed in the United States of America

ISBN 978-0-578-65326-6

Cover design by Melissa Williams Designs

Author photo by Ricky Codio Photography

This book is dedicated to all survivors of trauma.

I see you, I hear you, and you are not alone.

For Debora

Author's Note

There are highly debatable "hot topics" and sensitive subjects throughout this book. I want to be clear that it is not my intent to push an agenda or message regarding themes that can be found throughout the text, specifically abortion and immigration. These are only discussed because they are a part of my story.

Table of Contents

Author's Note vii

Prologue xiii

Part 1: Ravel 1

Chapter 1: Conception from Chaos 3

Chapter 2: Foreign Baby 11

Chapter 3: Rittenhouse Street 15

Chapter 4: Debora 21

Chapter 5: Marie 25

Chapter 6: My Hero 29

Chapter 7: The Monsters 45

Chapter 8: The Greatest Monster of Them All 49

Chapter 9: Meet Lorenzo 53

Chapter 10: The Change 59

Chapter 11: Normal 65

Chapter 12: Rhythm of the Night 71

Chapter 13: Somers Road 77

Chapter 14: 68th Ave 93

Chapter 15: Marie's Home 101

Chapter 16: Nedro Ave 107

Chapter 17: Church 117

Chapter 18: Playing with Fire 129

Chapter 19: Mr. Glasses Man 133

Chapter 20: Marie and Me 139

Chapter 21: Just Me 141

Chapter 22: The Gallery 145

Chapter 23: Q 149

Chapter 24: Moving Backwards 157

Chapter 25: Normal Love 173

Chapter 26: My Sister's Father 175

Chapter 27: A Shift 181

Chapter 28: Bitch 185

Chapter 29: The Choice 197

Chapter 30: First Step 203

Part 2 Unravel 209

Chapter 31: Triggered 211

Chapter 32: Second Step 217

Chapter 33: Conversations 223

Chapter 34: My Joy 231

Chapter 35: The Great Depression 233

Chapter 36: I'm Fine, Officer 239

Chapter 37: Never Alone 251

Chapter 38: Welfare to Work 253

Chapter 39: Starting Over 261

Chapter 40: Confronting Chaos 265

UNRAVEL

Chapter 41: Lorenzo 271

Chapter 42: Freedom 285

Chapter 43: Home... 287

Chapter 44: Higher Learning 293

Chapter 45: Not Without My Sister..................................... 299

Chapter 46: The Cycle Is Broken... 311

Acknowledgments... 321

Prologue

Through all of it, my sister was by my side. Time after time I was 302ed and institutionalized for trying to hurt myself, she was there—either making the calls to 911 herself or getting the call from my friends who bore witness to my breakdowns. She was the one that did the research and made the phone calls to get me into rehab. She found the best clinic my insurance would take. And it was a really good one.

In the dead of winter, we packed up my bags, and my sister drove me to the mental health facility, seemingly in the middle of nowhere. It's a night I will never forget. It's almost as if the universe wanted me to always have this special memory of me and my sister, side by side, in the thick of it and making it work. The way it always was and the way it should have always been.

Freezing rain and snow created a slush of a mess as we slowly traveled towards the facility. The 40-minute drive turned into two hours. My sister seemed more patient than ever, never losing her cool, just slowly driving, making sure we stayed safe and got to where we were going. The sleet and snow made it hard to see the roads, and she made a wrong turn into a dark road just feet from the actual entrance of the middle-of-nowhere facility. When she realized we made the wrong turn, she tried to make a U-turn to get us back to the main road.

We got stuck in the mud.

For 30 minutes, we tried to push her out of it but instead managed to dig the tires of her minivan deeper into the slushy mud. Concerned that I wouldn't make it to the clinic in time to be checked in for the night, my sister grabbed my overnight bag, smiled at me, and said, "Come on. We'll walk it." The snow started to come down harder as we trucked our way up a muddy hill on a long windy dark road. I don't know how we managed not to get tired and irritated from the hard freezing rain hitting our face, or from the pain of our frozen fingers and toes, but I do know that we were joking and laughing the entire walk. "Good thing we got all that practice walking through blizzards when we were kids," my sister said sarcastically.

I giggled and agreed. "Yea, they had no issue sending two small children in the middle of a storm to get milk and cigarettes."

"Guess we were preparing for the worst of it." My sister chuckled as she described trying to carry a milk jug that was the same size as she was while being blinded by the whiteout of snow. "All I know is, I slid from the store to the house, snot running down my nose, feeling like my arms were going to fall off, just to be yelled at when I finally got home because we took too long and the milk was starting to freeze." Our inside jokes kept us laughing as we treaded up the snowy hill.

It was how we coped, how we survived. We laughed at our pain and reframed the ridiculousness of what were our childhood experiences. Being with my sister made things real, and somehow, it made things right. There was always something about when me and my sister were alone, just us against the world, that always made me feel safe.

I checked myself into the clinic that night and did an inpatient stay for 30 days. After I got out, I did another two weeks

UNRAVEL

in a day program where I could go home at night. When it was all said and done, I was diagnosed with post-traumatic stress disorder, which included panic disorder, major depressive episodes, anxiety, suicidal ideation, and dissociative disorders. During my rehabilitation, I learned what all of that meant and how to manage it. I discovered resources and tools to monitor myself and to regulate my moods and emotions, to train my brain. I created safety plans. I also discovered that there were no cures for my illnesses. I would have to live with them and manage them for the rest of my life. This was disappointing to learn at first, but I was grateful to understand why I was the way I was.

I was also grateful that I was not alone. My sister was with me, as she had always been since the day I was born.

We cannot recall the day we were conceived, the day we were born, or the first things we saw when we opened our eyes for the first time on Earth. We can only relive these events by the stories told to us. I was told that the weekend I was born there was a blizzard, a lot like the ones my sister and I used to walk through as children. The snow started with my mother's contractions on Good Friday and ended by the time I made my grand entrance at midnight on Easter Sunday. The winds of change were starting to blow in, and signs of spring began to emerge. My mother liked to talk about my birth as if it was some magical event, but my conception—all that led up to it and the days after—was anything but magical. Looking back at all of it, it makes me wonder why I even came to be.

FELICIA P. ROCHE

Where did the very essence of me come from? Did it choose the path on which I would arrive? Why was I born to the family I was born to? Who assigns that anyway? Why am I wired the way I am, and how much of all this can I change? Are humans simply beings floating through time and space, subject to the mercy of a random universe? Or are we more?

Perhaps I am not here by chance. Maybe, just maybe, I have everything to do with how I got here, who my family is, and how I am wired. They say you can't choose your family. So I often wonder, if I had the opportunity, would I?

Part 1

Ravel

Chapter 1
Conception from Chaos

July 1981. The crack epidemic had just gotten its wings and was about to take off. Summer nights in Philadelphia were filled with nothing less than raging energy. People were possessed by heat, drugs, and hormones. There was not a single quiet block in Germantown, one of the poorer sections of the city. Boom boxes boomed from dusk till dawn and from block to block. Stoops were covered with folks talking until their lips gave out. Little boys and girls rode bikes in the middle of the street, dodging cars. The sleepy cries of toddlers and babies rang from the sidewalks, parents too enthralled with the feel of summer nights to take them inside, afraid they might miss something from this party without walls: gossip, strong drinks, and loud music. Joe, the neighborhood dog, ran from door to door, chasing the kids on the bikes and stealing bones from off finished plates when they were put on the ground.

Marie rarely got to partake in these carefree summer nights. She was always on the prowl for some kind of way to make money. She was an immigrant without a work visa and was constantly hunting for under-the-table jobs like housekeeping, bagging groceries, or babysitting. In order to eat, she had to hunt for work nonstop. Marie had come from Haiti some three years prior, pregnant with her daughter Debora. And now the two of them lived amongst a group of other immigrants in a boarding home, which had far more people than rooms. It was a big stone house with a front porch and other houses attached on either side, known as a rowhome in Philly. This boarding house that Marie and Debora lived in was one of the busiest in the neighborhood. It was crawling with people coming and going. It was known by those who lived in the neighborhood as "The Big House" on the small block of Bayton Street.

Most of these summer nights, while Marie was still working at whatever job she secured, Debora ran around Bayton Street unsupervised. She ran up and down the block until she grew sleepy and found an adult to lean against, hoping they'd take notice and clean her up and put her to bed. When no one took notice, she did what two year olds did: cried for her mommy. "Mommy, I want Mommy," she would whisper between sobs. Eventually she would find her way into the boarding house and search for a place to lay her head—a couch or an empty bed spotted through an open door. She'd put herself to sleep, sucking her fingers and clenching her eyes real tight, wishing her mommy would come back soon, before any of The Grownups would come and bother her. Even at two years old, Debora knew these people couldn't be trusted. Why hadn't Marie known?

One particular night, the sky fell fast. The sounds of crickets filled the air, and the neighborhood was quieter than usual. Lightning bugs twinkled, and folks gave into the cool breeze to settle in for a good sleep—relief from the heat wave that just passed. Debora found her way into the house before anyone noticed she was hungry or sad or even there. As people started to

UNRAVEL

gather in the house on Bayton Street, she crawled up into a couch in the living room and tucked herself between the cushions for comfort. She fell sound asleep within moments, wiped out from crying all day.

Marie was offered extra hours of work that day and she never said no to a job. When Marie got to the Big House on Bayton Street that night, the house was as usual, swarming with people. Kids ran in and out from the porch while most of the adult tenants huddled around the TV in the living room or in the kitchen, drinking and cracking loud jokes. Debora managed to stay asleep through it all. When Marie walked in, she barely took a glimpse at her sleeping baby on the couch before she headed into the kitchen to light a cigarette and catch up on the day from her housemates. As soon as she walked through the kitchen door, a glass was pushed into her hand. "Hey! Maria's home!" one of her housemates shouted as he grabbed her and twirled her around. He tried to get her to dance salsa with him. She pulled way. "Oh, Lorenzo, please! I'm tired," Marie said in her heavy Haitian accent. She sucked her teeth and slouched in a chair at the table. She decided she would just have one drink and one cigarette before heading to bed.

Lorenzo was the only housemate who was not Haitian or American. No one understood Lorenzo when he spoke, but in the year since he migrated from Cuba, he learned to communicate with others just enough to get what he wanted. And on this night, he wanted Marie.

"Lorenzo, leave me alone." Marie rolled her eyes, a hint of a smile behind them. He was staring at her and making comments she couldn't understand, perhaps flirting. Marie did her best to ignore Lorenzo and focused her conversation on the four other people in the kitchen, her Haitian housemates, as they continued gossiping about the drama in the house. After 30 minutes of chit chat, she finished her cigarette, drank the rest of her cherry Kool-Aid, stood up, and stretched. "I am so tired!" Marie bid a goodnight to everyone and lazily walked to her room down the hall, feet from where Debora lay on the couch. Lorenzo peeked out of the kitchen door, staring at her every step. Barely able to stand long enough to change out her work clothes, Marie plopped onto her bed and passed out from exhaustion.

Minutes later, Lorenzo boldly walked into the room where Marie slept. He sang her name in a whisper, "Maria... Maria..." Marie moaned and sunk deeper into her covers. Lorenzo was now sunken into the covers too.

The next morning, Marie woke up to the sounds of her two year old playing in a mess of shuffled papers on the floor by her bedside. *She must be hungry*, she thought with her eyes still closed, followed by, *I'm so tired*. She was exhausted before the day even started and begrudgingly opened her eyes. She was instantly startled by the sight of another body in her bed. She froze as her heart pounded. She clenched her eyes as hard as she could to try and remember. *What is he doing here? What happened after I got home last night?* She opened her eyes again and reached for a cigarette. She thought about how people slept any and everywhere in the house and privacy was a misnomer. Marie felt distressed with trying to figure out how and why Lorenzo was curled up sleeping in the bed with her and decided right then and there that it would be easier to ignore this confusion. Instead, she shrugged at the sight of her clothes in disarray, straightened herself up and called for her baby. "Debora, bring Mommy the lighter." With a cigarette in her mouth, Marie got out of bed and walked to the bathroom, leaving Lorenzo in her bed asleep. When she came back in, he was gone. She never once questioned him about that night.

About a month and a half later, Marie began to have a familiar feeling. *But how?* she wondered. Marie hadn't been with anyone in so long, she just knew there was no way she could be pregnant. She waited another month to see if she would get her period. Nothing. The truth was becoming clearer. She became petrified and confused. She wondered if this was some kind of miracle baby. Finally, she decided to go to the clinic to find answers. Her worse fears were confirmed, she was in fact pregnant. Her follow-up question to the confirmation she dreaded was one of urgency. She wanted to know what her options were for getting rid of the confusion that grew inside her, to abort the pregnancy and the shock that came with it.

Marie spent the next week drawing into herself, wondering how such a travesty could happen. Weeks before she found out she was pregnant, she had contacted Debora's father, who was still in Haiti. She wanted him to take care of Debora, to be her father and relieve her of this burden of single motherhood. She wanted to go home. Marie was slowly realizing she was in on over her head. She had no money and was tired of working like a dog. Day after day, she worked for what seemed like pennies. Some of her jobs paid $25 a day, others $5 an hour. By the time she paid

$100 a month for the room she was renting, she only had enough for transportation. She and her baby relied on the food from the boarding house so they wouldn't starve. She didn't come to America for this. But now, her pride and embarrassment spoke to her louder than the cries of her baby and her growling stomach. *You can't go back to Haiti like this,* is all she heard.

Marie couldn't afford the abortion she had inquired about at the clinic, so she consulted a Haitian doctor who had a private practice. Dr. Jerome saw a lot of the poorer immigrants in the neighborhood. He was their trusted physician and accepted private pay for private treatments, at a discounted rate. He prescribed Marie a concoction that was to rid her of this unwanted pregnancy. He told her to give him whatever she had. She gave him 50 bucks, her last.

Marie immediately took the concoction and waited. Weeks went by, and there was no change. The pregnancy didn't end as she hoped. Marie grew bigger, rounder, and came to the conclusion that she indeed would soon have another child. She felt more lost and more afraid than she could have ever imagined. Most of all, she felt crazy. *Yes, that's what it is! I am losing my mind*, she decided. So much confusion, all from a life growing inside her.

Marie was never taught the science behind conceiving a child. But having had a baby already, she pretty much knew that at the very least, it for sure took two people for it to happen. She almost busted a brain vessel thinking long and hard about this. She had to dig deep, deep in the corners of her brain where guilt, regret, and stress were swept away and buried. Finally, in a moment that

UNRAVEL

hit her like a tractor trailer, she remembered the morning she woke up next to Lorenzo.

To prepare to write this story, I interviewed as many people as I could to better understand my conception and the events that followed. Since I was a child, I have heard varying stories. My father has always contested that he actually dated my mother and that he only questioned her pregnancy because he thought my mother was having an affair with her boss, the Chinese man she spent so much time with. She says she did not have an affair and has never changed her story—that she was single and never knowingly had sex with anyone around the time she got pregnant. She insists that she was confused when she found out she was pregnant and the only time she was near a man was the morning she woke up to find Lorenzo in her bed. I am here, I exist, and Lorenzo is my father, so some version of that story must be true. My mother and father somehow conceived me.

    I questioned my mother time and time again about the events because frankly, they made very little sense to me. As I continued to push, I had to let my mother know I was not questioning her claims to make her feel like she was crazy or lying—too many people had done that already. I know that is one of the many reasons many victims don't come forward. I think about how horrible it must have been for her that no one believed her. How awful and lonely it must have been to be that confused, and that violated. But I wanted, *needed* the whole truth. So I pushed.

FELICIA P. ROCHE

After years of pushing, my mother eventually shared more details. I wish she had left out the part where she took some sort of drug that Dr. Jerome prescribed her to kill me, but I am grateful she found a way to share more about what she thought happened. Not so much for the sake of my desire to know, but more so for the sake of her own sanity, her own healing, and maybe even for the sake of justice. Marie believes that she had to have been drugged that night Lorenzo came into her bedroom. Bayton Street had a lot of drug activity; access to opioids and cocaine was in no way sparse. My mother says that she, my father, and the Haitian couple that owned the house were probably the only people who did not engage in recreational drug use. But being drugged, in her mind, is the only way to make sense of her lack of memory of the night my father raped her, the night I was conceived.

Chapter 2
Foreign Baby

The day Marie brought me home from the hospital, The Big House on Bayton Street was in more chaos than it had ever been. Many of the tenants openly smoked crack on the stoop or in the living room. There were couples beating on each other and occupants stealing from their roommates. All hell broke loose while Marie was giving birth, and from the looks of it, hell was here to stay.

"You are going to have to move," Mrs. Delair, the landlord, announced to Marie during the ride home from the hospital. "We bought another house around the corner on Rittenhouse Street; that's where you are going to live now," Mrs. Delair explained. Marie attempted to ask questions, but Mrs. Delair was not delivering the news in such a way that left room for a conversation.

Mrs. Delair had become somewhat of a mother figure to Marie. The Delairs had taken her in when she first arrived in America, and Marie didn't have anyone else helping her figure out life in this new country; she needed them.

"It will be better; you and the girls will have your own floor," Ms. Delair continued. Marie couldn't argue with that. She looked down at the baby she was holding while riding in the front seat of the car and then turned to look at all the items the hospital donated piled in the back: a car seat, a basinet, blankets, and diapers. She wondered where it was all supposed to fit. More space and some privacy would be better, she decided. In a matter of hours, after they arrived on Bayton Street, all Marie's belongings, including Debora were around the corner in the house on Rittenhouse Street. The first face she saw when she walked into that house was Lorenzo's.

"Why is he here?" Marie asked as she and Mrs. Delair carried in bags.

"He's fixing the place up," Mrs. Delair explained. "He's good with his hands; we are turning the house into apartments, so everyone will have their own space. Loco can do it." Loco was what everyone called Lorenzo, a term of endearment attempting to rationalize how he was seemingly both insane and sweet.

Marie's concern was not whether or not Lorenzo was good at construction. She could care less if he was there to improve her new home. All she wanted was for him to admit to taking advantage of her that night. She wanted him to acknowledge that the new baby she had just brought home was his. Lorenzo would do no such thing.

Marie began the process of caring for a new baby while settling into a new home. Eventually, the three-bedroom house on Rittenhouse Street was converted into a nine-bedroom boarding house. Lorenzo was better than anyone could have imagined with carpentry. He surprised even himself. The Delairs wanted to keep him around as long as possible, offering room and board as payment for all his hard work. And so, Marie and Lorenzo were once again living under the same roof.

UNRAVEL

Lorenzo stayed in the basement that he turned into a two-bedroom apartment with a private entrance. He and Marie could go weeks without running into each other. In the first few weeks after I was born, every once in a while, Lorenzo would sneak in a good look. And every time, he went running to folks to tell them his theories. His most popular one was that since I was so light, and since I had such thick straight black hair and those newborn, slanted eyes, that I had to have been a product of the Asian man Marie had been working for. Lorenzo spread the rumor that Marie had had an affair with her married boss.

A few months had passed when one afternoon Marie left me with Mrs. Delair, who couldn't help but pay a visit to Lorenzo. "Hey, Loco, come here... Look at your baby!" Mrs. Delair never once questioned if I was his; she never had a doubt, which is why she convinced Marie to name me Felicia. She knew that was Lorenzo's beloved mother's name and that I would one day be his beloved child.

Lorenzo didn't hesitate to take a good look at me for the first time in months. And for the first time, it was clear to him. He could see that I had his nose, his feet, and his crazy look in my eyes. My complexion had started to darken, and my hair started to curl. Lorenzo took one look at three-month-old me and called me his baby. There was just no denying it. I don't know if he previously denied that he was my father to cover up the rape, or if he truly just did not believe he could have possibly gotten my mother pregnant. Either way, he had finally resolved to the truth. I was his.

From that point on, all the people who lived on Bayton and Rittenhouse Streets knew that I was baby Felicia, my mother was

FELICIA P. ROCHE

Marie, my father was Lorenzo, and my sister was Debora. It didn't make sense to anyone, but not much did in those days.

Chapter 3
Rittenhouse Street

In spite of Lorenzo's efforts at home improvement, the house on Rittenhouse Street was an old, broken-down, dirty place filled with the lowest life forms—there were roaches and rats too. None of the furniture matched, but there was a lot of it, like a secondhand furniture store. Almost all the tenants at Bayton Street moved into Rittenhouse at some point or switched back and forth for various reasons. Those reasons mostly involved who could live under the same roof without killing each other, or who could pay the Delairs the highest rent. From month to month, the highest bidder got first dibs on the best space.

The earliest memories I have of living on Rittenhouse Street are fogged scenes of being shielded from bullets flying through the basement windows, my babysitters having sex in the same bed as me, and being too afraid to get a glass of water from the kitchen at night because turning the light on would mean a standoff with thousands of bugs and scurrying rodents. Marie was always yelling at different people as she came and went. It was all in creole, so I could never get a good grasp of what was happening.

Marie would get into physical altercations with other tenants on a regular basis. It was her way of guarding her territory in a space she had no choice but to share with others. I have one memory of her arguing in creole with one of the Haitian men that was our housemate. I'm not clear on how it started, but I do know she threatened to beat him over the head with a hammer. He must have stolen something from her because I can remember her standing there, hammer in hand, screaming one phrase in English: "Where is it?!" her eyes bulging like they were going to pop out of her head, a growl in her voice. My mother could be very scary when she yelled like that. She seemed to grow 10 feet when she was enraged.

Marie was short, just about five feet tall, but she was strong. She was muscular and yet extremely curvy; the term "brick house" comes to mind. To me, she was beautiful, with smooth cocoa skin and full cheekbones that widened with her pretty smile. She had a big laugh that seemingly showed all her teeth, which shined bright white in a perfect row, and made her big round eyes squint into perfect almonds. I thought she was the fiercest and strongest person alive. She seemed invincible to me. All that rage and fire, screaming and cussing with no thought of safety. Surely this had to be what bravery looked like.

I learned to be brave from Marie. And I had to learn to be brave because the house on Rittenhouse Street, where I lived for my first five years, was a scary place. It was so scary that I often question if the memories of it are nightmares that somehow got mixed in with memories of real life. Because things got pretty dark—wicked dark. Maybe it was the violence, or the hunger, or even the exposure to all the drugs, but looking back, I still can't decide if I was hallucinating from the trauma or if there were indeed evil spirits in the house. Based on how everyone treated me and my sister, I have landed on the latter.

UNRAVEL

I remember my nightmares vividly. The most reoccurring one was where my mother and I would come home from some sort of outing, like shopping or playing at the park, just Marie and me. We would walk through the front door of Rittenhouse and up the first stairwell to our section of the house. Suddenly, I would fall through the stairs. I would be hanging there in the balance, stuck in the stairs while my mother kept walking. I would scream for her, but she would never come. That nightmare seemed to have been a foreshadowing of my life; hanging in the balance, waiting for my mother to rescue me. She never came back. She never even noticed I had fallen, that I was stuck in the dark.

The most disturbing reoccurring nightmare I had was that Marie was in some horrible accident. I found myself collecting the pieces of her at a junk yard, desperately trying to find all of her to piece back together. Like a game show, I was running out of time, and every night I would wake up in tears. And so on and so on, night after night, as a four-year-old child, I was frantically trying to find the pieces to make my mother whole—another foreshadowing of life to come.

Debora had nightmares too. Many nights she would wake up screaming and pointing. Whatever grownup was around would check on her, and she would tell them that the lady was right there... right there! They never saw anything. When Marie was around, she would put a Bible under Debora's pillow and demand she sleep. Debora did as her mother ordered, only to find nightmares waiting to greet her. Her most reoccurring nightmare was one where tiny red, yellow, and green stick-figure people held hands forming a circle around her. The little stick-figure people would chant in deep, growling voices: "We're gonna getcha mommy, getcha mommy, getcha mommy!" Debora would wake up crying. She eventually learned to comfort herself back to sleep.

During sleep was not the only time I experienced horrors. Around the corner from Rittenhouse lived a girl named Hoakie. She was always hanging around Debora and me, although neither of us fancied her much. She was a little older than I, maybe seven at the time, and she was pushy. She tried to play with us even when we said we didn't want her to. She came over all the time, and we would tell her to go home because she smelled weird. Even though Debora would play with Hoakie outside sometimes, she would always leave the room when Hoakie came over. That's when I was left to play with her, alone.

One afternoon, Hoakie and I were playing Jacks in the hall on the second floor of Rittenhouse. It was my turn, and I bounced the ball, ready to pick up four jacks and catch the bouncy ball all in the same hand, my record high. All of a sudden, Hoakie stands up, walks to the other end of the hall, and then collapses back to the floor. I walked over to her and told her to get up so we could keep playing. She sat up, stiff as a board, as if someone else was controlling her body. She was staring past me, or rather, through me. I called her name and shook her shoulder. "Hoagie... Hoagie! (Which is how I knew to pronounce her name) What's the matter with you?" She just kept staring.

"I'm gonna tell," was the only thing I could think to say to get her to stop scaring me. I began to walk down the hall as a means to show her how serious my threat was. But when she stayed quiet, I stopped at the end of the hall, realizing that my threat was not working. Once I turned, I stood there, looking at Hoakie sitting upright at the other end of the hall, staring with terror in her eyes. Then, suddenly, her head was on fire—actual fire, big red flames. In shock, I watched Hoakie scoot down the hallway towards me in the same upright position, screaming in horror with her head on fire.

My memory ends there. Everything went dark, and I don't remember ever seeing Hoakie again. The only mental residue I have from that event is that that hall was never the same to me. There were days I would walk through it and I swear I would see a gigantic, black, moving hole. It looked like a portal. I would see it, act like I didn't, and rush past it. What else could a do?

Years would pass before I ever even questioned if what I saw was actually there or not. It's still hard to decipher, but in an attempt to make sense of all I saw, I eventually shared my memory of Hoakie with Debora. She told me she had a similar memory but couldn't remember the details, only that there was some sort of situation where Hoakie's hair had caught fire at Rittenhouse. Maybe my four-year-old perception of the incident makes it far scarier than it actually was. Still, the darkness of Rittenhouse stays with me, and my imagination still runs wild when I try to remember living there.

As an adult, I drove through Rittenhouse Street and I swear I saw Hoakie poke her head out the window of what was an abandoned house. The damn place still made me hallucinate. My early childhood seems to remain there, trapped in darkness for eternity.

What's trapped at Rittenhouse is still in my psyche. I have flashbacks that still take me there. But there are no flashbacks for the times I went to The Dark. The Dark is blacked out, just space and time meant to exist only to protect me, to help me get away from the reality that was Rittenhouse.

Chapter 4
Debora

Our early days in Germantown on Rittenhouse Street weren't all bad. In fact, the summers were the best. There were always other kids in the neighborhood, who weren't Hoakie, to play with, so Debora and I played outside A LOT—sometimes from dawn till dusk. The Grownups never wanted us in the house unless we were doing something for them. So, we woke up early and watched our cartoons: *Tom & Jerry*, *Thunder Cats*, *He-Man*, *Care Bears*, and so on. Our morning cartoon lineup held us over from the time we woke up 'til The Grownups started to rise from their drunken or depressed slumbers. As soon as there was a hint of movement from the grouchy adults, we got the hell out of there, dodging their complaints and requests.

Most mornings Marie was fine with us playing outside—as long as we brought her whatever she needed from the kitchen into her bedroom before we went out. Once she had her coffee and cigarettes, we were free for the most part. On an occasion, we would hear her yelling out her bedroom window while we ran up and down the block. "Debora! Ven la!" ('Come here' in creole.) Debora would run in the house and come out a few minutes later to tell me to walk her to the store. "Mommy want me to go buy her some'n."

Debora had a best friend named Amie, who lived around the corner on Bayton street. Mrs. Delair's youngest son, Freddie, lived on Bayton Street too. They would often join us on our walks to the store. The four of us would saunter down the middle of the street with Joe, the protective dog he was, zigzagging through our gang formation. As we got closer to the store, other neighborhood kids would emerge from their houses and join us with no question, no greetings, and no hesitation. Just laughs and kid talk.

We called the bodegas on what seemed like every corner in Germantown "the Papi store" or "the corner store." No summer day was complete without a trip to one for candy or popsicles. As we all trickled in, the owner of the store would usually watch us closely, yelling at every kid who wasn't buying something to get out. Most kids only had pennies, just enough to buy penny candy. Debora had bigger responsibilities. "Can I get a pack of Virginia Slims?" Debora would ask the store clerk, barely tall enough to reach the counter. The clerk handed her a pack of the cigarettes as she slammed the money on the counter. "Virginia Slims…LIGHT!" she would remind the clerk as she rolled her eyes and shook her head. She thought the clerk was an idiot. How could he not know what kind of cigarettes she came in for by now? Marie would always give Debora an extra 10 cents for her trouble. "And a pack of cherry NOW&LATERs," she would demand.

Everyone called her Debbie. The adults called her little Debbie because they thought they were clever. She hated it. My sister Debora was wise beyond her years. She looked like a tough kid too, sturdy like her mother. She wore pigtails and barrettes, which always seemed out of place on her oval face and against her strong jawline. She was a pretty little brown-skinned girl, but her childlike features didn't fit her adult-like demeanor. Even more out of place were the too small clothes she had to wear since Marie couldn't afford to keep up with her growing children.

Debora had to watch me, her baby sister, at all times. From the time I was a baby, she had to feed me, clean me, and make sure she woke Marie up on time for her shifts at work. Debora was shockingly and inappropriately good at taking care of a baby. She was only out of diapers two years when Marie taught her how to change mine. Right about when Debora started kindergarten is when Marie would leave us in the house the entire day while she went to work, or went to the grocery store, or went to visit with friends—locking us in so we couldn't get out and, more importantly, no one could get in.

Our little section of the boarding house at that time was just one bedroom for the three of us. We had to share a living room, kitchen, and bathroom with other tenants. In order to get around to these rooms, we had to pass the bedrooms of the other housemates. On occasion, they invited us in their rooms. The older I got, the more secluded we became because my sister instructed me to stay out of other people's rooms and only to hang out in ours. Debora figured out ways to keep us safe all on her own. When people would come knocking on the front door of the house looking for Marie, Debora would stick her little hand out the mail slot and yell, "She ain't here!", never opening it for anyone. As she got older, she realized it was better for strangers to think we weren't alone. "She here but she busy!" she learned to lie.

Debora continuously did her due diligence to figure shit out. She knew that not having an answer to a question my mother asked her could result in a backhand across the mouth. And the more answers she had, the more Marie trusted her to take care of other things. By the time she was seven years old, she was buying groceries for the house, fixing meals for herself and me, and making calls to government agencies for Marie. Once Debora could read and write, she was expected to answer any question Marie had about a bill or letter she had received. Marie could read, write, speak, and understand English perfectly fine, but for some reason, she thought Debora had more knowledge than she. Maybe it was the pressure of having to help Marie all the time, but somehow, Debora became the adult in the house. She was more mature, more responsible, and more serious than all The Grownups. She took on the responsibility of watching over me for fear that she would be yelled at and beat if I got hurt or cried for something. I knew my sister loved me, but I also know this fear and pressure made her resent me at the same time.

As good as Debora was at taking care of me, and things around the house, all the work she did was kid-level quality, which sometimes was good enough for Marie and sometimes not. There were times where she bought the wrong kind of milk or brought home the wrong amount of change. There were times that she didn't remember to change my diaper or I got hurt from a fall because she didn't watch me closely enough. These were the days Debora had to face Marie's wrath. It wasn't discipline that brought the belt out; it was usually just Marie's frustration.

Chapter 5

Marie

My mother was born in Port-au-Prince Haiti in 1956. She was born frail and sick and was abandoned by her parents for that very reason. A wealthy woman named Lucienne Roche decided to rescue her. She would give my mother a chance, a shot at this random world. Lucienne had never married and never had babies of her own, but now she could be a mother.

During an era in Haitian culture when it was unheard of for women not to be married, Lucienne was powerful and feared. She was strong, intelligent, and independent. Those who criticized her independence from a man had no choice but to, at the very least, acknowledge her success. She had earned a fortune as a seamstress and created somewhat of an empire.

Lucienne's wealth afforded Marie a comfortable life growing up. Self-proclaimed as born with a silver spoon, my mother had a carefree childhood. She was always very silly and somewhat mischievous. Once, she tied the headmaster's shoestrings together under a table at school. When he tripped and fell, she ran, laughing, and kept running all the way out of school and into the streets. She hid most of that day until her driver came to pick her up. She eventually got into trouble for that, but it didn't stop her from having fun and laughing. Laughing has always been what Marie does best. If I understand nothing else about my mother, I know that laughter is the breath she takes to live.

Growing up, maids, butlers, and cooks filled Marie's large homes and conveniently doubled as playmates. She was never alone. What she didn't realize, though, is that she was never left alone because Lucienne didn't trust her. Lucienne noticed that Marie's way of thinking just wasn't like the other kids her age. Marie was slower. This frustrated Lucienne to no end. The only way she knew to fix the problem was to beat Marie into thinking right. It was the way of the land.

Being wealthy did not save Marie from the brutality of Haitian culture. Most Haitian people during those times disciplined their kids using corporal punishment, including in the schools. Lucienne was no different. My mother's scars tell the story as well as she does. I would run my fingers over them when I lay next to her as a child. "Where did these come from?" I'd ask. Unaware of my innocence, my mother thought it best to quench my curiosity with a detailed description of the tool used to create the indentations in her skin. "A whip, like animal skin, like leather, tied to a big stick," she would recount to me in her thick Haitian accent. Her voice was animated as she spoke in admiration, as if she was taking delight in the whip's beauty. This confused me because the description of the whip and how it was used made me afraid. It also disappointed me because my child's imagination had already decided that the wounds on my mother's deep brown skin were imprints, beautiful birth marks, like mine but deeper. I was a baby asking her mommy for confirmation of what I thought was beautiful, but what I got was something too horrible to fathom.

UNRAVEL

The thought of mother's scars being beaten into her hurt me, and I wondered how she survived. *Why wasn't she upset about them? Why wasn't she crying or ashamed?* I wondered, and I wondered a lot—too much time wondering. Curiosity got the best of my small, developing brain and so, despite my emotions and fear, I went back for more. The question and answer sessions became quality time.

Marie told me all kinds of stories of the types of whippings she would get, like bedtime stories. Children in Haiti, little boys and little girls just like her, would have to strip down naked, fetch the tool made of animal skin, and stand on one foot in front of their master—their teacher or parent or guardian. They would be asked a question: "Èske w konnen poukisa wap resevwa bat sa a?" (Do you know why you are getting whipped?)

Good little boys and girls would always know the answer.

"Konbyen ou pral pran?" (How many lashes will you receive?)

Good little boys and girls were never to assume too low a number. The counting would begin. The wounds and the scars they left were reminders for the children of Haiti to always know the difference between right and wrong. My little mind had to believe that the children in Haiti always remembered and never had to get whipped more than once. Anything more would be too hard for me to process.

Because these types of whippings were standard discipline growing up, my mother did not think much of it. She knew Lucienne whipped her because she was being a good mother and for no other reason. The term "abuse" was never used when she described her upbringing, despite the scars. Those scars represented a life she loved and, as it seemed to me, a life she missed.

Chapter 6

My Hero

All things considered, I guess Marie was doing her best as a single mother of two, with little resources, education, or common sense. She tried to make sure we were cared for, even if she wasn't doing the caring. And maybe it was better that she wasn't always around. Her rage from the frustrated life that she never planned for was the perfect storm for two little girls to be verbally and physically hurt all the time. Debora bore the brunt of this. She was my caretaker, but that did not mean she would escape the same neglects and mistreatments that I did. In fact, hers were worse. She got more beatings because she was older. She got yelled at more because she was in charge of me and had more to answer for.

    I could tell Debora was always annoyed with me. But she was my savior. I never wanted to be without her. My intuition told me my survival depended on her and no one else. Where she went, I went. But where I went, she didn't always go. The Grownups liked to take me places. I was the cute little light-skinned one with the long hair. Debora was the bigger one, with short coarse hair, and she was heavy. Not physically heavy, just her aura. She didn't smile when people smiled at her. She called adults on their bullshit by staying silent and rolling her eyes, knowing it would be followed by a slap across her face. The

Grownups were very demanding and used children to weirdly stroke their egos; make them feel more important than they actually were. Debora challenged this; she saw right through them, and they hated her for that. When Debora had to get one of them a glass of water, it had to be served on a saucer. She obeyed the rule, but the way she chuckled and shook her head as she served the drink just made The Grownups aware of how silly it was. Whenever kids walked into a room where The Grownups were, The Grownups would stretch out their hands, signaling us to kiss them. We were to kiss their hands as if we were greeting royalty, almost bowing to them. They felt empowered, and we felt smaller than we already were. Debora, however, quickly swiped her face against their hands, no pucker and no actual kiss.

I, on the other hand, was the pleaser, unaware of all that Debora was protecting me from. I would gladly kiss every hand, smile on cue, say something cute and funny, and give the adults whatever pleasantries they desired. So, they took me places. I got taken to WWE matches while Debora stayed home. I would go over to people's houses for slumber parties. The Grownups would even bring me to their jobs to show off how cute I was. They would buy me outfits, and occasionally Debora would get a matching one as an afterthought. She begrudgingly accepted them and gave nothing more than a sorry "thank you," the minimum required not to get hit. Debora gave everyone but me, her baby sister, the minimum required.

But I don't think Debora ever envied the time I spent with The Grownups. I think she was relieved that she didn't have to spend as much time with them and that I was able to get out and enjoy myself from time to time. The only time she ever showed

UNRAVEL

real outward resentment towards me was when her friends were around. She would try and run out of the house to play with them but couldn't without hearing, "Hey, wait for me!"

Debora would make the "shhh" gesture, finger to lips, so Marie wouldn't hear.

"But I wanna come!" I'd proclaim.

"Debbie! Take your sister!" Marie would yell.

She didn't have a choice.

All her friends, the neighborhood kids around her age, would be waiting outside the house, all disappointed when they saw me, the four-year-old big baby, following behind. They would start running up the block, all bigger and faster than I was. It was hard to keep up.

We would stop at the playground only feet from our house. I had a Barbie doll in my hand, so while the big kids swung from the swings, standing on them and flipping off, I kneeled on the ground, pretending Barbie was having a night out on the town. In the months since Barbie had been gifted to me, all her clothes seemed to have disappeared, so I wrapped tissue around her to make her look like she had on a white dress. "Doodtidoodidoo..." I whispered as Barbie pranced around. There were these little glass tubes lying on the ground where we played. I picked one up and pretended it was a tall glass for Barbie to drink out of. The kids around me laughed. "Debbie, your little sister is making Barbie use a crack pipe!" They all laughed and ran again, as a pack—running down the streets, dodging cars, jumping fences, and finally through the abandoned parking lot. I couldn't keep up. But I knew where they were going. Bayton Street. Our whole social life was on Bayton Street. Amie's house, the old boarding house, and the Delair's third house, their actual home, which was not a boarding house, all were on Bayton Street. So, I just met them there.

Amie's house left much to be desired for my curious four-year-old self. Her mother, a big woman, seemed physically incapable of getting up from where she lay in front of the TV. The place was full of kids, mostly boys. Amie had a lot of brothers, and their friends doubled them in numbers. The boys would always be jumping off furniture, tossing the smaller of them to and fro.

Debora and Amie retreated into a free room and played whatever it was big girls played, leaving me to socialize on my own. I would try and be a big girl too, not caring that the person I felt safest with was ignoring me at the time. I stayed away from Debora but still in the house for as long as I could. But the house had a stench so bad it made my stomach hurt. I would cringe as I watched dishes being dried with dirty socks and broken toilets overflowing with poo. One day, I watched a little boy, smaller than me, stick his hands in the overflowed mess and then in his mouth, sucking off the sloppy treat he discovered. That did it. I was outta there! This may have been Debora's best friend's house and her chance at some kind of fun, but I hated it. Once the girls were in their zone, I made my escape up the street.

I liked going to the cleaner house on Bayton Street where the Delair's lived. Their son Freddie had so many pets. There were chickens in the backyard, turtles and gerbils in his room, and cats and dogs all around! I skipped up the street with a smile on my face because I was about to visit with my cool big cousin.

UNRAVEL

Freddie and I weren't blood cousins. Marie had no blood relatives in the states. But growing up black in Philly there was a cousin culture that everyone adhered to. There was no doubt that Freddie and his big brothers, Mike and Al, were me and Debora's big cousins. No blood relation needed. Our families were close. We shared bathrooms and dinner tables, and nobody better mess with us or we would get our big cousins. They scared us, locked us in dark closets while making wolf cries, mugged us when they walked by, and told us to stay out their rooms whenever we came over—cousin stuff. I loved my big cousins and just wanted to hang with them. Besides, they were the only males at the time that didn't touch me in a way that made me freeze or make me do things I didn't like doing. When I got up the block, the Delair's door was open. The door was always open. I ran upstairs and right into Freddie's room.

"Whatchu doing?" I asked, hanging on his doorknob.

"Hey, little Felicia," he replied. "I'm just looking at my comic book. I'm bored though. I'm about to go ride my bike. Wanna come outside with me?"

Freddie was cleaner than most of the kids in the neighborhood. He had nice clothes, nicer than what I was used to seeing anyway. He was tall for a 10 year old, and very thin. His brown-skinned, lanky body looked even thinner when he wore his fitted striped polo shirts, which is what he always wore, even on hot days like this one.

Before I could answer, he flew past me and down the stairs. "Yea, I wanna come!" I shouted, moving my little legs as fast as I could, trying to catch up to the six steps he jumped before flying out the door. By the time I got to the front door he was already on his 10-speed, headed down the hill, towards the end of the block, past Amie's and around the corner. I caught up just in time to see him turn that corner, placing my hand over my eyes to shield the blazing sun, to see as far as I could. I was winded. I slapped my knee and cracked up laughing at how fast we ran out of the house. Running always made me happy.

Here he comes! He rode all the way around the corner and was headed back from the top of the block, straight for me.

"Wanna ride?"

"Yea!" I said with no hesitation.

"Okay, get on."

I hopped on the front bar, held on to the handlebars, and off we went—my small hands holding on tight next to Freddie's. I slouched to fit between his shoulders and underneath his underdeveloped chest. He was still so much bigger than me, and so cool. He had a 10-speed bike and could ride like no one I had known.

Here we goooooo!!! We went speeding back down the hill, towards Amie's house at the bottom of the block. We started to approach the corner when Freddie said something I couldn't quite make out. I always wanted to please my big cousin; he cared enough about me to want to give me a ride. I didn't want him to think I was dumb, so even though I didn't really hear what he would said, I guessed at it.

I guessed: "Get off."

He actually said: "Hold on."

And he was saying that because he was picking up speed and about to make a hard turn at the corner. As we approached the corner, I followed my big cousin's direction and started to tilt towards my right so I could be ready to jump off once he slowed down. But Freddie didn't slow down. The closer we got to the corner, the faster we were going. My tilt was far enough that my head caught the side of a light pole that we were zooming past. My head hit that pole so hard it swung me clear off the bike, flung me a full circle around the pole, and landed me face down on the corner. Everything went black.

Debora and Amie had made it to her front door just in time to catch the show. I was face down in a puddle of blood. Everyone who was outside ran over and huddled around me. They just stared and screamed, too afraid to turn me over. I was for sure a goner. When I came to, I felt like I had come back from another place.

I don't know where I went, but when I got back the only thing I felt was warm. My face on the concrete was warmed by the sun. I opened my eyes and saw grey. Then I looked around a little and saw red, lots of red. The blood pouring out my head was warm too.

I managed to flip myself over and, much to my surprise, I was surrounded by a large crowd of people, staring at me with horror on their faces. I watched a lot of scary movies at that age. I saw Jason and Freddy, and these people had the same expressions as the people who saw those monsters—terror. What were they looking at that made them so afraid? Were they afraid of me? I started to panic. I didn't feel any pain, but this crowd was blocking the warm sun that invited me back to consciousness, and the way they were staring at me freaked me out. I started to cry and almost screamed in terror myself, a knee-jerk reaction to the crowd.

I caught a glimpse of my sister's face, and it had more fear on it than I had ever seen, worse than the fear from when we watched *Nightmare on Elm Street*. Her eyes were stretched wide and they started to turn red, filling with water. Her hands were over her mouth, but I could tell it was wide open, frozen that way in shock. I was calling out to her, but my mouth wouldn't move, and my brain couldn't form the words. I kept trying to get another glimpse, but I couldn't find her again. I closed my eyes, and all I could think about was how good she was at hide-and-go-seek. *She's the master.* And then I thought: *I'll ask her to play tag with me; we'll both feel better if we just play.* My thoughts started to wander.

Spit, spit, you are not it. Why can't I get up? So many kids out here—let's just play!

My mother and your mother was hanging up clothes. My mother punched your mother right dead in the nose. What color was the blood? RED—you're it!

Wait... RED. Blood! That's what's all over me. That's why Debora's face was like that!

I must have been going in and out of consciousness because with that thought, everything went black again. I was gone.

Debora was more scared and confused than she had ever been. *What just happened to my baby sister? Did she just die?* She went into action. Her instincts told her to run to get Marie. *Mom needs to be here. She has to take care of this. Not me; I'm just a kid.* Her little legs ran across the street and through the abandoned parking lot as fast as they could. She ran so fast and was so shaken, her brain forgot to tell her to breathe. She felt a sigh of relief when she saw our mother already walking towards her.

UNRAVEL

By coincidence, Marie was already on her way to visit with Mrs. Delair on Bayton Street. She spotted Debora running towards her, covered in tears and snot and out of breath. "What! What is it? Speak girl, speak!" Marie's voice was panicked, and frustration was starting to take over. She gripped Debora by the arm to shake her out of it. Finally Debora was able to get out one word, "Felicia!" That was enough for Marie. With that, they both took off running towards the accident.

By the time Marie and Debora had gotten back to me, Lorenzo had already found his way down the block. He was doing some roofing work on The Big House on Bayton Street, a bird's-eye view from where I lay. When I fell, Freddie had jumped on his bike and gotten to Lorenzo in seconds. "Loco! Come quick! Hurry, it's Felicia!"

When Lorenzo got to me, I was still dazed and confused—in and out of consciousness and crying. By now someone had called 911 and the sirens were in clear range. My dad scooped me up and jumped in the back of the police car. As I was hauled off, I caught a glimpse of Debora and Marie rushing over to me; they looked out of breath. I couldn't tell if the wet on their faces was from sweat or tears. Debora pointed towards me while saying something to Marie, like she was explaining to her what was happening, as if she couldn't figure out herself that I was hurt and my dad and the police must be taking me to the hospital. That one last glimpse of my big sister made me smile. I knew everything would be alright because she always made it that way.

After we sped away from the scene of my accident, Lorenzo was crying and telling me to hold on. As I lay across his lap all I wanted was to feel that warm again. I wanted to go back to where

I was, on the corner of Bayton Street, where my sister was, where I could play. I stared at Lorenzo; he was in tears, telling me I was going to be okay. I stopped crying, thought about playing with my sister, and closed my eyes.

When I regained consciousness this time, there was nothing warm, just pain. I woke up in the middle of getting stitches on my head. It stung like a bitch. It was the worse pain I had experienced up until that point, at least of what I could remember anyway. I already had stiches on other parts of my body from when I was younger but I don't remember why or how they got there. I have a nasty scar on my wrist and as the story goes, I was about one year old and asleep, napping on a couch in The Big House. No one was watching me, but they think I rolled over onto a glass table and my wrist was sliced. I was rushed into a bath to wash off all the blood, and my skin was hanging from my wrist like a banana peel. A Grownup, I don't know which, finally took me to the ER where I got the hanging skin stitched up. In another version of this story, one of the male Grownups (who wasn't around anymore) was bouncing me on his lap and dropped me on that glass table. He was afraid he would get in trouble so he hid the whole incident from my mother and father until after a visit to the ER and he knew I would be okay. That's the reason no one close to me knows exactly what happened. In any event, I have no memory of it, but the scar on my wrist tells me the injury was as bad as it sounds. And I am glad I can't remember the pain from it because getting stitches on the day my head split open is something I will always remember. Clear as day is the moment I woke up to the feeling

UNRAVEL

of a needle going through my skin, back and forth, over and over again.

The only thing that was worse than that pain in that moment was the confusion of why I could see my mother laughing at me through my tears. I don't know where Lorenzo had gone at this point, maybe just away from Marie since they could never stand being in the same room, not even for me. But it was just Marie and Mr. and Mrs. Delair in the room as I screamed in agony. And they were all laughing. Maybe they were just happy I was alive, but I wanted their laughter to stop as much as I wanted the pain in my head to stop.

The accident produced a lot of blood from the gash in my head but little other damage. At least to the naked eye. The doctors felt comfortable stitching me up and sending me on my way. A few hours later, we piled into Mr. Delair's car. I was in the back seat with Marie. I was so relieved that we were going home and that my pain had stopped. The sun was setting, and I laid my head on my mother's bosom. Thank goodness it was still the most comforting place on Earth. But the comfort was short lived. I was suddenly extremely dizzy and nauseous. It was either a side effect from pain meds or just the trauma of that day—or, most likely, a symptom from a concussion. I had to lean over off of Marie to vomit. I tried to communicate to her to open the door, but she just said she couldn't because the car was moving. I didn't say why I needed her to open the door, but she soon found out.

There was vomit everywhere: all over the back seat, the back door, and on Marie. I just knew I was in for her rage, screaming at me for making such a mess. But much to my surprise, Marie did not get upset with me. She didn't yank me like she normally would. She didn't yell at me or spew angry words at me in creole. She just asked for some of the newspaper that was in the front seat to clean it all up. I couldn't have been more pleased or relieved with her reaction. She cleaned up and covered the mess as best she could while we were still riding from the hospital. And before we got home, she even let me lay on her again. I was warm again. I was warm like I was on the ground. I looked up at my mother's smiling face and could tell she was happy I was here. She loved me. She really loved me. It was worth the blow to my head to finally know this. With all the pain and trauma I experienced that day, there was nothing I needed, or wanted, more than Marie, my mommy.

After my accident, I started to become as quiet as Debora. I wasn't the happy one anymore. We were the same. The sadness and darkness consumed us both. When Debora went to school, I stayed home and sulked. I couldn't wait for her to come home because she was my only friend, the only real friend I had to talk to. When she wasn't around, I talked to myself. I said the things I would say to her. "Mommy gonna be mad if I get into another accident. I can't go outside no more. Mommy gonna hate me if my stiches don't get better." My conversations with myself went on like this for hours every day.

For weeks after the accident, the entire left side of my face was covered in horrible sores and scabs. I thought I was turning into The Thing from the Fantastic Four in Cousin Freddie's comic books. The dark brown color and the thickness of the wounds compared to the fair bright skin on the other side of my face made it look like I had on half a mask. There was a full-size mirror in a room of our little section of Rittenhouse; I would stare at myself in it for hours. I told everyone I was monster. I looked like one; I felt like one; I was one. I used to be the pretty little girl who could light up a room. Now whenever people saw me, they cringed. I stayed in the house, stared in that mirror all day long, and cried.

When Debora came home from school, she would do her homework and then we would play Barbie in our room, sometimes until the sun went down. I can't remember who bought them for us, but Barbie and her accessories were the only toys we owned. Barbie had a pool, beach chairs, and little Coca-Cola cans. Every day was a day at the beach for Barbie. I so wanted Barbie's life, and her looks. Long straight hair, beautiful clear white skin, and boobs! Debora always got tired of playing Barbie way before I did. The only time I stopped obsessing over Barbie was when I was called away from playing to perform some chore.

Some nights, when she wasn't too tired or didn't work a double, Marie would come home from work, cook for us, and we would all sit and watch TV together while we ate. Other Rittenhouse folk would join us in the living room. Besides playing with Debora, this was the only thing that could make me smile after the accident. But I still wasn't happy with me. I would look at all the fair-faced girls on all the sitcoms and commercials and feel a weird feeling in my stomach. It was like someone was kicking me. What was this pain? Shame. I was ashamed of not being beautiful anymore and not looking like the girls on the TV that everyone was staring at. These girls got everyone's attention. My mom, my dad, my sister, everyone *I* wanted attention from. I became obsessed with looking like the girls on TV, or rather with the idea that I could never look like them, and there wasn't anything I could do about it.

"I wish I could be on TV." I'd sigh and pout and mumble under my breath.

"You can, Felicia," one Grownup or another would say to me.

"No, I can't."

"Why not?"

"Because I'm black, and my hair is not straight." Laughter would ensue.

"You're not black, Felicia, and you don't have black people's hair," The Grownups would say.

Well, if I'm not black, and I'm not a white girl like the ones on TV, what am I? I never asked this out loud. I knew I would just get laughed at even more. So I never got my answer.

Debora never laughed at me though. She just asked me why I thought black people couldn't be on TV.

"I'on neva see'm" I mumbled.

"Yes you do!" she yelled.

"I do?" I believed whatever my big sister told me. She said black people were on TV and I could be someday too.

"I can?"

"Yup," she said. "All you need is long hair, like this…" She grabbed my hand, and we ran into our room. She laid a long towel over my hair and tucked it behind my ears. She did the same on her head. Mine was pink, and hers was blue. She handed me the roll-on deodorant, and she used a hairbrush. We looked in the mirror and started singing into our makeshift mics. "See, we are singers on TV!" We laughed, and I felt better.

UNRAVEL

For weeks after that day, while Debora was in school, instead of staring at my scars in the mirror, I would sing in the mirror, with a towel on my head—my long flowing hair. Each day I couldn't wait until Debora got home to sing with me. I was starting to feel like myself again when the scabs started to peel off and my wounds were healing and clearing up. The day came where in my regular routine of running to the mirror to examine my ugly scabs, all that I saw was the wound from my stitches, a scar near my hairline. My smooth skin was back; I compared it to Werther's Original candies: "Same color and it feels like it too!" I wasn't a monster anymore. But I still felt like I wasn't pretty enough to get the attention I craved.

"Felicia! Come here! Come quick! Look on the TV!" Debora called out to me one night.

I ran in the room. "See, look; she's black and she's on TV," she said, pointing at the television.

Janet Jackson was on stage singing her first hit, "Control." I was amazed. She was singing like we did in the mirror. She was pretty, she was my color, and she had thick curly hair like I did. She wasn't a white girl and she was on TV! Debora looked at me and smiled. "See... Told you."

I smiled back at my big sister and for some reason, in that moment, I felt seen, I felt heard, and I felt loved. Somehow, my sister always *saw me*. She was always coming to my rescue, always my hero.

Chapter 7
The Monsters

Time spent with my sister kept me in the light. But The Dark was always there. Nothing made me want to go into The Dark more than the thought of the two Haitian men that lived on the top floor at Rittenhouse. Of The Grownups, the two worst ones were Osini and Edovete. I remember their scents as Haitian food and musk, the spices from chicken and gravy mixed in with cheap bathroom cologne and man sweat. Everywhere they went their scent lingered. It's a scent that relinquished the appetite of four-year-old me. I turned my nose up whenever I smelled it and tried to use my sense of smell to guide me into the opposite direction from which the scent came.

The flashes I have of Osini and Edovete come with a feeling of disgust and longing to crawl in the black hole of the scary hallway in Rittenhouse. I don't remember much about them, just their names, their scent, and what they did to me. And I would do anything to forget it. I cry when I think of young me, a little girl, body so small and helpless, lying there shaking and scared under the weight of a grown man thrusting his man parts on me. I could see the looks on their faces of pleasure and shame. All I could do is lay there and try not to scream. They told me I was a good girl and they smiled. I always wanted to be a good girl, so I continued to lie still, never trying to leave.

I eventually learned how to disappear each time. I went somewhere else, somewhere into darkness. When I came back, I found myself being shoved out the door and told to go play. Osini would go out for the rest of the day, and Edovete usually hid away in his room. He barely ever came out. A few days would pass, and their desires for the flesh of a young child would call out again. Once again, I'd go into nothing and escape, into The Dark.

I don't know where I went, but when I got back my sister was always closely watching me to make sure I stayed away from Osini and Edovete. One of the greatest pains I live with today is knowing that these Monsters got to her too. Never screaming, never crying, never telling; my sister remained silent and sacrificed herself, hoping to keep The Monsters away from me.

Marie and Lorenzo never knew either. Lorenzo turned a blind eye to the same sick, pathetic, perverted traits he saw in The Monsters that were also in him. Marie just wasn't there. What would make The Monsters so sure we wouldn't tell? What security they must have had to so easily come and go as they pleased. The pedophiles couldn't help themselves, but The Grownups were helping them. Their silence was more nothingness, like the nothing I went into when these men lay on top of me.

Debora and I never talked in detail about what happened when we were separated into the rooms of The Monsters. We silently confirmed simply that it did in fact happen. Anything beyond that makes what happened too real. We can never chance the black holes in space and time being filled. There is no need to fill them with anything that only causes pain. Details would never help.

UNRAVEL

Perhaps Rittenhouse really did have a portal like the one I saw that day in the hallway with Hoakie. Maybe my sister and I both went there to get away from The Monsters. I can't explain how we got through from day to day besides this: We survived The Monsters because we had some sort of an escape.

But I did not escape when The Monster was my dad.

Chapter 8
The Greatest Monster of Them All

Growing up, I heard everyone call him Loco. I didn't speak Spanish so I had no idea what it meant. I sometimes wonder would I have looked at him differently had I heard everyone saying: "Here comes your dad, Crazy." Nonetheless, Loco seemed to suit him just fine. When I finally learned that Loco meant crazy, I wondered why people called him that. I don't wonder anymore. When I put two and two together and realized they called my dad Loco because of the things he did, I questioned WHY he did the things he did. WHY do crazy people do the things they do? He's not just some crazy person to me; he's my dad.

My own dad... I felt nothing when the rest of them did it, but my dad was my dad, and I loved him so much, adored him even. My dad was funny, charming, and charismatic. I don't know if I viewed him this way when I was small or if I just picked up on all this from my observation of how everyone around us interacted with him. Everyone was always laughing when they talked to my dad. People seemed to light up when he was around, like he was sharing some jolt of light and energy with whomever was in close proximity. People listened intently when he spoke, as if he was somehow wiser than them. His jet-black curly hair had lots of silver strands that made him look older than he was, and his beady dark eyes looked like they had seen a hard life. He seemed to always have a white tank top on, what we used to call "wife beaters," no matter what the weather was. He never didn't look like he was working on cars or doing a house remodeling job. His combat boots and jeans forever had paint and grease on them, as did his hands. He was small for a man of his strength, about 5'7" and thin, but I saw him lift cars and bricks that bigger men around him couldn't. He had a temper and a big personality. When he wasn't yelling in anger, he would be yelling terms of endearment at everyone around him, "You got it, smart lady!"; "There he is, the big man!"; or "Hello, beautiful people!" And all his greetings were delivered as if he were announcing them through a bullhorn, and always in Spanish. "Hola!" "Buenas Noches!" People were undoubtedly amused by him. Everyone, that is, besides Marie.

From what my mother tells me, she couldn't stand being in the same room as my father. She hated how loud he was and was annoyed with how everyone seemed to listen to him. Although they lived in the same house for years, she wouldn't be caught near him. When he walked in a room, she walked out. I have not one memory of my parents ever being in the same room. Not one.

I must have observed my dad a lot because I don't have many memories of interacting with him, but I have lots of him interacting with others, or of him working on a car, or handling tools. That's when I admired him the most, when he was fixing things. I knew everyone marveled at his abilities, and so maybe I marveled too. Whatever early childhood memories I have of my dad, interacting with me or otherwise, I know all are from before

UNRAVEL

I turned six. I know this because all The Monsters got to me before I was school aged. And my father left when I was five.

When my dad left, everything changed. I felt confused because parts of me were shattered. I wanted my dad and I knew I would miss him. Other parts of me felt relief—I would be free from him touching me.

I can't remember the first time Lorenzo touched me. But my first memory of knowing he was touching me is filled with a dreaded feeling of *Oh no, not again*. I remember pretending to be asleep because I didn't want him to "bother" me. I couldn't've been more than three years old. I was laying down in the basement at Rittenhouse, and I can clearly remember faking sleep while my dad whispered in a singing voice, "Felicia…. Felicia… Felicia…" I was so proud of my acting when he failed to wake me and left the room. I remember this like it was yesterday and the feeling is still here too—relief that I didn't have to do what he wanted that night. I felt victorious in the moment of not having to give into him.

I wasn't so lucky all the other times. I have memories just as vivid of other times he had his way with me, and it was a regular occurrence. I can't say for sure because I was so young, but it seemed to happen every other night, or at least every night my mother was not home, which was often. Marie tells me she worked a lot of nights during those days, overnight shifts as a housekeeper at a nursing home. So, it could have been as often as every night for a while.

And it wasn't just me.

Sometime after I was born, maybe a year or two later, my father met a woman named Doris. She lived on Bayton Street, and the two of them got pretty serious. Doris was such a well-put-together lady, and I thought she was so pretty. She had fair skin, long hair, and a high, soft, sweet voice. She reminded me of Paula Abdul, except she was a black woman and she was shy. And she was head over heels in love with my dad.

Doris had a daughter from a previous relationship that was the same age as me, Amber. People called us twins. We wore the same long curly pigtails, and both of us had caramel completions, small, frail bodies, and cute button noses. We played together whenever my dad took me over to Doris' house. Doris took some time to warm up to me, but by the time I was four years old, she was almost like a stepmother. I stayed over her house even when my dad wasn't around. Before long she was buying matching outfits for Amber and me and called *us* her girls. Amber and I did become somewhat sisters because we would eventually share a baby brother. A year before my dad left, he had a boy with Doris. They all lived together in the blue house on Bayton Street.

Inside that blue house is where my father molested Amber and me, together. He made us perform sexual acts on each other and then on him, together. When one of us said no, or cried because we wanted to stop, he would use the other one as an example of what a good girl would do. He used jealously and guilt tactics to get us to do what he wanted, and it worked. I always wanted to prove to Amber that I was Lorenzo's *real* daughter and that he and I were closer than they. I tried to do whatever my dad asked.

Loco was a monster. Lorenzo was my dad.

Chapter 9
Meet Lorenzo

Lorenzo migrated from Cuba in 1980 and immediately connected with a program for immigrants sponsored by the Lutheran Church. The immigrant sponsorship program found a rundown boarding home for Lorenzo to live in a likewise rundown section of Philadelphia called Germantown. But in Lorenzo's eyes, it was glorious, a far cry from the refugee camp he had just come from. He felt safe. Although he was surrounded by crack addicts and alcoholics, he knew there was no one there as crazy as him, and in his craziness, there was real strength. He saw his neighbors as weak, taken over by substances that controlled their behavior. *They'd never survive all the shit I've seen*, he thought. The only thing that controlled Lorenzo's behavior was his past.

Lorenzo found comfort in the small room he was given at the home. It was the very first time in his life he had his own space. There was just a small cot with blankets, a little nightstand, and a TV. He did not spend much time in his room though. Being in his room meant being alone with his thoughts and memories. His days were structured around walking over a block to the church for breakfast, lunch, and dinner. On his walks he crossed trolley tracks that made him have flashbacks of the tracks he slept under as a little boy, lost and alone in Havana. But as soon as those thoughts entered Lorenzo's mind, he would disconnect them, as if pulling a plug. He'd much rather stay present and observe the Philadelphians, who always looked like they were rushing to get somewhere, all of them with their heads down. Lorenzo almost took it personally when people zoomed by, never looking up to say a friendly hello. He wondered why everyone was so cold and so busy.

One crisp spring morning, Lorenzo grabbed a light jacket from one from the donation boxes right before he entered the church. "Good morning," Lorenzo greeted the staff and a few other residents with a heavy Spanish accent. It was pretty early, so the rush had not started and neither had breakfast. Lorenzo decided to take his less-than-Cuban-tasting cup of coffee out to the walkway in front of the church so he could people-watch. He had come to learn how to stir up conversations with any stranger that took notice of him. If he made eye contact, he initiated a greeting. Engaging in conversations, even if he didn't always understand them, was how Lorenzo kept the voices in his head at bay. Even the ones screaming at him about his past were starting to become background noise.

The streets of Germantown Avenue were made of stone with trolley tracks laid through them. There was a park across the street from the church with small benches and a host of small trees and bushes. The small trees were budding from the newness of spring. Lorenzo marveled at the pink and white flowers and how the sun made them glow. He almost didn't notice the homeless people laid across the benches near the flowered bushes. There were small blossoming trees lining the avenue, which was filled with shops, newsstands and bus stops. This time of the morning, kids of all ages were getting on and off public

UNRAVEL

buses and school buses. Lorenzo watched them all closely. He zoomed in on a young man walking with a dog. The dog looked like a stray he befriended back home, a golden retriever for sure, mixed with some other things. Lorenzo was curious. "Hey man," he said to the young guy with the dog.

By this point, Lorenzo had been in America a few months, and what English words he had learned had been hidden behind a heavy accent and the sociopathic speed of crazy talk. No one ever understood him the first time he said anything to them, so he was always prepared to repeat. But this young guy simply answered, "What's up, man?"

Lorenzo wanted to try him in Spanish, "¿Como te llamas?" he tried.

Without skipping a beat, the young man responded, "Al."

Lorenzo knew instantly he found a friend. He proceeded, "¿Hablas español?"

"No, I just know that." Al laughed, matching Lorenzo's glee.

"Man, why you here with the dog? No colegio?"

"No what??" Al squealed back.

"Hahaha!" Lorenzo was beyond giddy. "How you say…uh uhmm…school?"

"Oh! Naw man! I'm not with that shit today. I'm in high school. My school right up the block." Al pointed north on Germantown Avenue towards Germantown High School. Lorenzo started to pet the dog, who was obediently waiting for Al to finish his conversation. "¿Como se llama tu perro?"

"Huh? You gotta stop it with all that guala guala man." Al grew weary of the conversation.

"Dog…dog…his name?" Lorenzo yelled, frustrated at Al's unwillingness to improvise languages a bit longer.

"Oh! That's Joe," Al answered.

"He's a nice dog." Lorenzo could tell.

"Well, yea, I guess. He's dope. Real smart. Watch this." Al turned to face the dog. "Joe… Gimmie five. Up high. Down low. You too slow!" Joe did the trick perfectly.

"Whhhaaaaaa?" Lorenzo was amazed.

The two continued their conversation for about an hour. Lorenzo gave the highlights about his journey to America in broken English, and Al laughed at his expression and delight, not believing a word he said. "Man, you crazy! How you say crazy in Spanish?"

"Loco."

"Well, that's what Imma call you… Loco."

Lorenzo was tickled. "Man, you know my parents are immigrants too. Yup, they from Haiti."

"Oh yea?" Lorenzo pretended to understand.

"Yea, man. They have two houses around the corner. They rent out rooms and they might have some work for you. You should come around."

Lorenzo didn't quite understand much of what Al said, but with no real thought they both started to walk down the street together, conversing and laughing. A few blocks later, Al assumed Lorenzo had already decided to leave the home the church provided and take him up on the offer of his parents' boarding home.

Meanwhile, Marie had only been in Philadelphia a few months when she went to the immigration office in

UNRAVEL

Germantown. As she sat in the waiting area to be called, she wrestled with the idea of lying about why she was in the states and how she had gotten there. But Marie was too tired to lie. She told the case worker at immigration her whole truth. And just like that, the truth was enough. Marie was given a visa, temporary ID, and an appointment for state benefits all in that one appointment. Her heart felt like it was leaping out of her chest; she was so overjoyed. With the biggest smile on her face she left the immigration office and practically ran straight to the Delair's house to share the amazing news that she was granted a work visa. When she got to the corner of Bayton Street, she started to speed up. Her fast walk became a run as she passed by two guys walking up the street, not taking the time to even check to see if she knew them. Moments later, she burst through the door and right into the kitchen where Mrs. Delair was making a giant pot of red beans and rice.

"Marie Delair! Bum 'di ou!" Marie yelled in creole. "They gave me my papers! They gave me everything! I told the truth, and they gave me my papers!" The two started to laugh and cry and dance and hug.

At that moment, Mrs. Delair's oldest son came storming into the kitchen. "Yes! Mom, you cooked! Good, because I have a new friend and he is hungry" he said while squeezing between his mom and Marie to grab a plate. "Hey man! Come in here!" he yelled out. The friend peeked behind the kitchen door and slowly walked in.

"Who is this?" Marie and Mrs. Delair slowed Al down for an explanation.

FELICIA P. ROCHE

"Oh, this is my new friend," Al explained with a smile. "Marie, meet Lorenzo."

Chapter 10
The Change

Sometimes, I feel somewhat special when I think about how my parents came from different countries and had one crossing moment that produced me. Other times, I feel sick at the thought that I am a product of rape. Most times though, I understand how every single individual on Earth, myself included, is actually a product of a miracle. The miracle being that there had to be an insurmountable amount of tiny yet precise events that led up to the very moment you were conceived. All of us, every single one of us. When you put it like that, the way Marie and Lorenzo came to cross paths is both extraordinary and ordinary.

What is clear is that once their paths did meet, Lorenzo and Marie would be forever connected by me, whether they liked it or not, and they didn't like it. They would eventually make it so that they could forget each other, never seeing each other again. But at least for the first five years of my life that they lived near each other, at times even under the same roof, I would always remind them they there was no reversing the fact that I had come to be, forever reflecting them both. Although I have no memory of ever seeing Lorenzo and Marie in the same room, it's extraordinary to me that I have such distinct memories of both of them, never together, but always at Rittenhouse.

Our final days at Rittenhouse were filled with people screaming at each other, the smell of cigarettes, and never knowing who was going to come bother you. I was five now and I lived a life of fear—fear of getting hit, fear of getting yelled at, and fear of having a man three times my size overpower me and make me do things I didn't want to do. But that was all about to change, and Gustave was the one who was going to change it.

Gustave was one of the last people to move into Rittenhouse before we moved out. He and my mother seemed to be in love. He was always grabbing her, and she was always cooking for him. They laughed together, lit each other's cigarettes, and slept in the same bed.

Gustave was a tall man, maybe six feet or so. I always thought he looked like a giant next to my mother who was five-foot-nothing. He had dark skin, even darker than my mother's. He was very thin and lanky for a man—but he had muscles. He was maybe a few years older than Marie, who was 30 years old at the time. And he looked like his name; he had a strut about him and was just a smooth brotha. He always had a beer in his hand and he had the coolest car I had ever seen, a red and white Buick with white leather seats and a red steering wheel.

"Can I go with you?" I would ask Gustave whenever he grabbed his keys to leave. He was more careful with us than The Grownups. He would pick me up, give me a kiss on the cheek, and say, "Next time."

As Gustave and Marie got closer, I started to wonder why he wasn't spending as much time with us as the other men in the house did. How come he never took me out in his big fancy car? Maybe it was because we weren't doing what me and my dad were doing. He wasn't having sneaky time with me like the other men. So I figured I'd let him know it was okay.

One night while Marie was gone, I laid next to Gustave in the room he usually laid in with Marie. I started playing around with his hair, and then I grabbed his watch. When he asked me if I like his watch, I said "yea" and moved in for more. Before he had a chance to understand what was happening, I climbed on top of him and straddled him. I knew what he wanted because my dad wanted the same thing, and Gustave was with my mom now, which in my mind meant a new dad. Once I straddled him, I began moving the way my dad so often enjoyed. Gustave's body became cold. His loving eyes turned black.

"What are you doing, Felicia!" He grabbed my arm, and I reached for his belt buckle to show him I was okay with it. His grip became more powerful and the squeeze on my tiny arm began to hurt.

"Nasty girl!" he screamed at me as he tossed me to the side. "Leave! Leave right now! Get away!" I grabbed my bottom lip and put my head down in shame. I was in trouble and I did not know why. I left the room, tears in my eyes and wanting nothing more than a father.

Gustave was extremely disturbed by my behavior, and it only confirmed his suspicions about the behaviors he witnessed around the house. He paid attention to the way Osini and Edovete looked at us. He noticed how we ran out a room whenever they came around and the way we tensed up and sometimes even froze when they tried to be nice to us. Gustave saw us panic at the idea of being left alone in the house with either one of them. It was the last straw. "Marie, we are moving.

These people in this house are evil!" Gustave never told Marie what happened and never told her why they had to move. And Marie didn't ask.

Marie found in Gustave something she never had: a man who cared for her and her children. And so we moved. Gustave found a nice, clean two-bedroom apartment all the way on the other side of the city—a much better neighborhood in a much safer area. It was a whole new world for Debora and me. The days of sharing houses and rooms with child molesters and crack addicts were over! At least for now.

Wadsworth Apartments had a walkway leading to our front entrance. It was lined with bright, fresh green grass on both sides, and a beautiful tree was planted right at the curb out front. I looked out the window and stared at that tree for hours on end the first few days we lived at Wadsworth—almost as if I had never seen a tree from a window before. Had I though?

By then I knew I loved trees. Willow trees were my favorite. The Grownups always laughed at me when I called them girl trees. This was not a willow tree; it looked like broccoli to me and like it had a halo around it. On days it would rain I noticed a hue around it that changed to different colors of the rainbow, and everything around it would change to those colors too. One day everything was green: the leaves, the branches, the dirt it was planted in, and the sidewalks around it. Then, another day, after it rained, it was all pink: the leaves, the trunk, the street and the sky—everything. It was the most beautiful tree I had ever seen, and I wondered if it changed colors with my moods. It was my mood tree.

UNRAVEL

The apartment complex was a row of four three-story redbrick buildings. It was a very quiet block compared to Rittenhouse and Bayton Street. It almost made me nervous not hearing people yelling, loud music, or kids screaming. Behind the buildings was a large driveway. The first day we arrived I saw a kid quietly riding his bike back there, riding in small circles as he peddled. I instantly got excited, thinking I would ride a bike back there someday soon too. I didn't have a bike, but that didn't stop my optimism. In the corner of the large driveway was a large green dumpster. It was where tenants could throw out their trash for collection. I remember waking up to a loud machine sound the first morning at Wadsworth. I thought it was an airplane flying to close to the house, but then when the sound continued for more than a few minutes, I got up to investigate. I ran to look out my bedroom window and kneeled down to watch. With my face pressed against the window and my hand by my chin, I watched in amazement as the truck lifted the dumpster and flipped it to empty the contents inside the truck. I wondered if our trash would soon be in there. I wondered where all our trash went when we lived on Rittenhouse Street; there was no dumpster, and I couldn't recall ever seeing a trash truck. I had an overwhelming feeling that our lives were very different now.

In our new two-bedroom home, Debora and I had our own room to share. The privacy was shocking to me, and yet pleasant. Never before could we just be. No peeking out our room door down the hall to see if there were people around, something we used to do to make a decision if we would go to the bathroom or wait. No more listening at the door to see who was in the house— The Monsters or people we actually could stand to be around. It took a few days, but eventually we just walked out our bedroom door without peeking our heads out first. I eventually stopped tiptoeing to the bathroom. We adjusted.

It took a few weeks to settle in, but once we did, Debora and I started enjoying each other's company in a more relaxed way. We spent hours listening to our Whitney Houston and Michael Jackson vinyl records. That record player was everybody's at Rittenhouse. But now, Marie let us have it in our room—our own room! And it did not take long to get used to the good life. We shared a bed, but we felt entitled to our half of it. "Keep your stuff on *your* side of the bed!" Debora would yell at me. Neither of us ever made the whole bed. We only did our own side and left the other sister to make up their own. My side of the bed was mine, and I wouldn't allow anyone to touch it.

Chapter 11
Normal

As things started to quiet down for us, our spirits grew calmer and so did our days. Marie let us play outside just as much as she did before but now she was around way more often. She still worked a lot, now as a nurse's aide—a lot of overnight shifts and doubles. But now when she wasn't working, instead of leaving us with monsters, she was at home with us. And I loved it.

First grade had finally come for me. After spending the year I should have been in kindergarten at home, school was extremely nerve-wracking. I didn't know it, and neither did anyone around me, but I was having anxiety about the whole thing. I was going to be separated from my mother and sister five days a week out in the scary world. I needed my sister to protect me. I even believed I needed Marie to protect me. She was big and strong and fierce, and even though I was scared of her too, I knew Marie's fierceness could scare off anyone who might try to hurt me.

At McCloskey elementary school, my sister was in the big kids' classroom; too far away. I felt older than the kids in my class. I had done so many grownup things and was beyond them all. *Ugh, such BABIES!* My sister and I walked to school by ourselves just as we did everywhere else when we lived in Rittenhouse. Not like these babies. They had their mommies and daddies bring them into school. I could tie my shoe, and my sister knew how to braid her own hair. We were smart and tough and we knew more than these kids. My anxiety started to fade when I realized this. I felt like Debora and I were in charge.

Our resilience was evident as we adjusted to this new world. Within the first few months of living at Wadsworth, we were socializing with the whole neighborhood. I played outside with kids from the apartments from time to time, and Debora made a best friend. At Rittenhouse she had Amie; here she had Cassandra. Cassandra and Debora were so cool; I just wanted to be around them every day. And so I was. When they went to the corner store, I followed. When Debora went to Cassandra's, I walked in behind her, uninvited. I sat in the living room while they hung out in Cassandra's bedroom. I didn't mind. Her mother always offered me snacks and turned the TV to cartoons. I happily waited around for my sister to be done playing with her new best friend. This was a much better experience than waiting around for her at Amie's house. By sundown, we would walk quietly across the grass that separated our apartment building from Cassandra's to go home. Debora almost never mentioned me waiting around for her like some lost puppy.

"What do y'all be talking about for hours over there all day?" I'd ask. Debora would just roll her eyes and say nothing as she fixed me something to eat for dinner. She was only 9 or 10 years old around at this time, but as I reminisce about these days, she seemed like a teenager when she was hanging out with Cassandra or doing chores. But by the time we were getting ready for bed, she would be back to listening to records with me and laughing about something silly. That's when she would allow herself to be a kid again.

After school each day and on the weekends, we would go to cheerleading practice. Our squad was called the Angels and we cheered for the neighborhood's little league football team, The Saints. Most of the girls were Debora's age, and I was the baby of the group. I was shocked when I tried out and got in, no other first grader even tried out. I only did because Marie would not allow Debora to without me. But I was so glad I did. My teammates treated me like their little sister, encouraging me when I got frustrated and cried because I couldn't get the steps. They would pull me to the side and show me the steps after practice, slower than how we were taught by our instructor. Debora and I practiced at home all the time too. Being Angels made our bond even tighter. We knew we were a part of something special, together, and we carried ourselves as such.

Marie seemed to have enjoyed supporting it too, or at least she didn't hate it. Without complaining, she came up with the money for our uniforms and always made sure we had the money for the trips to our away games. She never showed up for a game but she did take us shopping. The most stressful part about this was trying to find the very specific items listed on our cheer contracts. I can remember Marie screaming at us in frustration in Kmart because finding nude stockings that matched our skin tones, a uniform requirement, was impossible. She told us we would just have to quit. We would do no such thing. There were a few games Debora and I went to bare-legged in the cold because Marie gave up on the hunt—and understandably so. There was no such thing as nude stockings for black girls. We eventually learned from the other moms that coffee was the best color to get. At some point, during weeks of practice and shopping and trying to convince Marie to let us stay on the team, we gradually acquired all the necessary items. We looked like professionals; everything was so new, clean, and fresh. I used to stare at all of it in the mirror—hunter green and white pleated skirts, white turtlenecks that went under our cheer jerseys, thick green and white tube socks, mismatched in style, and white sneakers. We wore our hair in ponytails held by green and white ballies. And I just busted with excitement the first time I got to hold our green and white pompoms. I got beside myself and started to think we were the most important thing in Wadsworth. It certainly was the most important thing in my life at the time.

We practiced every single day and eventually got selected to compete in the first round of a local cheerleading tournament. It was bigger than life to me. I can't remember if it was in an arena or stadium or just a local gym, but it seemed to be a massive space, maybe because I was so small. The bleachers were filled with people, and when I tried to see how far back the audience was, I was blinded by bright lights. Cameras and announcers were there, and I screamed to my big sister, "Are we gonna be on TV?" Debora said we probably were but not to get too excited.

Our team didn't display a lot of technique in the few rounds we competed in. We hadn't practiced any flips, pyramids, or jumps. Every other team there had all of that in their routine. We had songs and steps, closer to what would be considered a drill team. And most importantly, we had spirit. So much so that we won the Spirit Award in what would be our first and last competition.

UNRAVEL

The prize was a trophy for each team member. I couldn't believe we were leaving with actual trophies—trophies of a gold cheerleader, pompom in hand, one leg raised and chest sticking out in pride. I stared at my trophy for days, slept with it, shined it—loved it. I had never won anything before. I had never gotten rewarded for hard work and dedication. That trophy represented something I had never experienced before it was mine—pride.

A few years after we had won those trophies, Marie packed them up and sent them to Haiti. I guess as some sort of gift to family she had left behind. Debora and I were devastated. I still can't understand what the joy would be for someone living in Haiti to receive a trophy I had worked so hard to earn. As much as we tried, Marie never took notice of our hard work. Nonetheless, our cheerleading days were probably my best days growing up. In fact, all our early days at Wadsworth were the best of my childhood. No one was touching us, and I stayed out of The Dark for a nice long stretch, days on end.

I credit Marie's effort at trying to be a better mom for our better days. She seemed less angry and tried to assimilate to Wadsworth norms. In Germantown, she was surrounded by poverty, and it overshadowed all her experiences. She was also only around Haitian people, and the influence of the culture held tight. Since leaving Rittenhouse, she had more access to American people and began engaging in the leisure activities she observed them doing like taking trips to the mall, even if she didn't buy anything, and going to the beauty salon to get her hair and nails done. She started going out to restaurants with co-workers, who were now becoming her friends.

Marie even tried to give us our first Thanksgiving. She made a turkey and all the sides commonly found in traditional black family Thanksgiving dinners: baked mac and cheese, collard greens, sweet potatoes, cornbread, and more. This was so different from the Haitian meals of red beans and rice and stewed chicken that I was so very used to. She dressed the table really nicely and set it for four. Gustave didn't come home in time for dinner. I think that may have been why after she put all the food out, Marie just went to bed. Debora and I made our plates, and I enjoyed every bit of my food, not thinking twice about Marie or Gustave. "You like it?" I asked Debora. She nodded, mouth full. I smiled and kept eating.

Gustave showed up the next morning.

Chapter 12
Rhythm of the Night

A few months into living at Wadsworth, cable had just come out and we could afford our very own box. Debora and I spent a majority of our time getting lost in countless hours of MTV videos. I got lost in the wonderment of how the sidewalk lit up as Michael Jackson walked on it. I wanted to be in those videos with my idol Janet Jackson; I wanted to know what an escapade was. What was all this talk about dancing my troubles away? I was discovering that there was some sort of magic in dancing. DeBarge sang it, and it started to make sense to me: *When it feels like the world is on your shoulders and all of the madness has got you going crazy... I know a place where we can dance the whole night away...*

I was never bored, thanks to music and music videos. And thank goodness because once our cheer season was over, there really wasn't much else to do.

Marie would sleep all day since she worked overnight. Towards the evening she would wake up and cook dinner, shower, and get dressed for work. I loved watching my mom get dressed for work. She took her time, laying out her uniform and white stockings across her bed. I hung around her room while she dressed just to get a whiff of her shower gel and fancy body crème. Sitting on her dresser were the Imari perfume products that all came in the burgundy packaging which she faithfully purchased from Avon. To this day, it's one of my favorite scents.

Debora still had a ton of responsibility on her shoulders. She was still in charge of me and waking Marie up in time for work. She now had the added job of ironing Marie's uniform. And those uniforms were crisp white! God forbid she got something on them or that they weren't perfectly smooth. Debora was still screamed at constantly, even more than before, if that was possible. And the yelling wasn't directed only at Debora anymore, Marie screamed at me too. I still couldn't understand creole at this point so I never really knew why we were being yelled at. All I knew was that Debora was always doing something wrong. That's why when Marie did leave for work, Debora was her happiest. She was free to watch music videos all night.

Marie and Gustave started to have arguments. It seemed like with each argument, the intensity of their body language and the volume of their voices grew. A few times when Marie was off from work, Gustave would come in drunk in the middle of the night and Marie would interrogate. When the argument escalated to its peak of Marie's rage, Debora and I would be awakened from our peaceful sleep by her screams and loud crashing bangs from the living room or their bedroom. We lay in our shared bed, clenching to each other in fear from all the noises. We would scream in terror, "God No! Please!" Glass shattering, furniture breaking, and my mother's body being slammed into the walls of what was supposed to be our safer home; these were the noises we'd hear as we screamed out for God's mercy.

UNRAVEL

The one time we ventured out of the bedroom during these violent nights, my mother told Debora to call 911. Marie knew Debora would always back her up, no matter what. While Debora tried to follow confusing screams of orders to clean up, call the police, or go fetch something, I slowly tiptoed out of our room to survey what was happening. I was petrified as I started towards the light in the living room. As I moved down the dark hallway, I could feel myself slipping. I wanted to go into the nothing, The Dark. But as I crept, a beat came to me...

... to the beat of the rhythm of the night, dance until the morning light.

I heard the music in my head and I stopped. Then I took a few more steps and stopped in the middle of the hall. I heard no one and saw no one. It felt like I had been listening to Marie being beaten for hours and now there was silence. *She must be dead*, I thought. I cried a little and froze. I clenched my eyes really tight, still standing in the middle of the hall.

... forget about the worries on your mind, you can leave them all behind.

I tiptoed some more. And then fear took over. I thought about what she might look like dead and I stopped again...

... tonight is gonna be a night like you've never known. We're gonna have a good time the whole night long...

I wiped my tears and found my courage again. Shushing myself, I tiptoed a little more until finally, I was standing in the light of the living room looking for my mother's body.

... Laaa la la la...

My eyes quickly scanned the whole of the apartment of Wadsworth Ave.

... the music's playing, it's a celebration...

The front door was open and most of the light in the apartment came from the stairwell of the complex. I saw Marie's shoes at different ends of the apartment, blood on the floor, and Gustave seated at the table smoking a cigarette. Marie was nowhere to be found.

I tried to find the beat again...

... forget about the worries on your mind, to the beat of the rhythm of the night, oh baby... forget about the worries on your mind...

Suddenly my loud thoughts drowned out the music that was keeping me present. *What happens when people die? Do they just go away?* With these questions and no one to answer them, no one to comfort me or reassure me everything was going to be okay, I turned and walked back into my room. I believed my mother was gone and all I could do was cry myself to sleep. I shook uncontrollably until I passed out, going into The Dark.

The rhythm that night was gone.

The next morning Debora woke me up for school. "Hurry up so mommy can do your hair" she snapped at me.

She's alive! This was my only thought.

As I brought my mother the comb, brush, and grease for her to do my hair for school, I walked up to a face I did not recognize. *What happened to my mommy's face?* I handed her the comb.

"Sit down," she said as she turned to me while putting out her cigarette.

I understood this to mean, *"Don't ask me no questions. I'm fine."*

She did my hair, and I cried. Not for the usual reason, which was because it hurt to get my hair done, but because my mother's

UNRAVEL

face looked like it hurt. I remembered how dark it was only hours before, how lost I was with a dead mother. Now, I couldn't help but be grateful that she was still here with me. She wasn't dead now, and I felt complete. I had my mom, I had my sister, and I always had my dark place to disappear to. I knew I would be okay.

After about a year and a half at Wadsworth, Marie and Gustave, for reasons I didn't know, decided it was time for us to move again. I was happy for it. The violence that stained the walls of the apartment on Wadsworth made the place feel less liberating. It was becoming just as suffocating and anxiety inducing as Rittenhouse. I hated being nervous and scared all the time, always holding my breath for when Marie would get beat up by Gustave or have a fit of rage. I had my first real break from it when we first moved into the apartment and I thought that moving again would mean getting another break. I wanted the newness of the first day we moved in, how I felt when I saw the color tree out the front window. Now when I looked out that window, all I saw were bare branches, no more color—the withered imagination of a little girl who was once filled with so much hope.

Chapter 13
Somers Road

With a new address came a new school. We were transferred out of McCloskey in the middle of the year and I had to finish up the 2nd grade at Penny Packer Elementary School. As my sister and I walked the few blocks to school we would pass the library and Papi stores. Gustave made sure I was never in short supply of dollars or quarters so that we could stop in for candy and snacks. Marie and Gustave were fighting less, and things were starting to look up again, just like they did when we first moved into Wadsworth. Feelings of being a kid started to creep back in; laughing and playing started to feel okay again.

Marie was still working double shifts at the nursing home, and Gustave was still always in and out. For the most part it was me and my big sis. The peace we found was short lived, but while it lasted, Debora and I went into ourselves. We never talked about the past. We didn't mention the beatings we watched Marie take from her lover, or the beatings that we watched each other take from her. We avoided discussion of men stealing our innocence. We never mentioned the terrors, The Monsters, and the violations. And it was good to suppress these things. For now, we simply did not have the ability to process them. Our brains were still growing; those parts weren't developed. For now, our days went quiet. We did our chores, we went to school, and we did our homework.

For now, we walked on eggshells, making sure we did not wake up the rage that was sleeping in Marie.

For now, like always, we did what good little girls did.

But later, we found out the real reason we moved into The Bigger House on Somers Road. And everything changed.

The house we moved into on Somers Road was the biggest house we had lived in up to that point. And once again, it was all ours. Three bedrooms, a living room, a dining room, and a kitchen was just right for Marie, Gustave, Debora, and me. The kitchen had a little shed in the back, and we had a big basement and a front porch. Our very own porch.

But all of this, as it turned out, was not just for us. We moved to The Bigger House on Somers Road so that Gustave could achieve his dreams of having *his* children come to the land of opportunity. All this time, through all the fights, yelling, and staying in a miserable relationship, it all came down to this: Gustave saw opportunity in Marie, a means to a better life for his children. Gustave did not work much, but he needed the funds to send for his kids and he needed a house for them to live in when they arrived from Haiti. Marie's endless hours of working doubles provided it all.

Gene was the first to come. Gene was Gustave's eldest son—twice Debora's age—and it did not take long for him to fit in with my sister and me. He was like a big brother or cool uncle. He didn't need much from our parents and within the first few months of him moving in, he quickly learned English, went to trade school, and got a job as a cook in a fancy restaurant downtown. He treated us a lot like Gustave treated us, but better because he didn't fight with our mom. He took us to the park

UNRAVEL

and to the movies. He bought us Disney records, more music I got lost in. Gene never violated us and was always kind. He was drama free. So I wasn't too concerned when Yanny, Gustave's oldest daughter, came to live with us on Somers Road.

But Yanny was different. She was not like a big sister or cool aunt. Not the least bit—unless your big sister or cool aunt was a wicked witch. She was close in age with Gene and she made her presence known. She took charge when Marie was at work and Gustave was out. She felt like an ugly stepsister and made things miserable for Debora and me, always yelling and making us clean things that weren't dirty. We had to scrub a clean bathtub, wipe down spotless walls, or rewash silverware already put away. She called us names like "lazy" and "dumb" and told us we were spoiled bratty girls who would never find good husbands. I felt green eyes on me whenever she was around. Resentment and insecurity projected from her every insult.

Marie told us to be respectful, so we just took the insults and the side eyes. All of a sudden, I was interested in learning creole. "What did she say?" I would ask Debora as we left rooms Yanny walked into. Debora always translated the insults under her breath but told me not to listen. Her insults bothered me, and her presence made Somers Road cold. But Yanny was a delight compared to what was coming.

In a matter of months we were outnumbered. Gustave sent for more of his children in Haiti. Holston, Rita, and Edman all came at the same time. They were closer to Debora's age and came to go to grade school in America. Holston and Rita would go to Penny Packer with us, and Edman would go to the middle school grades above us. At first, we were like a family, eating together at the table, waiting for each other in the mornings so we could all go to school together, and then walking home after. Debora looked out for them in school, checking in with their teachers, because she knew they knew very little English. We helped them with their homework and always asked if they understood what we were saying to them before we walked away from conversations. I quickly learned to speak creole, and Debora no longer had to translate for me.

The number of children in the house drove my mother to be less patient and just meaner than ever. We barely saw Marie anymore and when we did it was because we were all getting in trouble for something. Something was broken, or missing, and or not cleaned. The truth never came out about who did what, so we all got beat. Debora and I grew resentful because one of them was usually the culprit. But we never knew how to tell. Before long, a divide started, and jealousy ensued. Rita and Yanny became territorial with their father and the house. Debora receded even more into herself, ever the more distant.

I was in trouble more than I was before. I began having uncontrollable impulses that grew stronger and stranger. Things in the house felt totally out of control, and I started to lose control of myself—or at least of what little control a seven year old has. I started having disturbing thoughts about wanting to feel pain. My thoughts would get so overwhelming that I would pinch myself really hard in an attempt to quiet them. Then, my thoughts started becoming behaviors that were downright wrong. I engaged in behaviors that made me feel something, anything, besides the anguish of my overwhelming thoughts. There was a cat in the house. I wouldn't say it was our pet because people treated pets like they are a part of the family. This cat was just in the house. We never named it, and it was mistreated. Gustave's children threw the cat around the house, did cruel experiments on it, and otherwise tortured the poor thing. I felt bad for the cat, so I wanted to show it love, the way my dad had showed me love. I missed my dad. The cat was not the only thing I handled inappropriately. When I was alone, I explored sexual feelings and when I remembered where those feelings came from, I would smack myself, pinch my skin near my privates until it bled, and fantasize about cutting into it. When I wasn't alone, I picked at the skin around my lips and got yelled at for it daily. Within months I was covered in self-inflicted scratch marks.

As the months went on, all of us began to live as siblings. Bickering and annoying each other. Gene moved out and the boys shared one room for the two of them and all four of us girls shared the other. The master room was for Marie and Gustave. The Big House didn't feel that big anymore.

The boys showed me more attention than the girls and sometimes even made me feel special. I didn't really know what it meant for boys to like girls, but the energy I would get from them reminded me of romantic scenes from movies. *Why were they looking at me like that?* Everyone said they were now my brothers. I never had a brother before, so I wondered what brothers did to their sisters.

I made the mistake of venturing into the boys' room one night and found myself alone with Holston. I sat on his bed, and he leaned in for a kiss. I was thrown off. *What was that? No one had ever tried to kiss me on the mouth!* I turned away, and in that moment, I realized I had some power, power to reject. It was the first time I could do it, and so I did. Holston got aggressive and pulled me in to touch me. He was aroused and tried to press himself up against me. I pulled away, and he jumped back and laughed like it was joke. I got angry and left the room. My little heart was pounding. *What had just happened? Am I going to get in trouble now for embarrassing him? Did I do something wrong?* Even though it was the first time I had fought against being violated, I was more afraid about someone finding out than I was proud that I said no. Once again, I did what I was trained to do: tell no one.

My secrets had no end.

In the girls' room there were two beds. Debora and I slept in one while the other sisters slept in the other. Yanny and Rita were two peas in the pod. They were relentless with their insults. They called us dirty and ugly and laughed at any troubles that came to us. If we got yelled at, they were filled with glee. If there were whoopings to be handed out, they pushed us up front and they would do anything to make sure we stood out as the troublemakers in the house. They told on us every chance they got. "Felicia left a mess on the table"; "Debbie threw away her food"; Felicia and Debbie came home late from school today."

I was surprised when Rita called me into the boys' room one day to come hang with her. The boys were gone, and Yanny had taken Debora out to get groceries for the house. Gustave was out cruising the streets as he always was, and Marie was where she always was: work. I was prepared to sit alone watching TV until someone got back home because Rita and I were not buddies. Instead though, she called me up and told me to lie in the bed next to her.

"Vein la," she said in creole.

UNRAVEL

"Why?" I asked.

"Cushe la mere di!" Her voice was a bit raised and very stern.

"But I'm not tired," I tried to negotiate.

Maybe I can find that same fight in me that I used against Holston, I thought. *Maybe I can keep protecting myself.* Rita sucked her teeth and rolled her eyes. I knew I didn't want any trouble from her. *Why was it so easy to pull away from Holston but not stand up to Rita?* I didn't care about what Holston thought of me, but Rita, I wanted her to like me. I didn't want to be the butt of her jokes anymore. I didn't want her to get me in trouble with my mom all the time. And she intimidated me. I had no power. I was afraid but I was also tired. I was tired of worrying about who was going to take advantage of me next. I was tired of trying to come up with ways to get out of being touched. I was just seven years old and already mentally exhausted.

I got in the bed next to Rita. We laid still for a while before anything happened. I lay as close to the edge of the bed as possible, facing the wall and away from where Rita lay next to me. I started to shake. A girl had never touched me. But I knew this energy and I thought I knew what was coming. But I didn't know. I knew what men had because they always rubbed it against me or made me hold it. And I knew what girls had because I was a girl. *What will she want me to do with what we had?* I started to tremble. Rita grabbed a peach-colored sheet and covered us from head to toe. She lay behind me and assumed the big-spoon position.

I had on shorts and a t-shirt, and so did she. After she covered us with the sheets, she made her way into my shorts with her hand and started to fondle me. I knew this part well; they all did this. I lay there stiff and petrified, disgusted at the thought that a girl was touching me. I froze. This was not like how I froze when my daddy made me please him. Because then I moved, I was just frozen in my mind, in my insides, dark and gone; I went away when I was with Lorenzo. No, it wasn't the kind of frozen I was with The Monsters at Rittenhouse. No, this was a different kind of frozen.

When she knew I was good and frozen, she turned me over and climbed on top of me. It only took her a couple of minutes to finish her business. Climaxed and satisfied, she got off from me, moved the sheets off of us, and left the room without a word. I lay there frozen, in shock and completely confused about what I should do next. I slid off the bed and on to the floor. I picked the skin around nails and pinched at my mouth, squeezing until it bled. *What have I just done?* Shame overcame me, and I wondered why there was no power like there was with Holston. I wanted to die in that moment. But then I wanted my mom. I wanted my sister. I wanted comfort. I wanted anything but the shame and disgust I felt sitting on that floor, lost and confused. All alone and with no one to comfort me, I simply went where I knew to go; into The Dark. I disappeared.

When I came back, I heard the front door slam shut. Life came back to me; my heart was beating again. I heard my sister's footsteps. She went in our room, and I rushed in after her. I lay in our bed and pretended to go to sleep while she put away some of the things they bought from the store. "I'm going downstairs to put away the groceries. You okay?" "Mmmhmm," I mumbled from under the covers.

UNRAVEL

The house started to fill with even more sounds as people came home one by one and flooded the house with all kinds of energies. Hours passed, and I pretended to be asleep, listening to every footstep and every voice, wishing I could rejoin the world. But my stomach was twisted, and I started to shake from fear. I was gone again. I don't know where I went, but when I was back, I was numb as ever.

The next morning, Marie was still in bed when I went to ask her for a hug. I remembered the feeling I felt that day in the back of the car after getting my head stitched up. I remembered being comforted by Marie and knowing that she loved me. I remembered she didn't punish me or yell at me when I messed up. I wanted to feel that again and I knew I would if I could just get back in her arms. Then as I stood at her doorway watching her sleep, snoring to the gods, I suddenly realized that I couldn't remember the last time I had hugged her. We didn't hug, and she did not show me any other affection. I was lucky on the days she looked at me with anything other than frustration and disgust. I turned from her door and wondered where I could find the comfort I used to find in her. There were no answers, so I wandered on.

It was common practice in a Haitian upbringing to come home from school, take a *toilette* (bird bath/wash up), change out of school clothes into "house clothes," and then do homework. Once homework was done, we were free to go on the porch or watch TV until dinner. After dinner we had to wash up again and then get ready for bed. This was a new routine for Debora and I and only became the standard after all of Gustave's kids had moved in. We learned the drill quickly and did our best not to mess up. Messing up, missing even one step, meant we would get a beating or had to do extra chores. The pressure and stress to keep up with these demands was enough to make me physically ill. I became extremely thin—seven years old with the weight of a typical four year old. I grew to hate living at Somers Road so much that I had completely lost my appetite. I just stopped eating. Anytime someone noticed, I was threatened with beatings to make me eat. I would throw up and get hit for not finishing my food. I was sad and sick all the time and I wanted to run away from home. I wanted to die. And I wasn't the only one who had a particular disdain for our life on Somers Road.

After Gene moved out, Edman became the oldest boy in the house. He looked exactly like his father, spitting image. And he liked to break the rules. Edman would cut school, use his bus fare money for everything else but getting to school, and come home at all times of the night. Edman would only get away with his rule breaking until Gustave got home; then there was hell to pay.

The typical beatings we got were with a belt or an extension cord, and there was an occasional sandal here and there. We normally got about 5 to 10 good lashes, about a good full minute's worth of whips, depending on how still we were. A bad beating would be more dramatic. Those were the ones when conversations happened in between, an interrogation. If we were deemed to be lying, a minute-long beating could turn into three or four of those one-minute rounds in a beating session, interrogation happening between each round. These rounds continued until the adult giving the beating was satisfied with the answers to their questions. I remember there being times when I just lied in the end, just so I could stop getting hit. I told the truth in the beginning but was tortured into lying because my mother or Yanny didn't believe the truth.

On occasion, a really bad whooping escalated into an outright chase around the house. I have memories of Holton doing laps around the house, up and down the stairs, trying to outrun Gustave with a belt in his hand. Gustave never beat Debora or me, but his kids were a different story. Beatings in our house were so common, we would get up to get them like we got up to do some chore we hated, huffing and puffing and eventually just accepting it as the norm. At some point, Edman became so numb to our beatings that he just shrugged them off. He had lost the fear that was normally associated with them, the fear we all typically displayed with tears or begging for an alternative punishment. Edman's fear seemed to dissipate, as if he had been pushed to his limit.

Edman started to rebel against Gustave's authority and sized him up every chance he got, testing his boundaries. He had a particular anger towards Gustave and almost dared him to try and discipline him. I think this had less to do with our family's strict ways and the beating and more to do with the pain and resentment Edman was harboring from watching the father he adored move away to another country while he was just a little boy. Then, he was finally reunited with Gustave only to find out his beloved father was living with a whole other family the entire time, shacked up with another woman, a woman who was not his mother. The truth was Gustave was still married to the mother of his children, who was still in Haiti. Marie was his girlfriend.

Gustave took notice that he was becoming powerless in controlling Edman and became more and more violent towards him. When whooping him with a belt just wouldn't work, Gustave resorted to acts that can only be described as attempted murder.

One cold, rainy fall day when Marie was at work and Gustave at home, I heard him talking to someone on the phone about how he had gotten a call from Edman's school saying that Edman had been missing a lot of days. I sat up from the couch and started pinching my skin when I saw Gustave pacing in and out the house and talking to himself in creole. My anxiety was beyond me. Gustave kept cursing and rambling on and on—something about giving Edman money for school tokens for the bus but him never getting the tokens or getting on the bus. Gustave made it clear that this was the last straw. I don't know why this was the last straw but I do know I wished I had never witnessed it breaking the camel's back, or Edman's.

The sun started to set. *Why is he so late? Why out of all days would he come home so late TODAY!?* I thought as I bit my nails and stared at the door. Gustave retreated into the basement; none of us knew why. Everyone but Marie was home and tried to act like they were preoccupied, but you could feel the anticipation, the fear—the wishes that today would be the day he just ran away. *Don't come home, Edman.* I wanted to shit myself. I knew what it felt like to get in trouble when you walked through the door. I knew that feeling of your stomach twisting because you knew the belt was coming. They ask you questions; they torture you with the questions, and then they let you know how much pain you are about to experience. When Marie used to tell me the way Haitian kids got whipped when she was growing up, I never

UNRAVEL

imagined the fear of impending doom that could twist your insides into unyielding knots.

Finally, a key in the door. When I saw the knob turn, I rushed to it. My little legs ran to warn Edman, but my brain forgot to make the rest of me work. I opened the door and just stood there, looking up at him, my eyes filled with worry and my mouth open, frozen.

"Where's everybody?" Edman asked.

I looked around and saw an empty living room. "Gustave is home," I responded in a panicked voice, eyes wide. Edman shrugged and started to put his things down. I could tell he was nervous, but he wasn't afraid. Not like I was. Soon everyone came through the living room, just to see how it would go down. Holston pretended to want to see what was on TV as he plopped down on the couch. Debora shouted some directions at me about doing my homework from the stairwell while Yanny and Rita walked to and from the kitchen, pretending to fix food. Then Gustave emerged from the basement with a cigarette in one hand and something else in the other. It was a 2x4 piece of hard wood, with nails. Gustave asked Edman where he had been. Edman looked like he was torn between believing his dad may actually use that 2x4 and saying something clever to test him. He chose to be a wise guy.

"School, where else?"

"Liar," Gustave growled.

"Man…. Whatever, I went to school."

"Where are your tokens?" Gustave shot back. Edman sucked his teeth and attempted to walk away. Gustave grabbed him by his neck and told him he had one more chance or he was going to teach him how to respect his father. Edman called his bluff. He rolled his eyes and yanked himself away from Gustave, ready to put up a fight. What happened next was something no one should ever witness, especially not a child.

I watched Edman's skin being torn apart by a board with nails in it, blow by blow. I began to wail. When Gustave noticed we were all watching and Yanny tried to intervene, saying that Edman clearly had had enough, Gustave moved the beating into the basement, where we couldn't witness the bloodshed and no one could stop him from killing his son.

Gustave threw his son down the stairs, and we continued to hear the most gruesome cries a teenage boy could possibly get out. Gustave came back upstairs, his hands and clothes stained with blood. Debora was on the phone with Marie by this point, asking if she should call the police because Gustave had lost it. Then she hung up and didn't pick it up again. I guess the answer was no. Gustave took a shower, grabbed a beer and a pack of cigarettes, and was gone for the night, then days. Edman did not emerge from the basement. Rita and Yanny went down to help care for his wounds, both the internal and external ones.

The next day, Edman moved into the basement, and we barely ever saw him from that night on until one day he just disappeared. I started to miss him. Before he disappeared, he would buy me Twizzlers and watch cartoons with me. After I was amped up on sugar, he would do what big brothers did: toss me around, using my body for karate and wrestling experiments. He was gentle, but there was always a lot of horseplay, and tickling. When I would laugh and tighten my body, he touched my privates. When I straddled him as he tickled me, I could feel him erect. He had no idea that I was a pro at being sexually abused by then and knew exactly how to make him okay with what he was doing. I acted like a little girl that was totally oblivious to him taking advantage of our play time. I wasn't disgusted with Edman and somehow reasoned with myself that he wasn't as bad as everyone else. He wanted me to laugh and be happy. At least he wasn't being outright forceful like the others had been.

After Edman was banished to the basement, Somers Road became a house even more divided. Marie began to take notice of the withdrawal Debora had been displaying since Gustave's kids moved in, and how now she almost never spoke. She called us into her room for private conversations and asked us if we were okay. We just said yes because we believed that's what we were supposed to say. By now, we were trained to answer questions according to what we thought she wanted to hear in order not to get hit. Marie may have been looking for reasons to pull away from Gustave and his kids, or she may have actually cared about our wellbeing; either way, I think she knew we were lying when we said we were okay and began to show us favor. We drew closer to her, and her to us.

Meanwhile, Gustave gave less and less attention to Marie. Finally, she was fed up. She started to question why she was even sticking around anymore. For everything she had done for him, all the money and time she sacrificed to provide a better life for him and his children, there was no return, and Marie wanted to cash in.

The move was as abrupt as a move could be. No planning and even less warning. After an argument with Gustave about how unfair he had been towards her, Marie ordered us to put all our things in garbage bags. With just our clothes and a few knick knacks, we were headed out the door. With all the rushing, yelling, and intense energy surrounding us packing our things, I panicked at the idea of never coming back to that house and was overcome with racing thoughts. My emotions were so mixed up. I was going to miss my "step brothers and sisters." But I hated them and I wanted them to pay for hurting me. I loved being a part of a family, but I just wanted to be with the only two people I knew could protect me, my mom and my big sister. I loved being in a big house. But there was no room here.

Being all mixed up made me feel like my world was being pulled from under me. I had no foundation and even less protection. I floated and I was gone. I don't know where I went but when I came back, the three of us were living in a bedroom at a stranger's house. One day we were living with a whole other group of people as a dysfunctional family and the next, it was all over. Finally, it was just Marie, Debora, and me.

Chapter 14
68th Ave

We moved into a room in a nice house on 68th Ave in a section of Philadelphia known as West Oak Lane. It was about 20 minutes from Somers Road, two short bus rides away. The area was considered to be a black middle-class family neighborhood, nice and safe. And the owners of the house were nice too: a Haitian couple who were new to the states and just starting a family. They were kind to us, and everyone pretty much stayed out of each other's way.

Sharing a room with Marie and Debora wasn't easy. Marie's snoring was at a devastating volume, and sleeping was impossible. She was gaining a lot of weight, and her breathing was different—but she was still strong, beautiful, and fierce. I liked her even more now because after leaving Gustave, she was standing with her head a little higher.

After the breakup, Marie and Gustave both pretended to be caring parents to all nine of us. Both Gustave and Gene picked up Debora and I for visits. We spent time with Rita and Holston at Gustave's new two-bedroom apartment. Even then, he left us while he went and did whatever it was he did in the streets of Philadelphia, "taking care of business" as he called it. We would just sit on the couch in his very cramped living room for a few hours, silently watching TV, waiting for Gustave to return, which he did only to take us back home. I guess Gustave thought he was giving us a chance to continue our sibling-like relationships. We all never even looked at each other in the face.

Those visits didn't last long, maybe once weekly for a month or two. Marie tried to stay close to Gustave's kids too. She tried to help Edman as best she could by giving him leads on jobs or telling him about a school program whenever he called her. He graciously thanked her but never followed up on her suggestions. He was a homeless teen now, couch surfing and staying with relatives from time to time. He always said he wanted to go back to Haiti, I don't know if he ever did.

Marie also spoke with Yanny often and then became close with her sister Dolores, Gustave's middle daughter, the last of his children to come to America and who was living with Gene at the time. She had moved in with him when she first got to America, about a month before we moved out of Somers Road. Gene had a live-in girlfriend, and she and Dolores did not get along. Marie just couldn't help being helpful and suggested that she rent a room in the house on 68th Ave.

Dolores rented the finished attic and moved in only weeks after we started living there. Her space, with its private bath, was large in comparison to the one room and tiny bathroom I was sharing with Marie and Debora. I don't know how she could afford to move into the largest private space of the house because Dolores did not work; she spent all her time with us. She didn't seem to have much of a social life either. She was in her early twenties and had a small frame but a manly build. She looked strong. Her skin was beautifully toned, a shade darker than

UNRAVEL

Marie's. Her eyes were like amber flames, and when I looked into them, I shivered.

Marie was relieved to have someone there to watch after her children. Ever since Rittenhouse, she believed she was so fortunate to have live-in babysitters. She didn't want to take this opportunity for granted. "Look after my girls, and I'll take care of what you need," she told Dolores. Dolores used this as an advantage to be supported while she got adjusted to life in America. She saw it as a real job, a job she took way too seriously. She acted as if she was our prison guard. She watched us like a hawk and questioned our every move. Debora and I had not changed. We were the well-behaved Roche girls: Marie's daughters, cute and quiet. Debora, the older and sterner one; Felicia, the small one with sweet cheeks who was ready to please. All the while, what we really were, were two little girls scared shitless, too scared to do anything, ever.

The measures Dolores took to enforce her control were unwavering, relentless, and soul crushing. Nothing we did was right. She timed the minutes it took to walk home from school. If I got home 15 minutes after what she timed as a 10-minute walk, I was in a heap of trouble. She would yank me as soon as I got through the door and tell me I was on big trouble for being late. I believed her. I wasn't allowed to watch TV or go outside; I had to just sit in our room, do my homework, and wait for bed, staring at the walls, nervous about what would happen when Marie got home. Dolores would tell me my mother would beat me once she found out I didn't come straight home from school. I begged her not to tell. She agreed as long as I did everything she told me to do for the rest of the day. When I wasn't sitting in the room, I was washing dishes or doing some other chore Dolores had assigned. The Haitian couple we were renting from thought I was such a good little helper around the house.

Dolores wasn't as tough on Debora as she was on me, not at first anyway. She almost ignored Debora and put all her focus on me. She was obsessed with my hygiene. I had to brush my teeth for five minutes exactly; otherwise, I would be yelled at and called a pig. "Did you wash your privates when you got home? Did you wash up before you ate? Did you pray your filth away before you laid down? It's 8:00 a.m. on a Saturday; why aren't you up cleaning?" There was no rest, no fun, and flaming eyes always on me.

When Marie was home, it was like a vacation day. I could lie in her room and watch TV. I could play outside, feeling the sun on my skin and taking in the wind. I would sit outside, away from Dolores, and just be. Every once in a while, Debora would join me on the front stoop and show me how to play the big kid hand games like "numbers"—it took me weeks to get to 10. Debora's hand game lessons could take hours at a time, and I was happy to do anything to escape the gut-wrenching fear from knowing what I had to return to. Marie never took more than a day off at a time; it would only be a quick break. By the next day, I would be back under Dolores' command.

When we first moved to 68th Ave, I was midway through the 3rd grade and transferred to Ellwood lower school. The following year for 4th grade, I moved to a new building five blocks away at Elwood upper school. The longer distance allowed me some free time after school because Dolores believed it took 20 minutes longer than it actually took me to walk home now. I also had

UNRAVEL

more projects in the 4th grade, so I was allowed to meet Debora at the local library more often too. Debora was in middle school and, for the first time, traveling somewhere different from me every day. She took public transportation to school, and I was in awe. I thought my sister was all grown up.

I wanted to be grown up too. I started to tell stories to myself and to my 4th grade classmates as a means of escaping my reality and portraying myself as such. I told the kids my family was different because we were Haitian and we knew how to do voodoo. I noticed this frightened some of them. I liked it.

I stole cigarettes from Marie and snuck them into my book bag from time to time. After school, I would walk slowly down the block with an unlit cigarette in my mouth. Almost all the kids in the neighborhood went to the Papi store before or after school to buy chips or candy. Instead of buying penny candy, some days I would buy a 5-cent matchbook, in front of as many kids as possible. I was determined to make the other kids believe I actually smoked cigarettes, that I had real-life grownup stress, and that I was a serious person. They didn't know I never actually lit a single one.

These bizarre behaviors made most of my classmates pretty uncomfortable around me. But there was one girl who found me interesting. Perhaps she got a good laugh from my outlandish stories, or maybe she was just intrigued. But she would hang on to my every word and allowed me to indulge her. "I'm pregnant and it hurts," I lied to her one day as we were walking to the local library from school.

"Who the daddy?"

"This boy I had sex with. But he don't want the baby, so I don't know what Imma do. But it really, really hurts!" I grunted as I pushed out my stomach as far as it would go. I could tell this girl really believed me, and I started to believe myself. Reality set in when I remembered that I was walking to the library to meet up with Debora. I had to figure out a way to get out of this ginormous lie. I didn't want her to ask my sister if I was really pregnant, so I came up with a plan. When we got to the library, I went to the bathroom and stayed in there for probably 15 minutes, pretending to be sick. "I'm not pregnant no more," I told the girl when I emerged, sitting down with her at a table.

"How that happen?" she asked, sucking her teeth.

"Stop asking me so many questions. I don't want to talk about it!"

I walked away from the girl and over to my sister and her friends. I pulled Debora to the side and asked, "How you find how to have a baby in the encyclopedia?" I spent the rest of that afternoon reading about just that.

Dolores' mental and emotional abuse continued the whole year and half we lived at 68th Ave and peaked at the halfway point. As Dolores' control increased, our access to Marie decreased. We barely saw her and were almost never allowed in her room. There was a lock placed on the door when she wasn't home, and when she was home, Dolores stood guard. "Leave your mom alone!" she would threaten. When Marie worked the night shift, her room was free, but I was still forced to sleep in the attic with Dolores. Debora got the big bed in Marie's room, because she was older and I had to respect that, according to Dolores.

UNRAVEL

But I would have given anything just to be safe in that room with my sister at night. Dolores used the time alone with me in the attic to her advantage. She and Rita had the same methods. The only difference was that Dolores would wait until I was asleep to molest me, but I only pretended to be asleep. It was easier to act like I was asleep than to face it. I was older now and knew I should be ashamed and embarrassed. But what was I going to do, confront her? No, I wasn't. I never did before, and that wasn't about to change just because I was older.

Marie started to show real signs of resentment for what was now a life of a hardworking, single, and lonely woman. She stopped going to the mall. She stopped going to restaurants with her newfound friends, her co-workers. She didn't get her hair and nails done anymore and she seemed exhausted all the time. All she did was work doubles, sleep, repeat. "Sometimes I hate ya'll" were the words she used to express this resentment whenever we spent more than a few hours together. We were just reminders of her responsibilities, the reason all she did was work. I never believed my mother hated me. I knew she was just tired and frustrated. But that didn't change the fact that it hurt like hell to hear it.

After almost two years on 68th Ave, the time had come when we somehow had overstayed our welcome. The Nice Haitian Couple came up with a story about there no longer being enough room for us. When Marie protested and said she needed more time to stay, they forced us out by other means. There was no formal lease or contract between Marie and the homeowners, just a verbal agreement that we could stay as long as Marie paid her rent. With no legal way to evict us, they simply turned off our water supply. They claimed the city did this and they didn't know when it would be back on. After two days without water, Marie confronted The Nice Haitian Couple because she noticed they conveniently did have access to water. They were turning the main supply on and off on an as-needed basis. When she made the accusation that they were turning the water off on purpose, they laughed at her. Marie retaliated in screams and curses, telling them her life was not a joke. She screamed about how she had two daughters who needed a place to stay, it was the middle of winter, and they needed hot running water. She screamed about how she was a tenant who had paid her rent and she demanded they respect that.

The Nice Haitian Couple was not amused with Marie's screams and demands. They told her to move out immediately. When she refused, the next day they changed the locks so she couldn't get in after her shift at work. In the cold of a winter's night, with feet of snow covering the ground, Marie found herself, once again, homeless and alone.

Chapter 15
Marie's Home

The first time Marie found herself homeless and alone, she had just arrived to America. It was 1978. A dear friend of hers had made arrangements for to stay in New York with his relative, but this person did not take too well to Marie's high-status demeanor. She may have been wealthy and carefree in Haiti, but in NY, she needed to take a look around and take notice of where she was.

The apartment she was staying in was tiny and not the cleanest. The dust bothered Marie, but she didn't do anything about it. She wasn't lazy, but she never had to clean up for herself. In Haiti, when she got up from the table someone cleared her setting. She never had to worry about a clean plate or clean underwear. When she needed them, they were just there. So, when her new and very temporary roommate saw her leave messes and became less than kind about it, Marie was confused. *What is her problem?* Marie just figured the girl didn't like her. The stay only lasted a week before she was asked to leave. Marie left the displeased roommate and checked into motels by the week. Soon she realized that she was running out of money. After about a month, she felt like she was only just settling in. She needed more time to experience this captivating freedom called America, and she needed more money. So, she set out to find work.

The area was crawling with Haitian people and even more foreigners from other countries. Marie was living in an area where helping immigrants find work *was* a business. At first, Marie did $25-a-day housekeeping jobs that were posted around the city. Then, she made friends with a group of Haitian people at a diner she ate at every night. They all worked at a perfume factory that hired immigrants with IDs and a social security number. Marie wanted to make things more stable and permanent for herself so she gave her last few dollars to a guy who would get her a social security number.

Within a few months of leaving Haiti, Marie got a job and was settling in. She had grasped the street lingo of New York well enough that the mannerisms used to bum a smoke or flirt with a guy came easier than speaking her native tongue. English came pretty easy too.

Marie had been working for the perfume factory only a short time when she started feeling pains and weird stomach movements. The feeling was familiar, but in her mind, there was no way. The only man she had ever been with was far away, left behind in a life she so desperately wanted to escape.

Marie noticed she put on some pounds but no one, not even she, could recognize pregnancy as the culprit. She just didn't look pregnant. She chalked the extra weight up to the fast food she had been eating every day since she had arrived. Time had run so fast since she arrived in the states she hadn't kept up with her period. But the truth was slowly unfolding.

Her friends at work laughed at her when Marie told them that she thought she might be pregnant but in the same breath said she hadn't been with anyone since she left Haiti. "Crazy Marie"

UNRAVEL

became her nickname. Marie started to feel crazy. Finally, during a visit to the local clinic, a nurse took pity on the crazy lady and gave her pregnancy test. "Listen, sugar, whatever man you are trying to trap, it ain't worth it if you have to trap him." Marie resented the nurse but was grateful someone was finally giving her a test.

The idea of trapping a man was the opposite of Marie's intention, and she wished these people only knew all she had been through—all she had already had to bear. Having a baby for a man was the very last desire she had now. No one believed she was already a mother.

"Whelp, lady, you're definitely pregnant," the nurse proclaimed with all surety.

Marie had heard about how people got rid of pregnancies in America. There was no way she could have another baby. She had come so far to get away from all that was holding her back in Haiti. This baby couldn't happen, not now.

The doctor that Marie followed up with thought she was just as crazy as everyone else did when she asked, with all innocence and true curiosity, about an abortion at almost seven months pregnant. After testing her for drugs, the doctor explained to her, through an interpreter, how far along she was and that she, in fact, would be having a baby very soon. Marie was in shock. *How could I have not known for seven months that I was pregnant?*

Marie lost her job at the factory shortly after that. She started to run out of money much quicker than she imagined she could. Budgeting was not something easily grasped by a rich kid in a foreign country. One day, Marie woke up, looked in her wallet, and saw she only had 20 dollars left. That wasn't enough to eat for the day and get a room for the night. *Where will I sleep?* She walked the streets, knocking on the doors of the few friends whose addresses she knew. No one answered. She spent most of that afternoon in the local diner she and her friends frequented, hoping and praying they would come by so she could ask to borrow money or let her crash on their couch. They never showed up. Suddenly pregnant and homeless, Marie had nowhere to go and no choice but to rest on park benches, bus stops, and finally the hard concrete.

For the next few weeks, Marie claimed her spot on the avenue and set it up with all she had: a suitcase, some blankets, and a smile. She maintained her beauty, always staying clean and nicely dressed, washing up in the bathrooms of restaurants and department stores. She ate off of people's unfinished plates at the diner after they left their tables, and the sidewalk is where she laid her head at night.

One night, as she set herself up to sleep, Marie came across a Haitian man who seemed concerned for her safety. "What are you doing here on the street? You look like you will give birth any day," the man asked with a warm look in his eyes.

"I probably will." Marie gave a sweet chuckle and a silly look. Her naive demeanor caught the unsuspecting man off guard. He just couldn't leave her. He told her to grab her things and he brought her to his home for dinner. By the end of the night, Marie had found her way into the man's heart. An instant friendship was sparked, and the man let Marie stay with him while she got ready to bring a new life into the world.

On July 18, 1979, my sister was born.

UNRAVEL

The man Marie was staying with knew he couldn't support her and her baby for long. She had been staying in his home just a few weeks after Debora was born when he started to panic about the situation he was in. His brother and sister-in-law, The Delairs, were visiting from Philadelphia, and he turned to them for advice. Mrs. Delair took one look at helpless Marie with her baby and instantly came up with a solution. She asked Marie if she would be willing to come back to Philadelphia with her and start a new life there. She offered her something no one else had—not a job, not a place to sleep, not food or anything else Marie had been searching for. She offered Marie the one thing she could yet find in America: a home.

On the drive to Philadelphia, Marie stared out the window the entire time, silent, tears streaming down her face, and amazed at how quickly things were changing. In less than a year she left the only home she knew, was completely on her own, and birthed a new life.

What is this thing called life? How had it come to this? Where is it going to take me? She had been through so much that she couldn't imagine going through more. Things had to finally be right. Things would just have to work out now. There was no way they could get worse.

Chapter 16
Nedro Ave

After Marie was kicked out of 68th Ave, Dolores acted as if she was some sort of saint when she told her she would allow Debora and I to stay with her in the attic until Marie found a new place to live. A few days later, Marie moved us into a co-worker's basement where we would stay for the next few months. For some strange reason, Dolores joined us. There was no escaping the hell that was her, until finally the day had come. All the hours Marie had been working were for this moment; for the first time, Marie did something for herself, by herself. She had saved up enough money and taken the steps to purchase her first home.

Our new home was 10 minutes from 68th Ave, one bus ride away, and it was beautiful. The first thing I noticed when we first went to see it was the door: a big heavy wooden door with a gold doorknob and a stained-glass window right in the middle, the colorful ones you see in the church windows. My skinny, nine-year-old legs almost gave in when I stood before that door for the first time, not just because it was so beautiful but because Marie made it clear that it belonged to us. This house was ours. Not like Somers Road where it was kind of Gustave's too. Not like the other places we shared with strangers. Nope, my mom was the queen, and this was our castle. I felt like a princess for the first time in my life and I just knew that everything would be perfect and new. I was so very proud of my mother and I couldn't wait to finally start the life that we had always been waiting for. Not just in a big pretty house, but the life I closed my eyes and prayed for so many nights; the life that I cried myself to sleep for so many times; the life that was just Debora, Marie, and me. Finally, just us.

Walking into the house on Nedro Ave was almost as magical as standing in front of its great big beautiful door. The floor looked like sand as far as I could see. I had never seen such clean floors, wall-to-wall, beautiful light tan carpet. The first room covered in this carpet was a small den area that opened into a big living room. The living room sparkled from the sun shining through the window and bouncing off glass. I looked at my sister, who had just walked in after me with big brown eyes, jaw dropped. "This is a palace!" I exclaimed.

She smiled. "This is nice," she said less enthusiastically, ever the realist. Debora was always careful not to give The Grownups the benefit of the doubt. She knew that if it seemed too good to be true, it was. Still, to hear her agree with me about the house being nice was something good. It felt like permission to be optimistic.

"We are going to love it here! We gonna have our own rooms. This is so nice, we rich now. Mommy is going to be happy now, and we not goin' to be gettin' in trouble and—"

Debora stopped me, "Okay, Felicia."

We both turned to look into the biggest mirror we had ever seen. The entire living room wall was a mirror. In it was the reflection of two little brown girls beaming with hope, reeling from devastation. I held my sister's hand and prayed inside, *God, please let this be real. Please let us be happy.*

UNRAVEL

Next to the mirrored wall was a staircase, which was also covered in the sand-looking carpet. We slowly climbed the stairs, not believing this was truly all ours. Marie came through the door, trailing behind, talking to a Haitian friend who was helping us move in. We ran the rest of the stairs when we heard her coming in; we didn't want her to stop us.

The sand carpet covered the upstairs hallway and ended there. A room was on each end of the hall with a bathroom and another bedroom in between. We looked at each other, giggling with our eyes about which room we were going to run to first. I ran to the master room while Debora checked out the back.

It's so big! was my first thought. The next thing I noticed was my echoed footstep. "Hello." I tried to hear the echo again. The floor was hardwood, and three huge windows canvassed the front of the room. Outside those windows was the roof of the den. "Debora, come here! Come here!" She came strolling in as if she had lived there for years.

"Oh, this is nice," she said as she slowly walked around.

"Come and look at this! It's a roof, but you can go on it," I explained.

"Oh my god, no you can't." She rolled her eyes and turned away from the windows. "But look at this!" she said, changing her tone. The room had two exits, one that led into the hall and one that led into the smaller bedroom next to it. "Now this is cool," she declared.

"Oh wow, I can't believe the rooms are connected! This gonna be my room!" I proclaimed.

"We'll see," Debora said as if she was in charge.

When Marie called our names to come downstairs, my stomach immediately dropped. There was a tone of disappointment in her voice, and I was preparing to hear the worst; that this really wasn't our house and we really weren't moving in. I dragged myself, ready to mope, prepared for the letdown I was used to. We got to the bottom of the stairs, and Marie looked tired, but all she said was to go outside and start helping to move the boxes. She seemed sad that it was only boxes, no furniture. I could care less; looked like we were staying!

The first few weeks we slept on the living room floor. All we had were blankets, a small black and white TV, and each other. I was still the happiest I had ever been in my nine years of life, at least of what I could remember. There was a permanent smile on my face that no one could remove. The first bit of furniture Marie got was a bedroom set, and she set it up in the master bedroom for herself. But since she was still working nights, it became where we slept. A few weeks later, Debora got a bed, and it went in the middle room. I slept in Marie's bed, and Debora in hers. We were apart but still connected with the door open so we could talk with the lights off. "I really like it here, Debora. You like it?"

"Yea," she responded tiredly.

"But Mommy has to work all them shifts just so we can live here," I said with a question in my tone.

"Yea, so?"

"So, I can't be sad that she's not here right?"

"Right."

"But I am sad, and I feel lonely."

"Go to sleep, Felicia."

UNRAVEL

The joy of moving into Nedro lasted only a few months before my anxiety started to creep back up. My nights became sleepless as my mind wondered about all the bad things that used to happen. Things were too quiet now, and it scared me. *When is something bad going to happen?* It had to happen soon; it was too good for too long. Maybe my mom was really going to die, like in my nightmares. It's what I had always feared. Maybe now was the time. Or maybe someone was going to try to get us. *Are we safe?*

My fears were legit. It wasn't long before all-too-familiar havoc came back into our lives. Although I feared something bad happening, I wasn't anticipating it the way Debora was. She never allowed herself to feel the few weeks of joy I felt when we first moved in. She knew something was coming, a storm of some sort. She didn't know when it was coming or how much damage it would cause, but she knew it was coming. She waited for it, and once it arrived, there was no question it was the disaster she expected.

Dolores was back.

Marie needed help, again. The bills and mortgage turned out to be higher than she anticipated. She would never save up enough to buy furniture. Dolores offered to rent a room and look after us, again. Marie saw this as an opportunity and a blessing, again.

The room situation got weird once Dolores moved in. Soon we couldn't tell whose room was whose. Debora did a good job of holding onto the middle room. I slept in there with her on nights Marie didn't work, or I slept with Marie in the front room. Dolores pretty much stayed to herself in the back room, and I avoided her at all cost. She became territorial and put a lock on her door. The only phone in the house was in her room, and she made sure it stayed locked away from us. This may have been Marie's house, but Dolores was making her presence and power known.

Dolores immediately returned to her abusive ways. She would search for things to yell at us about, blowing the smallest mishaps, like spilled milk or leaving a light on, out of proportion. But more often she would just lie. She would yell and hit us for no reason whenever we would come home from an outing. When Marie would come in tired and frustrated from working long hours, Dolores would spew crazy accusations, saying we stayed out past curfew or disrespected her in some way. This infuriated Marie so much that she would lash out and beat us even more than Dolores did. We were now suffering twice the physical punishment we had been before. My sister's anger about how unbelievably unfair this was reminded me of Edman's protest of his injustices. I remembered how he carried himself when he was at his wit's end, when he had had enough. Debora had had enough now too. I noticed she refused to cry whenever we were beat. She stood strong with every lash, waiting to cry when she was alone. She rolled her eyes at Dolores when she started her whipping, looking at her like she was small and insignificant. Watching Debora's body language showed me that Dolores couldn't break her. But Dolores was certainly going to give it her all. And just like with Edman, Debora's protest would be met with a wrath so great, it would change my sister forever.

On a night after working a 16-hour shift, Marie wanted nothing more than to come home, slip out of her uniform, take

UNRAVEL

a hot bath, and sleep. But Dolores found no rest and wanted to make sure none of us did either. Before she could even take off her coat, Marie was subjected to one of Dolores' daily reports. Marie! kite m 'di ou ('let me tell you' in creole) Debora is the worst!"

"Ay yayai!" Marie yelled. "What??? WHAT!!!! What now???"

"You have to do something about Debora! She comes home from school whatever time she wants; she disrespects me and lies about where she's been. Then when I try to tell her what to do, she rolls her eyes and ignores me! I can't discipline her, Marie. She's out of control!"

Marie couldn't engage. She knew the only way to please Dolores was to beat Debora. That's all Dolores wanted. So, Marie beat my sister. She called Debora down from her bedroom into the living room and she beat her, and she beat her, and she beat her. She beat Debora until she was black and blue. The belt dug deep into her young, beautiful brown skin. I listened and I wept thinking about the scars that were forever embedded in my mother's skin, now tough and worn. I hid in Debora's room, standing behind the door, listening to every word, then every scream, then every lash.

Debora came back in the room, red. She didn't look sad. She looked furious. She was breathing so hard, seething with so much unleashed anger, I swear smoke was coming from her ears. With her fist balled up she looked down at her wounds—the bruises and the blood. She looked at me in the shadow, shrugged, and shook her head, as if to say… *What can we do?* She shrugged again, then she looked up to the ceiling, sat on the bed, and started to think. Maybe there was something we *could* do. Parts of me felt like she would finally save us; other parts of me just wanted her to hide away—*Leave. Save yourself, Debora*. She looked at me again, and I knew there was no way she would ever save herself without me. She put on what looked like a new face; it suddenly appeared resolved, like she had come to a conclusion. With calm eyes, she wiped her tears and stood tall, walking towards the door. Without saying a word to me she headed to do the unthinkable: confront Marie.

There may have been two or three occasions between the two of us where we attempted to speak up for ourselves. Marie considered this "talking back" to her. Expressing our displeasures as children was completely disrespectful in the time and place we were growing up in. Speaking up for yourself in our culture was cause for a serious whooping. I had a sandal leave bruises on my thighs once because I stomped up the stairs and slammed the door. It was seconds before Marie was up those same stairs and stormed right through that same door. I had my arms crossed and pouted so hard my face hurt. But I knew when I heard those steps behind me that it was over for me. I could have peed myself I was so scared. But still, I tried to stand firm by my decision to stomp, and pout, and slam a door. Marie whooped me bad, and I never stomped, pouted, or slammed a door around her again. My sister did, though; she stood up to Marie a few times before and on this night, she was giving it one last try.

Debora stormed right out her bedroom door, back down the stairs, and directly to Marie, who was trying to finally settle in from work. I never left my spot from behind the door and listened intently, biting my nails, my little knees knocking.

UNRAVEL

"Mom, I can't take it anymore!" Debora protested. "I haven't done anything but suffer! Suffer, suffer, SUFFER!" Marie was silent. I imagined she was just staring at her with those Roche eyes, the stare that can send you running and hiding.

"Mom, I have to tell you something." Debora's voice became calmer. "When I was little, I was abused. Osini and the other men in the house, they touched me. They molested—" No sooner than I heard those words come out of Debora's mouth did I hear the terrible sound of her body hitting the floor. Screams and more screams followed. Even Dolores, who was watching the whole time, thought it was too much.

"No, Marie... Don't hit her in her head like that! You will kill her! Stop, Marie STOP!!!"

"Yes! Yes... I will kill her!" Marie shouted as she stormed off after being pulled off of Debora. "Don't ever say those lies to me again! You makin' up lies to make me feel bad!? You want me to hate myself? You are the troublemaker!" Marie sounded manic. Debora was silent, and I was gone. In that very moment, I knew that parts of my sister had died. Her spirit was broken, we were broken, and there was no saving us in sight. I detached, I went into The Dark and disappeared.

I don't remember what else happened that night, how it all ended. I don't remember the next day or how we managed to go back to our regular routines. But I do remember that at some point after that night my sister became deeply depressed. She stayed that way for a long time. I barely saw what was left of her because all she did was go to school and sleep. There were parts of her I knew I would never see again.

I learned that night that I had better never try to tell my mom that Dolores, and Rita, and Holston, and Edman, and Edoveet, and Osini, and my dad had all molested me. The night Debora told was the night I decided I would lock that truth away forever. I planned to take it to the grave.

That night made Marie different too. She seemed regretful after the whole ordeal. She became quieter. I barely heard her complain or yell anymore. I think allowing Dolores to get under her skin to the point where she completely lost her temper and beat her kid into a bloody pulp was when Marie finally realized Dolores was not good for our little family. I'm glad she finally realized it because a few weeks after that night, she asked Dolores to leave. But I think in many ways, it was too little too late. So much damage had already been done.

Dolores would eventually move out a few months later, and we would never see her again. I guess in some ways, my sister did save us. We were free from Dolores, and it was because Debora was brave.

Chapter 17
Church

Church played a major role in my adolescent development. It shaped me in ways I now both appreciate and regret. I found faith there but also experienced a lot of shame. I did my best to do all the things that church taught me to do to be qualified to get into heaven. I read my Bible, I prayed, accepted Jesus Christ as my personal savior, and repented for all my sins. But even as I did all of these things, I never once believed there was enough repenting and praying to remove all the dirt and stains left on me by those who violated me. But nonetheless, there I was, a faithful servant, trying my damnedest to get qualified for God's love.

Debora had a best friend in middle school, Shanae. Shanae and her family were faithful members of a small storefront church in North Philadelphia, which was 20 minutes from Nedro Ave, one bus ride away. Shanae always went on and on about her church to Debora, about how they had a great youth choir, and how awesome her pastor was, and on and on and on. She insisted Debora come visit, convinced she would want to join right away. And she was right. After Debora's first visit, she got on the bus every Sunday morning to attend service. Marie told Debora if she wanted to keep going to this church, she would have to let me tag along. Before I knew it, we were full-fledged members of Sprit & Truth Church of God In Christ. And I loved it.

FELICIA P. ROCHE

A few years in and Spirit & Truth became like a second home. It was a Pentecostal, Holiness, black church. This meant we were in service A LOT. Every Sunday we were there all day—10:00 a.m. for Sunday school, 11:00 a.m. for morning worship, a break for lunch (we all ate together), 5:00 p.m. evening worship, Tuesday night Bible study, Friday night prayer and fellowship, Saturday afternoon youth choir rehearsals, and finally, once a month, we had shut-in. Shut-in was fasting and praying on steroids. We would live at church from Friday evening to Sunday evening and we could only drink water. The idea of having a two-night sleepover with church friends was actually exciting for me. How many young people got to spend that much unsupervised time with their friends and, in some cases, their crushes?

My crush was Deon.

One shut-in weekend when Friday night service was over, the gang, a bunch of us teens, decided we'd all walk to McDonalds to eat dinner before fasting started at midnight. We wouldn't be able to eat again until after Sunday morning services. My stomach was doing flips as we walked as a group. Deon was so close behind me, and I knew he was looking at my legs. I wanted to cry because I also knew they were boney. I was 13 now, and things on my body had grown, just not as much as the other girls. Most of the girls were closer to Debora's age, 16, and had curves. So I couldn't believe it when I started catching Deon staring at me. There was no way he liked little boney me. *Does he?*

When we got back to church that night, Deon wanted to make it clear that he did like little boney me. Or at least he wanted me to know that he knew that I liked him. I had spent two years staring at Deon; just staring, every single service. I'd stare at the door the entire service if he wasn't there, praying he would walk through at any moment, squealing inside when he did. Although Deon was three years older than me, I started to shoot past him in height. He was dark skinned with a low cut and he was talented. He could play the drums and the piano, and I could not wait to get to choir rehearsals just to hear him sing. I would wish to God he would sit next to me in the church van when we traveled to other church services as a group, anything for our legs to touch. Every night, I wrote in my journal the fantasies I had about kissing him. I thought about it every day, obsessively. Maybe the time had finally come that he noticed.

Everyone found their quarters for the night. Spirit & Truth had about 30 or 40 members at the time. Most members slept on the sanctuary floor during shut-in, wrapped up in sleeping bags or the blankets they brought with them to service, ready to pray hours into the night. There were other rooms for people who wanted more privacy. Deon and I found ourselves together in the choir room. I couldn't believe it.

He made it simple. He grabbed a blanket and said, "Come here. Lay with me." I obliged with no hesitation, no questions. We spooned, and I stopped breathing. And just that fast, my excitement turned to dread. All I could think about as we lay there was the magazine I had just read about giving guys the "green light." I wondered what I did wrong because I had apparently just given it to Deon. I didn't want him to, but within seconds he had put his hand up my shirt and fondled my small, developing breast. I froze, squeezed my eyes, and prayed he would stop. Finally, he did. Without a word, I got up, walked out the door, and made my way to the altar to pray and fell asleep. I avoided him the next morning and the rest of the weekend in church. It took months for me to able to look at Deon again.

After the night in the choir room, Deon always ignored me at church. I was confused because I knew he liked me, but parts of me thought maybe he had violated me too. *Should I even want him to like me anymore?* I couldn't tell. I had no way of being sure. It was a great ball of confusion, hormones, and trauma all wrapped up in the bleeding heart of a now 14-year-old girl.

Seemingly out of nowhere, Deon quietly invited me over to his house one day. He passed me a note during worship telling me to meet him there afterwards. He lived two blocks from the church, and I just had to go. I was nervous but I wanted to feel like being around him was okay. I wanted to let my guard down. When I got there, he led me down to his finished basement where he had Christmas lights hanging and a keyboard set up. We listened to music and without a word, started kissing. And I liked it. My first consensual kiss.

I felt all the things I read about in teen magazines. Fireworks, butterflies, sparks—it was all there. I felt like I was in control of my sexuality, for once. Kissing Deon came so natural; we did it any chance we got. We snuck out of church services to kiss in the choir room or run down the street to his house. I loved the excitement of sneaking out of church and getting back before people noticed. It was only a matter of time before our raging hormones got out of control and we wanted more. Deon asked me to cut school so we could see each other on non-church days.

The first time Deon asked me to cut school, I was a freshman. I went to the roughest middle school in my neighborhood, so when it came time to apply for high school, there was a lot of

UNRAVEL

pressure and competition to apply to the top schools in the city. I was on honor roll, but that wasn't saying much for my middle school. Still, my teachers thought I was bright and helped me apply. Only a handful of students from my school would even qualify for consideration. Imagine my surprise when little ole me, scared, poor, and misguided, got accepted into one of the best high schools in Philly: Carver High School for Engineering and Science—the small school with a big name.

I hated it.

I did not belong there. I didn't have the discipline, resources, background, or knowledge to excel or even get by in a school like that. I knew I was in over my head on the very first day of school. So, I did what I did best; I disappeared.

Deon asked me to come over to his house while his mother was at work. I obliged and cut school to spend the day in his bedroom. For weeks, the days I cut school to be at Deon's house were spent making out. Every time things got hot and heavy, he would stop because he didn't want to "break my heart" if he took my virginity. *Break my heart how?* I was so confused by this sentiment. I thought that maybe Deon must have known he had no plans on sticking around because he already knew he was going to "break my heart." The thought did not persuade me to back off though. I was a tough girl who couldn't be hurt as much as I had already been. I didn't think Deon had the power to destroy any parts of me that were left. So I lied. I told him I had already had sex and was no longer a virgin. I convinced him I was a mature and experienced woman. Not too far from the truth in reality. It was all he needed to hear. We had sex; my first consensual experience.

We had sex all the time. Deon was an only child, and his mother worked every day, so the house was ours. Nearly every day of my freshman year was spent in bed with Deon, barely talking, just having sex and watching TV. And it seemed that every single day when it was time for me to leave, I would find something to be upset about; something to cry about. I had no idea at the time, but the emotions I had tied to sex were already hard-wired. There was a road mapped in me that drove intimacy directly to feelings of emptiness, fear, pain, and confusion. From The Monsters on out, that's what sex was. And yet, I believed it was all I had to offer. And I offered it as much as I could to Deon, just to keep him around. I needed a friend.

Deon eventually grew weary of this exchange of sexual pleasure and grief. He got quite tired of me lashing out at him after every encounter. I made threats of never speaking to him again because I knew he didn't really love me. I made it clear that I knew he was using me. I needed him to be aware that I was aware. But we both knew I was always going to come back for more. I was addicted to sex, heartbreak, and drama—anything to feel.

The peak of my rejection always occurred as we were wrapping up for the afternoon. I despised the feeling of being dismissed after sex. It made me feel used and unloved. Just like I felt after The Monsters got finished abusing me. How could I convince Deon that I was worth more than that? Would I ever know my worth? My father never knew it. The Monsters never knew it. I didn't know how to be worth more than what they used me for. But I knew more than anything, I wanted to be.

UNRAVEL

I eventually flunked the 9th grade and I didn't care. Before freshman year was over, Deon broke things off with me. I cried. All. The. Time. Nonstop. I listened to sad music as any normal teen would. That was the most normal part of my adolescence, a broken heart. But it was what Deon did next that began a pattern of treatment I seemed to always attract.

A few weeks had passed since Deon and I broke up when he asked me to come over. He said he had something he wanted to ask me. I had longed for this call. Without hesitation I cut school that day and immediately went to him at his home. Maybe he had finally felt the love I had for him, my version of love. God must have finally heard my prayers and allowed him to love me back. My mind, body, and soul were desperate to feel what love was.

Deon opened the door the same way he had hundreds of times in the past, nonchalantly. Dressed in sweats, he turned and walked from the door before I could even get through it. As usual, I felt dismissed. But I wanted to be there, so I followed him upstairs and into his bedroom. As I walked in and sat on his bed the first thing my eyes landed on was a picture on his wall, a picture of Shawn Whitaker.

Shawn Whitaker was a girl who attended our church. She and Deon had been friends for years, longer than I had even known him. They never dated before, but it seemed Deon just woke up one day and was totally smitten by her. He was intrigued with the fact that she was basically an adult, completing her year first year of college. She was mature and she had her stuff together. She was also one of the only virgins among us young people at our strict holiness church, and this was the highest level of honor for a woman. Holiness or hell. In our church, being "pure" was the goal, and for that reason, I could never compete. Deon's mom, the head of the youth department, made sure I was clear on that fact every chance she got. She wanted me to stay far away from Deon and asked for Shawn to come to all group outings. Shawn was good enough for her son, and I was not. Eventually, after he dumped me, Deon made the wise mama choice to date the pure girl. He asked Shawn out, and they started dating. So why was I in his room, sitting on his bed?

"What's up?" I asked, attempting to mimic his nonchalant attitude. "Why did you call me over here?"

"I have something I want to ask you," he responded.

"Okay....??? I'm listening"

"Well, you know I've been seeing Shawn, right?"

"Yea... I know that's your girlfriend."

"Yea, but you know she's a virgin, right?"

"Yea...??? Soooo????" I was growing impatient.

"Well I'm not a virgin," he replied.

"I know you're not a virgin, Deon," I said with a smile. "So what?"

"So, I don't think I can go without sex."

"What does that have to do with me?" I asked as my smile faded.

"Well, you are the last person I had sex with, and since we were already having sex...well..."

"Deon, what are you saying to me right now?" My emotions started to rise.

"Aww man," he stuttered. "Ugh... I can't say it."

UNRAVEL

"Well, you need to say something!" I started to scream. "I didn't come all the way over here for nothing!"

"Okay, okay, okay... Let me write it down. It will be easier." He handed me a piece of paper that he clearly had written on already. And it read: "Will you be my sex partner?"

"What does this mean, Deon?!"

"What you mean?" he said, laughing.

"So I'm good enough to have sex with but not be your girlfriend!?"

"I'm not saying that! Don't be so extra. I'm just saying, we was already having sex, so we should just keep doing that. Do it for me."

The words I was hearing were shocking to my ears but were not at all unfamiliar to my spirit. I knew what it was to want to be used for my body. I tried to act like I had some dignity. I knew there was some inside of me somewhere. "Wow, you really don't care about me, do you?" I got these words out as if I was acting.

"Yes, I do!" he responded. "You're one of my closest friends, and I miss what we had. It's just that Shawn is my girlfriend now. Nothing really has to change, not really."

Every day before this moment, I had tortured myself by stalking Deon and obsessing over his relationship with Shawn. When I spotted him at the mall, I followed him and watched him pick her up from her job at the food court. I watched him wait there for her until her shift was over, hug her, and walk to the train with her. All I could think about was: *Why wasn't I ever worth that?* Deon never took me anywhere, never met up with me anywhere. It seemed like he never wanted to be seen with me in public. *Why wasn't I good enough to be in public with?* The only answer I could come up with is that Shawn was pure and I was not. I was all used up. And here I was being used again. *What else am I good for?*

Determined to show him I wasn't the overly emotional wreck he dumped, I continued to act. I acted like I believed him when he said he still cared about me. I acted like I wasn't bothered by him claiming Shawn as his girlfriend in public but secretly having sex with me. I acted like I had a one up on Shawn because her boyfriend was cheating on her with me. And I acted like I wasn't disappearing into myself when I laid down and let Deon have his way with me that afternoon.

The treacherous rain that entire day was the perfect setting for how I felt. I walked out of Deon's house that day feeling less than human. I had to be rushed out right after we had sex because his mom would be home soon. He used me and kicked me out into the rain. I cried from the moment he shut the door until the moment I had reached mine. I cried on the train. I cried on the bus. And then I cried myself to sleep that night. I believed with everything in me that I was trash. To be used and thrown away. I continued to have sex with Deon for a long time after that terrible and sad, sad day. I became desperate for his attention and found myself crying every day as I left his house. I kept going back because I was addicted to the abuse.

A few weeks into this pattern, Debora noticed how sad I was and checked in on me, sitting by my bedside one night. "What's been going on with you?" she said seriously. Without a word I got up lazily, walked over to my book bag, and pulled out the note Deon had given me asking me to be his sex partner. I was embarrassed, but she asked, and I wanted her to know.

UNRAVEL

She and Deon had considered themselves best friends at the time. They hung out together outside of church and talked on the phone a lot. She knew we were seeing each other and on a number of occasions warned Deon that he'd better not ever hurt me. She told me it was a bad idea to get involved with him but pretty much kept quiet about the situation. When I showed Debora the note, she had no verbal response for me. She sighed, walked out my room, and I could hear her talking to someone on the phone downstairs in the living room beneath me. I closed my eyes and tried to forget. I wanted her words of guidance right then, but I don't think she had any. I was left to figure it out on my own.

I found out later, Debora had no words for me because she believed she made herself clear to Deon on the phone that day. I don't know the details of the conversation, but Debora tried to protect me. She ended their friendship that day has never spoken to him since. Not even once. She completely cut him off. I am grateful for that now, but I couldn't feel it then. I couldn't feel the love my sister had for me, or anything for that matter. I was depressed and numb and just kept going back to Deon to *feel*.

Chapter 18
Playing with Fire

The days that I couldn't indulge in drama by seeing Deon were the days I would find other ways to feel. I started cutting into my arms and getting into fights at school. I gained a few reputations at school that had nothing to do with who I really was. I was considered dumb because I never went to class. In all actuality, I was pretty smart. I was called a slut because I showed a lot of skin and all the boys looked at me. In all actuality, I never touched even one boy in school. I was the carefree girl because I ran the halls and always played around. In all actuality, I was dying inside and was just trying to survive.

The one reputation that I did deserve was the one no one attributed to me. I had moments where I would be in class, dazing off into thoughts of wishing my life were different, that I was someone else, staring at another kid who seemed to have the perfect life, and the next moment I would be in front of a burning trash can in the girls bathroom or an empty classroom, staring at flames. The smell of smoke always brought me back. *Did I just light this fire???* With a lighter in my hand and no one else around, I knew the answer.

All the teachers were tasked with assigning lessons that would teach students what an arsonist was. I knew the arsonist was me, but I didn't feel like it was me setting the fires because I didn't remember setting them. I was gone when the fires were set; I was somewhere in The Dark. When I got back, I completely disconnected from feeling responsibility for anything. I didn't feel a thing when we had those discussions in class. And no one ever found out it was me.

The more disconnected I became, the more erratic my behaviors were. I started joyriding in cars with strange men. I would lie down on train tracks for hours and smoked cigarettes, for real this time. I stole money from cash registers when no one was looking and I took pills to see if I would stay asleep or die. I lied and did anything for attention. I wanted so badly to no longer be me. I let someone else take over. I was a girl I no longer recognized. I didn't know it at the time, but I was developing dissociative identity disorder.

The persona I created to protect myself made up any and every lie imaginable just to keep my life in an uproar. She came up with the most elaborate way to keep Deon's attention. She lied and told him she was pregnant. She told everyone she was pregnant. She told me. Everyone believed me/her. I believed me/her. I believed with everything in me that I was pregnant. I was amazed at how excited Deon was. I was taken aback at how supportive everyone was. Even Marie.

When Marie and I sat down to talk about how things had gotten to this place, I told her about The Monsters, and she believed me. She didn't yell, or hit me, or do any of the things she had done to Debora when Debora told her. I was in shock. My new personality, this other me, was a genius. She was making things right. She knew how to protect me. She knew how to talk to everyone around me so that they would listen, so that they would love me.

UNRAVEL

With all the attention that came with getting pregnant at 15, being sexually abused as a child, and needing support from all my family and friends, I was able to finally breathe and focused on being better. Within weeks I started going back to school, got a job as a cashier at a beauty supply store, and I never missed a church service. I was taking control of my life and wanted to get things right.

But with this newfound stability also came the expectation that eventually a new baby would be in all our lives. In reality, no baby was coming.

I had no way of fixing this. But my other personality did not disappoint. She reminded me about the lie I told when I was nine and what I learned at the library that day. Together, we came up with an elaborate story about how I lost the baby. We executed the lie beautifully.

I couldn't have imagined just how sad everyone would be about the loss. Guilt started to creep up, and I wanted to tell the truth. But my other personality warned me that if I told the truth, everything would go back to how it was before the pregnancy, when I wanted to die. And so I kept quiet.

Chapter 19
Mr. Glasses Man

The news that there was no baby made no one sadder than Debora. But I could tell that it wasn't from the disappointment of there being no new baby coming. She felt sad for her little sister. She thought I was devastated, and she hated to see me hurting. I wished I could have told her that I was actually relieved that I was getting away with a big fat lie and wasn't sad at all. But I was a scared little girl, a coward in my own right.

By now, Debora and I weren't as close as we had been, but I knew my sister was still my protector. I was getting nervous about the fact that she was about to be turning 18 and graduating from high school. She was barely around anymore. She kept her head low at home and steadily got through school while keeping a part time job. The older she got, the more she disconnected from the life that was ours. I wondered if she planned to leave me after high school, but I was too afraid to ask. Perhaps I developed this new personality to help answer the question: who would look after me if Debora wasn't around? I felt like no one could take the place of my hero. Debora stayed strong and brave through every situation I had ever seen her in. She stood up against The Grownups and The Monsters, she confronted Marie, and she stood her ground with Dolores. She even took on a relentless stalker once, who could have very well killed her. Debora had to rise above all fear when she had to face Mr. Glasses Man.

Mr. Glasses Man first appeared in our lives about two years after we moved into Nedro Ave. I was around 12 years old and Debora had to be about 15. The first time we saw him was at night outside our living room window. It was just Debora, Marie, and me watching TV when all of a sudden, a dark figure appeared at the window.

"Go answer the door, Debora," Marie demanded, although there was no knock.

Debora went to look through the blinds next to the door as she grabbed the knob. Before she could turn the knob, she saw the figure run down the front stairs. "I don't know who that was, ya'll," she said seriously.

"What do you mean?" I asked.

"I don't know who that was, but they ran."

We all shrugged it off as the wrong address or some kid playing ding dong ditch. But the next night, the figure was back—just a shadow of a man. This time we could see him putting his hands up to the window, trying to see inside. Debora and I were home alone, sitting in the living room, and we became afraid. It was evident that whoever was outside the window was trying to see inside our house. Unable to move, we just stared at each other, eyes wider than ever. I giggled a little from the frights. We looked at each other and remained still until he left.

Debora wondered if this was the guy who had been walking closely behind her after school. She attended Central High School, one of the other top high schools in Philly. It was three long blocks from our house, about a 10 minute walk each way.

UNRAVEL

Most kids who attended did not live in the neighborhood, and Debora walked alone. She walked in from school complaining one day, "Ugh, Imma have to get a knife or something. Some creep keeps walking behind me for like my whole walk home!"

I don't know if the man in the window actually was the same guy that followed Debora, but the next time I saw the shadow at the window, there was no giggle. It was around eight o'clock at night, Marie was in bed, and Debora was not home from her 5:00 p.m. to 9:00 p.m. shift at the sneaker store yet. I was reading a book on my bed when Marie called to me and asked that I bring her a glass of water. That meant going downstairs, where all the lights were off. I turned on the upstairs hallway light, which lit up the stairwell too. The next light switch was in the dining room. I crept through the dark living room and approached the dining room when… there he was. The tall dark shadow in the dining room window looked like the boogie man. That window faced an outdoor staircase that led to our back door and driveway. The shadow walked up those stairs and positioned himself against the window, determined to see someone inside. I ran back upstairs and told Marie what happened. She fussed at me for not getting her water.

After about a year of regular visits from the shadow, it seemed that Marie and Debora felt no fear from his presence. Meanwhile, I thought I was going to shit myself anytime I was home alone or had to go downstairs by myself. I couldn't understand their fearlessness. I was fearful every day.

Even though Debora believed this guy posed no threat and was just a creep, she felt violated and grew tired of his shenanigans. One day, as we noticed his shadow appear, Debora told me to stay still while she slowly crawled to the door. She swung the door open as quickly as she could so she could catch the weirdo. He ran, and she chased him down the street. I have no idea what she thought she was going to do if she caught him. I stared at the window, frozen and counting the seconds until my sister got back, praying she wasn't hurt; angered that she left me alone. When she got back, she was out of breath. "Dummy got away," she said, irritated.

"What'd he look like?" I asked because I had only ever seen his shadow.

"He's tall and skinny," Debora responded. "Oh, and he wears glasses."

The years went on, and we started to call the shadow "Mr. Glasses Man." He became as much of a nuisance to our home as the mice. I still got nervous about seeing his shadow but, like Marie and Debora, I believed he was harmless.

Eventually, Mr. Glasses Man either became frustrated that we were ignoring him or he thought he could use it to his advantage. Our guard was down after years of his visits. We were unalarmed and unsuspecting the night he broke into our home. It was the middle of the night, and I was awakened by the loudest scream I had ever heard. All I could do was clench my covers into my fists, squeeze my already shut eyes tighter than they had been in my sleep, and scream too. I didn't even recognize my own sister's voice. These screams were something right out of a horror film, and I just did not want to look.

After nonstop screaming, I heard footsteps run down the hallway stairs and a big boom. Marie came running in to see what all the panic was. She turned on the lights, and I leaped up to find my sister screaming on her bed, holding her covers, and pointing at the door. "He was in here. He's in the house! Mr. Glasses Man! He's in the house!" Marie did not hesitate to run down the stairs to catch the fool. But she was too late. He had broken the back door to escape out of the house and was gone.

Mr. Glasses Man climbed in through the living room window that night. None of us were smart enough, or scared enough, to make sure all our windows were locked before bed. We made it easy for the lunatic to get to us. When the police came, Debora explained that he had been stalking her for years and that until now, she thought he was harmless. She said she woke up and saw him standing over her bed, just staring at her as she slept. That's when she screamed.

The police took the report and told us to get a dog.

Mr. Glasses Man stopped showing up after that night. For a while. But from then on, I slept so lightly I don't think you can consider what I was doing as even sleeping. Every creek of the house settling, every time the wind blew, anytime there was a sound outside my door, I stopped breathing. I never felt safe again. I started to have nightmares every night about Mr. Glasses Man and I didn't trust anyone who wore glasses.

I eventually developed PTSD and had panic attacks anytime I drifted off to sleep.

A few months before Debora was set to graduate from high school, Marie left us alone in the house while she took a trip to Haiti. One day, Debora was in the shower, and I went downstairs to get something to drink. I got to the middle of the hallway staircase, and there he was. Halfway through the front window,

Mr. Glasses Man and I locked eyes, and we both froze. He gave me a smirk, backed out of the window, and took off.

I was frozen from shock in that moment, unable to scream, paralyzed by fear. When I did move again, I ran back upstairs and told Debora. She simply got out of the shower, grabbed a towel, and marched straight downstairs to lock all the windows. She seemed over it; not afraid, just over it.

Debora *was* over it. After graduating from high school, she got some sketchy sales position and started working a nine-to-five. *A real grownup job*, I thought. A few months later, she saved up enough money to move out. She packed all her things without a word and just left. She didn't sit me down and have some heart to heart sister talk about how she would always be there for me even though she was moving out. She didn't give me a hug or even say goodbye. I sat at the top of the stairwell watching her and her new friends from work pack up a pickup truck, laughing and full of life. I sat at the top of those stairs wondering how I would survive everything I had just been through with Deon and the fake pregnancy, failing in school, and now having nothing and no one but Marie as my support. Debora was gone, and I knew I had to make the best of what I had left. Now, it was just Marie and me.

Chapter 20
Marie and Me

After Debora left, Marie became depressed and withdrawn. She had taken a fall at the nursing home she worked at while transferring a resident from a shower chair. She slipped, hit her head on a wheelchair, twisted her neck, and tore a ligament in her shoulder. As she waited for her workers comp case to process, she did nothing but take pain meds and lie in bed. She seemed to become virtually immobile. I hated her pain. With less mobility she gained more and more weight and became less and less the strong fierce woman I had always seen her as. I would have rather her wrath than her depression. It pained me to see her this way, and I wondered how I could help. My reoccurring nightmare of trying to piece my mother together had returned.

Marie could not work, and we had no income. What was once my bright and sparkly castle became a dark and gloomy dungeon. Nedro Ave was empty and cold. But as dark as things were becoming, there were parts of me that felt fulfilled. Before her accident, Marie was almost never home. Since we were babies, Marie was always gone. I always wanted her to stay, to not work all the time. I always wanted her to stop and pay attention to me. But I was quickly learning that her busyness was never the reason she didn't pay enough attention to me. Busy parents are not the reason for lonely children. Marie did not pay attention to her children because she simply was not capable of doing so. All these years, she subconsciously avoided us as much as she could because we were reminders of her misfortunes. Debora was a representation of her failed attempt at coming to America to find freedom. I was a product of the injustice she suffered, the recompense for her rape.

For an entire year after her accident, I did what I could to help Marie. I felt sorry for her and all her pain so I listened to her complaints, her moaning and discomfort. I fetched anything she needed. I did her shopping and brought her food. I lay in bed with her and I took part in her depression. We spent days laying in her bed together, talking and watching countless hours of TV. She slept, and I stared at the ceiling, listening to her snores. I never wanted to be alone in the house because I was afraid of Mr. Glasses Man coming back. My mother's snores were impossible, but at least I wasn't alone. I gave Marie massages every time she ached. And all she did was ache, and wallow, and worry, and wonder. So did I. This was us, and this was all.

Marie in all her misery only seemed to be concerned about her own woes. I began to feel lonely even with her next to me. I missed my sister and I yearned for any days from the past, no matter how bad they were. I stopped going to school, and Marie didn't inquire. I never knew where my next meal was coming from, and Marie took no notice. When I did get out of the house, I was in the streets, car hopping, drinking, and smoking with kids in the neighborhood, in a fight every other day, and Marie had no clue. And she took even less notice when she left me.

Chapter 21

Just Me

A year into Marie's depression, all the days began to bleed together. If I ever mustered up the guts to think about my future, all I envisioned was a dark empty space. I wondered if that meant I would die young. I started to accept that that was going to be the case. I knew I would die young and I knew I would be the one to kill me. These thoughts and the deep depression I was in made me disappear into The Dark. This time when I got back, Marie was gone.

Just like that. I woke up to an empty house one day and had no idea how to contact my mother. The house was under foreclosure, and Marie, desperate to keep her first home, sought out advice from old friends. I didn't know it at the time, but Marie had kept in touch with the Delairs. She met some shady finance guy through them who they claimed helped them with all the homes they owned. The guy talked Marie into a scheme to save her home by temporarily renting it out to the government program, Section 8, and applying for the same program so that she could stay in it. She paid him to handle all the paperwork. It turned out he actually sold the house to the government for a small fee. He took that money, plus the money Marie had paid him, and he fled to Haiti. Marie went after him.

While Marie spent her time chasing a con artist in Haiti, I spent mine trying to find a means of supporting myself. I had already failed 9th and 10th grade, and there was no hope in catching up. I told my principal about how I was without a parent, afraid and alone. Her response was to let me transfer myself out of her wonderful school and go to my neighborhood school. Apparently, there was no room for parentless children like me at Carver.

I was down to nothing. A few friends let me stay at their houses, and their parents were nice enough to feed me, but I hated being in other people's homes. Hated it. It triggered the feelings of anxiety I felt growing up in boarding homes, being in other peoples' spaces. But I had to survive. The days I thought I would be okay on my own, I lay in my mother's bed and cried myself to sleep, praying the next day would be better and that no one would break in as I slept. I prayed my mother would come back, better than ever, ready to be my mother again. She never came. Instead, she called me one day and told me that Al, my godfather, was coming to take some furniture out of the house. She said he would give me a few dollars for the furniture and to use it to take care of myself. I didn't ask any questions.

Al came and took almost everything. He handed me 40 bucks and told me to call him if I needed anything. That night I slept on the floor in the living room. All I had was our old, small black and white TV and a blanket. I remembered sleeping in the same exact place just five years earlier, the first night we slept in Nedro Ave. I remembered how bright everything looked. I remembered the sand-colored carpet. I remembered looking at two little brown girls in that great big mirror wall; the smallest one looking back at me with so much hope in her eyes.

UNRAVEL

That was all over now. I missed that little brown girl. I missed her big sister. I missed her mother and I couldn't wrap my head around the fact that that life was over. This was a new life now. I would have to be stronger and braver. I would have to learn to take care of myself. I would have to protect myself. No more waiting for someone to come rescue me. No more going into The Dark to hide away. I had to be the only somebody I knew and trusted.

A few days later, a Haitian family showed up with a truck, ready to move into Nedro Ave. Whatever deal the con artist made with the government, it led to this family renting my home. I was happy at least to see that there was a girl my age in the family. She, her mother, and her four little brothers were all new to Philadelphia, from New York. Her mother was a mean woman in her demeanor but kind in her heart. She was kind enough to let me stick around while they settled in, considering I had no place to go and no one to take care of me. I smiled for the first time in months when the girl my age told me what school she was transferred to. We both were set to start classes the next week at Germantown High. Her name was Bianca, and we became instant friends.

Chapter 22
The Gallery

Bianca was dark-skinned, petite, and had the biggest eyes I had ever seen next to my sister. She also had the straightest and whitest teeth I ever saw on a human being. With all the white from her eyes and her smile, she literally lit up a room. The light came from within her too. She was as sweet and generous as she was cute, always laughing and smiling. She was easy to get along with, but we were both hurt, confused teenagers. Her parents were divorced, and every time I brought up her father, her usual giddiness disappeared. We found ourselves in each other, and that made things okay, or at least bearable.

Bianca and I wasted no time becoming the best of friends and did a lot of crazy things together. We began cutting school only weeks into our transfer there. We would walk the entire day away just to escape, sometimes 20 miles or more. We lied about where we were to her mother and met up with strange boys. We got drunk with these boys and had wild unprotected sex. I believed I had no one to answer to and I dared anyone to try and make me. I considered myself a free spirit. I told everyone I met I was "passionate." I had no idea I was just trying to survive. I don't think Bianca was just trying to survive. I think she was just along for the ride. She found me exciting. Looking back, I am just glad I had someone there with me. She kept me from going off the deep end, and we grew to really love each other. Love found me when I thought it simply didn't exist anymore.

As the months passed, most days Bianca and I cut school. We would use our school tokens to catch a bus and the subway to Center City Philadelphia so we could hang out where all the kids who cut school would go to hide—the Gallery. The Gallery (the same mall where I used to stalk Deon and Shawn Whitaker) was in the heart of the city, just a few blocks from City Hall. All local trains rode to and from it—the Orange Line subway trains (Philadelphians refer to this as "The Sub"), the Blue Line trains (endearingly referred to as "The El"), Regional Rail trains, and even New Jersey transit. Bianca and I caught The Sub to get there at least two times a week.

The first floor of the Gallery was underground, where all the trains let out. In the center of that first floor was a huge food court, next to an FYE music store, surrounded by smaller shops. The second and third floors were above ground and had tons of clothing stores. It was always extremely busy, crowded with folks hustling and bustling to and from work, school, meetings, and shopping. There was not a day of the week you wouldn't find the Gallery crawling with people, especially young people.

It was easy enough to blend into the crowds. If you were caught on the street during school hours, especially in Germantown, you were yanked up by cops and your parents were called. I had no parents, so this never made me nervous. Bianca, on the other hand… Her mother would lock her up and throw away the key if she was ever caught cutting school. So we hid as best we could. When there weren't enough people to get lost into or there were too many security guards and cops around, we'd ditch the food court and hide out in the department stores. The furniture section at Strawbridge's was our favorite. There was never a soul there, and we could hide for hours.

We sat on the couches on display and explained to each other which one we would be buying once we were adults and had our own places. I always picked the big bright red couch. We described in embarrassingly precise details what the life surrounding our couches would look like. Bianca had a husband and a few kids. I had a boyfriend and a dog. She was a nurse, and I was a supermodel. But we would still be the best of friends. Our lives were all planned out.

I never wanted to leave the Gallery because when we left, Bianca had a real family to go to. I would decide if I was going to stay at church, a friend's house, her house, or some random guy's house for the night. She thought it was cool that I had that choice. She never asked what I thought of it. The truth is, after a while, I didn't.

Another reason I never wanted to leave the Gallery was because there were always cute boys there. The day I met the cutest of them all is the day that would change the course of my life forever.

Chapter 23

Q

He was with his cousin, and I was with "my cousin" too. Bianca and I were sitting at a table in the food court when I saw what I thought was a fine specimen. At some point he must have noticed me looking because he started to put on a show—acting like a fool, laughing, and cracking loud jokes. We started to laugh too, and that gave him the green light. He walked over to us. "How ya'll doin? What's your name?" he asked with a smile.

"Felicia… What's yours?"

"Q."

Q was tall, about six feet, with a strong frame. I thought he was extremely handsome—beautiful olive skin with a touch of golden sun, perfectly symmetric almond-shaped eyes, high chiseled cheekbones, a pointed nose, and full, curved lips that looked soft as pillows— simply dreamy. It was almost too much that he was also charismatic and charming. I was swept.

We exchanged numbers, and I called Q a few days later, and then a time or two after that, but didn't reach him. Then, one day, April 20, 1999 to be precise, Bianca and I were hanging out at her house as we did most afternoons after school (or after cutting school). The Columbine shooting was being covered on every channel as Bianca and I watched in shock until we grew weary. After a while we changed the subject to what we always talked about—boys.

"Whatever happened to the boy from the Gallery, girl? He was cute!" Bianca said excitedly.

"He never answered the phone and he never called me. I guess he didn't really want to talk to me."

"Nah… I don't believe that. He liked you a lot. Just call him one more time and see what happens. If he doesn't answer, then forget about him."

"Okay, but this is for sure the last time." I dialed his number, and an older lady answered the phone, his mother I presumed.

"Hello, can I speak to Q?"

"Hold on… Q! PHONE!"

"Hello…"

Finally, I got to speak to what I thought was the best catch I ever caught. Turns out there was a sudden death in Q's family, and he was in the South for the past two weeks. He and his family had just got back that day. The timing for my last attempt at contacting him was impeccable. It felt like it was meant to be. We spoke on the phone that night until the wee hours of the morning. We connected on a level I didn't think was possible. He told me that he went to West Philly High but was at the Gallery the day we met because he hated his high school. He told me he was ready to drop out and get his GED so he could train full time and try out for pro football. He told me he felt like life was passing him by, even though he was only 17 years old, and he felt like an old soul. I told him I felt the same way. I got lost in our conversation and I wanted it to never end. It felt like Q was really listening, holding on to my every word. It made me feel like I was

UNRAVEL

more than pretty, or interesting. It was the first time I felt like I was special.

In the following weeks, we called each other every day and talked on the phone for hours on end. His mother consistently interrupted our calls in the middle of the night, saying that it was time to hang up. After she went back to bed, we were right back at it until the sun came up. Our puppy love was a whirlwind. I eventually started to go see him in his neighborhood. Q lived in West Philadelphia, and since I usually stayed on the other end of town at Bianca's, I had to take a bus, The Sub, and The El to get to him. I eventually became addicted to seeing his beautiful face and enjoying my time with him. I couldn't go a day without it. We cracked jokes and shared stories about our crazy teenage lives and our plans for the future. Our PDA was incessant and annoyed all his friends. "Get a room!" his homie from around the corner blurted out whenever he walked past us.

We spent most of our time on his stoop. His mother was always home and not open to him bringing a girl inside. We preferred the freedom of outside anyway. During our time on the stoop, all his friends stopped by at some point or another and would eventually become my friends too. They all grew up together in that same neighborhood, and their familiarity was mesmerizing. I couldn't comprehend knowing the same group of people, having the same friends and schoolmates from elementary to high school. I thought it was the best thing in the world. I started to feel like I belonged to something. On occasion, I would ask Bianca to use her allowance to tag along with me on one of my regular trips to West Philly, begging her to lend me bus fare at the same time. One of Q's friends took one look at

Bianca and was in love. He didn't waste time and made her his girl in a matter of a few of our visits. It wasn't long before we had the reputation in the hood for being Q's and Jason's girls. I was grateful Bianca let me borrow her clothes because all summer long we made sure that because we had this reputation; we always looked our flyest. We wanted all the boys to wish they were Q and Jason and all the girls to wish they were us. I think we succeeded.

There was a laundromat across the street from Q's house that we hung out at when the weather started to break. It was in this laundromat that I found out that Q was not as free as I was. One night while we were in there, a little girl, maybe about one year old, ran into the laundromat and right into Q's arms. His eyes lit up as he scooped her up and kissed her all over. I was confused. "This is my little girl, Laci."

Q was 17 years old with a one-year-old daughter. The baby's mother was a girl who had Laci when she 14. I was taken aback that Q was a dad, but it did not deter me from continuing to spend as much time with him as possible. I had become obsessed with spending time with him because it was the only thing that made me happy. It didn't matter how tired or cold I got, I stayed out there on that corner of 56th & Market until Q absolutely couldn't stay out any longer. Sometimes, that was as the sun was rising. He walked me to the train, and we kissed goodbye as I prepared for my sleepy hour-long commute back to Bianca's. Some nights, though, we found ways to sneak in and cuddle on his indoor porch, talking about life and cracking jokes. We would laugh so hard we would cry because we had to whisper and not laugh too loud. Other times we snuck in a little further and watched a movie on the couch in his living room. That always led to making out. It was exactly what young love was supposed to be.

Q wanted more.

I thought that what I was experiencing was true love because I had never spent time with someone who was attracted to me without having to have sex with them. I had never known someone to enjoy my presence and even my body without it becoming sexual. The innocence of it all was taking me into a light I had never seen, and my heart was filled. If only Q felt the same.

Jason pulled me to the side one day to let me know about Q's displeasure. I couldn't believe my ears. Q had been sharing his frustration with Jason about how unsatisfied he had been with our relationship. "All the guy wants is to be shown a little love and appreciation; he just wants to feel it." Jason explained. I looked up at Jason like he was crazy.

"What are you talking about? We spend all our time together and we are happy."

"He just wants to *feel* that though." I didn't understand. But I knew what he was saying. And so I gave in. The next time we snuck into his house after his mother had gone to bed, our regular make out session on the couch turned into our first time. Our first time led to many times.

Bianca and I continued to hang out and even got our first jobs together. We both filled out applications to work at Express clothing store. We interviewed at the same time and were hired on the spot. With cool jobs, hot boyfriends, and cute clothes to match, we thought we were the shit, and no one could tell us otherwise. To get to and from work, we took The El, which just so happened to be the same train that rode by our boyfriends' houses. On the way home, we almost never missed an opportunity to see them. How could we not get off when the train stopped at 56th Street? We never wanted to look like obsessive girlfriends but we just couldn't help but run to the train doors just as they were about to close; our hearts beating fast, almost missing the chance to see them again. Some days they expected us, but most days they just knew that we may or may not pop up. Popping up didn't always work out so well for Q.

Q, as it turns out, had other girls that liked to visit him on 56th Street. During one of our unscheduled visits, Bianca and I decided to pop up at the YMCA where the guys played basketball. Usually, if they weren't on the block, we knew we could find them up there, just two blocks away. They had just finished up a game and were walking out of the gym. Jason was happy to see Bianca and immediately went in for a sweaty hug.

"Ewww... Don't touch me!" she squealed.

"You know you love my sweat, girl! You see the sweat glistening all over my baaawdyyy," Jason teased. They laughed, and then Jason spotted me. "What's up, Felicia? Yo, walk with me real quick."

"Why. Where's Q?"

"Oh, he's coming. He told me to tell you to meet him on the block." I knew Jason was lying, so I lingered. Jason and Bianca tried to linger and walk too. It was just awkward. Within minutes, I saw Q emerge from the gym with a girl. She looked a lot like me, just shorter and thicker. He walked with her but not with her. He saw me and said what's up. We all walked down the

UNRAVEL

street, quiet, awkward, and making small talk. "Q, what you doin the rest of the day?" I asked to make it clear I was here to see him. The girl chuckled. I rolled my eyes.

Jason tried to interject. "Oh we prolly go to the fish store and grab some food and just chill... Maybe go to the state store and grab some 40s—"

"Jason," I interrupted, "I didn't ask you."

Bianca giggled.

Once we got to the corner of the block, the girl grabbed Q to tell him she was leaving. He brushed my hand and told me to wait for him at his steps and he'd be there in a minute. I acted like I obliged, satisfied that he had acknowledged me in front of the girl. But I actually stood behind the newsstand and watched their interaction so I could get the real deal. I watched them exchange words, a hug, and then a kiss. I was on fire.

"Fuck you, Q!" I screamed as I walked up to him and the girl. She showed her satisfaction at my outburst and smirked at me. I knew that anything else I would say would be at the cost of my own dignity. I was already embarrassed, so I just ran up the stairs to The El train. Jason caught the whole show and ran up after me; Bianca after him. We all had train passes, so by the time they had reached me, I was already on the platform, praying the train would come so I could leave fast, before the tears I felt coming could drop.

"Yo. Yo... Yo..." Jason grabbed my arm. "It's not what you think. She just a hype jawn! She just want him, that's all. Trust me, yo; he wouldn't never do that to you. Just come back down and talk to him." Jason was always so convincing. By the time we walked back down the stairs from the platform, Q was begging the guy in the cashier's booth to let him through just so he could speak with me. "I'm not getting on the train, man… I just gotta talk to my girl…"

"Ay yo, Q… She right here," Jason summoned. I somberly walked down to him. I stood on my side of the turnstile with my arms crossed and not needing to say a word because my face said it all: explain yourself.

Q came up with this elaborate story about how the girl was someone that he used to talk to and just really wanted to be with him. "She only kissed me because I told her you were here for me and she wanted to make you jealous. She waited until you were looking, right? That's because I told her you were my girl. She just wanted to break us up."

It didn't take much more to convince me. Q was all I knew and the only good thing in my life. So I chose to believe him and I spent the rest of that day and almost every day after that wrapped in his arms. He was my best friend, my lover, and my heart was his.

Chapter 24
Moving Backwards

While I was spending my days and nights getting lost in a teenage love affair, Debora was living a grownup life in Harrisburg. She had moved there a few months after she moved out of Nedro Ave. Her job, a huge pyramid scheme, promised her great success if she relocated. A naïve 18 year old with no one to guide her, she didn't hesitate. Debora was always a hard worker, and this company could see that. Always serious and always focused; she never looked back at the life that once was.

One of her close co-workers was the same way, and together they became leaders in the business, challenged with making the company's Harrisburg location a success. They worked non-stop and were forced into a roommate situation when they both relocated from Philadelphia to Harrisburg. Eventually, this perfect co-worker and business partner would become the perfect boyfriend. The relationship Debora and her boyfriend developed provided the support they both needed to help them realize their job was bullshit. They began to see that the financial output was not matching the amount of input. Their hard work and dedication was simply making someone else wealthy and would lead them nowhere. They decided it was time to go back home.

When they got back, Debora's boyfriend moved in with his mother in Northeast Philly. Debora knew coming back meant coming back to no home at all. I kept her up to date on everything whenever we spoke on the phone. She knew Marie lost the house and that I was homeless but lucky to be able to crash with the people who moved into Nedro Ave and had places to couch surf. The real reason Debora knew it was time to come back to Philly was because she knew I had no home, and no family. She knew she would have to come home and take care of her baby sister, again. Debora used all the money she had to rent two rooms so that we would have a place to stay. My heart was shattered. Not because we had to rent rooms, for this I was grateful—it would be so refreshing to have my own space, even if it was just a small room. No, my heart was shattered for a different reason. I was sad because we had to rent rooms at a boarding home in the same area Marie rented rooms all those years ago; the same place that still held my childhood captive. We were back to living in Germantown.

The boarding house we rented rooms in was old, cold, and run down. The tenants made it look like it was a halfway house. They looked like they had tough lives, strung out on drugs or just unable to maintain their own upkeep. They smelled like cigarettes and alcohol, the whole house did. They always looked upset, never responded when we said hello, never a greeting. I thought they were going to eat us alive. There was only one bathroom for each floor, and sharing it with the scary people made my anxiety shoot through the crumbling roof. Debora had a room on the third floor, and I was right under her on the second floor. But, I never saw her. Within weeks of being back, Debora started working two jobs to save up for us to get out of that hellhole. She got a nine-to-five office gig and then worked 5:00 p.m. to 9:00 p.m. at Pier 1. The commute was over an hour;

she was literally gone from 7:00 a.m. till 11:00 p.m. every day. When she was home, I never visited her in her room, and she didn't visit me either. I avoided her because every time I saw my sister she looked exhausted. I thought she was tired of taking care of me.

I also never saw her because all my time was spent with Q. He eventually got a job at the same mall where Bianca and I worked in the outskirts of Philly. The commute was brutal. Coming from Bianca's house, it would take an hour or so. Coming from my new place in Germantown, it was almost two hours. Just to work a miserable four-hour shift that paid $6.00 an hour; half of my check was bus fare. To make the commute worth it, Bianca and I would meet up with Q so we could all take the bus and train home together. It felt impossible for us not to get off with Q at 56th Street. Bianca went straight to Jason's, and Q and I found somewhere to hang until his mother went to sleep. Our lives were in West Philly. Our boyfriends' friends' girlfriends became our friends. We all got along pretty well. There were nights when just us girls would hang out, drinking, playing cards, and gossiping, while the guys were out getting into trouble somewhere—copping drinks and weed, playing basketball, or just handling some street drama.

Sometimes the street drama lead to losing one of our friends. Someone was always getting shot. Q was no stranger to this and shrugged it off every time it happened. He had been shot three times before I met him. It was just a part of the life in this neighborhood, and now it was a part of my life too. All the times we all ran in a house because somebody was shooting just made me feel more connected to the hood. Dodging bullets made me feel invincible. I had been dodging them my whole life. Our little bunch started to feel like family. I never wanted to go to my rented room. I don't know where Debora thought I was spending all my time, but it seemed like she didn't have the time to even think about it. I got really comfortable with Debora taking care of everything and hanging out with my new family. Eventually, my unpredictable part-time hours at Express dwindled down to just one or two days a week. I barely made any money, and all I wanted to do was hang out. No school, no work—just hanging.

Just about every day, I hung out at one of the girlfriend's houses. Her house was the hang out spot for the little family we created. We spent hours there, getting lost into each other, like the outside world didn't matter. The guys would huddle up in the kitchen after we ordered take out, yelling about sports or street beef. We listened, the girlfriends, looking at them like they were crazy half the time and the other half like we adored them. All of us played spades, drinking and yelling some more, laughing until we hurt. Sometimes, you could find all 10 or 12 of us jammed in one room watching movies, pair offing, all the couples cuddling.

The hang out house was right on Market Street, directly under the EL and one block away from Q's house. I sat on those steps most nights waiting for Q to get home from work. I knew which train was his and anticipated seeing him come down The El steps like a little girl waiting for her dad to walk through the door when he came home from work, ready to leap into his arms. And that's exactly what I did. It became such a routine that the neighborhood regulars knew what was about to happen. "He on his way?" an old man would ask as he walked by. "It's almost that

UNRAVEL

time," the lady on the stoop next to us would remind me. Every night, at exactly 11:30 p.m., my heart would leap out my chest and into Q's arms. He would catch me, spin me around, and kiss me on the forehead. It seemed like the whole world was watching in awe. I never felt so loved.

One night, to my unimaginable disappointment, Q did not get off the train. I waited the entire night, train after train, until there were no more trains running. I grew weary and curled up on a couch at the hangout house. I fell asleep just knowing that somehow, in the morning, I would spot Q on the block. The next morning I got up with the sun. I heard the first train go by and I stared out the window. It was raining, and I couldn't help but worry. I told myself to stay calm, that there had to be an explanation. By noon my thoughts had turned into anxiety. I decided to call his house, only feet from where I had stayed the night before. No answer. I decided to go over and knock on his door. No answer. Hours had gone by, and I grew hungry. I decided to walk across the street to the fish market to get something to eat. I gazed out of the store window as I waited for my wings and fries to get done, watching all activity on the block, hoping to spot my love. My hopes turned into reality because there he was. My hopes also turned into dread because he wasn't alone.

Q was with a tall, beautiful, light-eyed girl with long hair. She looked like brown magic floating alongside him. They were walking down the street laughing—her arm wrapped around his as if he was escorting her somewhere fancy. They looked like they were in love. I stopped breathing. I froze. I watched them until they were out of sight. I left my food and went straight back to the hangout house. I walked as quickly as I could, hoping not to run into the happy couple. I wanted to stick around to find out who the beautiful girl was. I felt desperate to know. Bianca would be coming around soon to see Jason, so I waited around scoping for her. The sun started to set, and I listened to every single train that went by, watching every person come down The El steps until I finally saw her. I knew she wouldn't let me down. I stood on the stoop close to the door, sure not to let too many people see me. When she got close, I shouted a whisper: "Psst... Bianca! Come here!"

"Why are you whispering?" She giggled as she walked over. I told her to come in.

"Is Jason here?" she asked.

"No, but come in." I was still whispering. She came in, and I explained in painful detail the last 24 hours, telling her she should have been there with me, adding friend's guilt to my plea. "Now I need your help."

"Okay, okay, I'm sorry," she whimpered. "What do you want me to do?"

Surprised my guilt trip worked, I became excited. "Call Jason and tell him to meet you in front of Q's house. Tell him you need to get something from me and that I'm over there and see what he says." My plan worked like a charm. I listened to Jason on the phone with Bianca, assuring her I definitely wasn't over at Q's house.

"Naw, Felicia ain't over there. I seen Q earlier with his baby mom, so I know Felicia ain't around."

My heart dropped. She was exactly what she appeared to be: important. I knew she was special, somehow more special than me. I motioned for Bianca to put him on hold. "What?" she asked.

"Tell him you already told me to meet you there, and I'm probably on my way already anyway." Bianca got back on the line and did what I asked.

"Aw shit. It's gonna be some shit jumpin off then" was Jason's response.

Bianca reacted wisely. "Well, don't say anything to him, Jason. Let's stay out of it."

I nodded my head and gave a thumbs up. Bianca had the same thought as me. *Let's just roll up and see what happens.* Bianca and I waited a little while so I could gather my thoughts. We also gathered my appearance. Together or not, if his baby-mom was going to see me, his new girlfriend, then I would have to be at my best. We made our way up the street. My heart was in my shoes. I wanted to disappear; I was so nervous. Going into The Dark felt tempting in that moment. Ever since I had met Q, I had no need for that place. I was hoping that wouldn't change now. As we walked up, I saw Q emerge from his door and down his front stairs. He saw me, and his face lit up. He cocked his head to the side and looked at me with admiration, desire. I melted. I walked up and embraced him. We hugged for three minutes straight. I closed my eyes and I exhaled. We spoke while we embraced. "What's up with you?" he asked, still holding me.

"Nothing. I just came with Bianca to see Jason. I figured you might be off tonight, but I wasn't sure." I lied. We unembraced, and he kept his arm around my shoulder as we walked over to Jason and Bianca, who had just met up at the corner. She debriefed him before we walked over. I thought against confronting Q about the beautiful girl. I had missed him so much the night before; I just wanted to enjoy the moment. I just wanted it to be like it always was. No drama and no weirdness. Just love and fun. We walked over to Jason's stoop, which was next door to the laundromat. A few more guys came around, and they started talking amongst themselves while Bianca and I watched. I didn't want to face her and the questions I knew she had brewing in her mind for me. I was ashamed that I was playing dumb.

There was a makeshift basketball court on the corner between Q's house and the laundromat. Most nights, even if I had heels on, Q and I would play HORSE. And I always won. The guys liked to give him a hard time about it. "Aye… Felicia, you not gonna whoop his ass tonight?" one of his friends said while tossing me the ball.

I got up and started shooting. He came up behind me, and right as he was about to try and grab the ball, the beautiful girl emerged from his house. "Q," she called out to him. "I'm about to leave. Your mom said Laci can stay the night." I tried to act like I didn't hear.

"Oh, alright." He said as he jogged over to her, not even acknowledging me. He went in the house, and she, with all comfort in her stride, walked right up to me and asked who I was.

I found my boldness.

"I'm Q's girlfriend. Who are you?" I made sure to say it with attitude, for no other reason than I believed that's how these types of interactions were supposed to go.

She gave a fake laugh. "Girl, please. Let me tell you something. Q done had a lot of girlfriends. I watched them come and go, and guess what? I'm always the one he comes back to. Have your little fun because what we have will never go away." She said this as she pointed to the tattoo of his name that completely covered the top of her arm.

I smirked and tried to show I was not intimidated. "Whatever."

She smiled and walked back to Q's house in a sexy 30-year-old woman kind of way. I was confused.

A few minutes later, Q came back out. This time my temper got the best of me. "Why the fuck did your baby-mom just come out here and tell me y'all will always be together? What did she mean, Q?" I demanded. He grabbed my hands to get me to calm down.

"Naw, it's cool. She knows about you. We ain't together. She know what it is." He kissed my forehead and tried to hug me. I was exhausted from the whole two-day ordeal and just wanted to leave. And so I did.

I was confused and relieved all at the same time. All I could think about on my long train and bus rides home was that everything was okay because I still had him. Q was still mine, and I would do anything to make sure it stayed that way. Q called me the next day and apologized for the "misunderstanding." He wanted to make it up to me. "Mom dukes is going down south for a week. You should come stay over. Just me and you for like three days straight. Come on. Come stay with me."

I could only imagine what that would be like. Q had never come over to my place because I was too embarrassed about where I lived. And we could only sneak a few hours of alone time here and there when I came to see him. Finally, we would have an uninterrupted love fest. I couldn't say no and I couldn't wait. Even though the words of his baby-mom resounded endlessly in the back of my 17-year-old mind, I moved past my insecurity and was determined to make sure Q stayed in love with me no matter what.

Staying at his house was just the opportunity. We made love endlessly. I got up early, cleaned the kitchen, and cooked breakfast. He came down and wrapped his arms around me and told me how perfect I was. In that moment, I closed my eyes and exhaled, an overwhelming feeling of peace coming over me.

We had a full day of watching movies, eating junk food, and more love making. We laid in bed after repeated sessions and talked about music—he LOVED Beyoncé from Destiny's Child; sports—he never shut up about the Eagles; and the future—he was going to be a pro baller no matter what. I never talked about what I liked or what my future was because I honestly didn't know what I liked and I had no clue what I wanted for my future, besides him. I was happy to just keep asking him questions and listen to him answer. When it came to the past, I had a lot more to say than he did. I told Q about my dad, and the abuse. I didn't tell him about The Monsters or Gustave's kids, or Dolores because I thought that would be too much. He already reacted strongly to hearing about my father. He stared at the ceiling in silence for what seemed like forever. It was as if he was processing anger. Just when I thought I saw a tear falling from the side of his eye, he pulled me close and said, "I'm so sorry you had to go through that." He held me tighter and whispered that he loved me. It was all I needed to hear to be okay in that moment of sharing.

UNRAVEL

Our talkathons went like this every night that weekend. On our second night we talked until we realized the trains stopped running. "I haven't heard one in like over an hour," I noticed.

"Yea... That means we been running our mouths past midnight." We both laughed, and the conversations continued until we heard the trains come by again. "Damn, that's the first train. That means it's 6:00 a.m.," Q informed me. "Yo, we really be running our mouths." We finally drifted off as the sun started to peek through the blinds.

I was awakened by a knock at the door. "Q," a man's voice called out. Q jumped up and ran to the door, blocking me from the man's view. "Yo, wassup, Dad."

"I came up here checking on you while your mom is gone."

"Oh, I'm cool."

"You got a girl in there?" he asked.

Q chuckled. "Yea, yea, Dad, but it's not like that."

"Okay, son." He chuckled back. His dad gave him some instructions, some cash, and was on his way. Q had a little brother and sister who had gone with their mom, and so his dad, who randomly came and went as he pleased, told Q to hold down the fort and make sure everything was exactly as they left it. Q jumped back in the bed and buried his head into my neck. "So, what we doing today?" I asked.

"Sleep!" Q answered. And that's exactly what we did that entire day.

The next morning, Q seemed distant. Every time the phone rang, he took the cordless phone and walked out to the backyard. I asked why he was being so secretive, and he said it was his mother who kept calling and he didn't want her to hear me. He said she was coming home early and was already on her way. "I'm sorry, but things got fucked up. Dukes is gonna be home tonight." I was disappointed but grateful for the amazing time we had had so far. I wanted to drag it out as long as possible, so I seduced him into making love one more time. We talked and laughed as much as we could in the few hours we had left. Q rushed all of it.

"Imma just leave when she get here," I said. At this point, his mom knew who I was, and even though she didn't seem to be onboard with our relationship, she tolerated my presence.

"Nah, that's prolly not a good idea. I don't want her thinking you was here the whole time," he explained.

I started to get agitated. "Well, let's sit on the porch. When we see her car, I'll just bounce. She won't even see me."

Q let out a heavy sigh and sat down. He was not good at getting me to do something I didn't want to do. In many ways he had spoiled me. It was a notion I had never known or experienced, but I got used to it quick. I was going to have my way. The phone rang, and Q said it was his mother and that she asked him to meet her at the gas station a block away to help her with something. Clever.

"Imma go head up the street to meet her. Just be gone before we get back in like five min," he said as he gave me a kiss on the cheek, anxious and scurrying away.

As I walked towards the El, a car pulled up. "Excuse me," the person in the back said. "You know Q?"

"Yea. Why?"

The front window rolled down, and I saw a familiar face. It was the hype jawn.

UNRAVEL

"Umm, well, you don't know me, but my name is Danni. I think I saw you before, that day we was walking back from the gym at the Y," she explained.

"Yea?" I said, confused as to why she was being so nice.

"Are you supposed to be Q's girlfriend?"

I said yes.

"Well, Q don't have no girlfriend."

I stood there, confused. The hype jawn proceeded to tell me how much of a player Q was and that she was there to see him.

"He told me to come over because his mom was out of town. He told me that you was over and he was trying to get rid of you so we could fuck." I stared and looked as dumbfounded as I was. The two other people in the car huffed and puffed and seemed to be over our exchange.

"She not gettin it, Danni. Just tell her to leave."

"You don't believe me?" she asked.

"I gotta go," was my response.

"Well, here, take my number and call me later. I ain't got nothing to hide girl. I can prove to you he's a player. I'm fucking him but would never claim to be his girl. He's playing you, girl. I'm just trying to help." She ripped off a piece of paper from a notebook and handed me her number. I walked away and up the stairs to The El. I looked down over the railing and I saw the car Danni was in parked in front of Q's house. I knew his mother was not coming. I knew he would not go back into the house until after he knew for sure I was on the next train. That way he could lie later. I knew that she wasn't the only person who had warned me about Q.

Maybe I was in denial before that night because there was something about that moment that felt like I had known all along that Q was a cheater. Maybe I just wanted him so bad, I wished for my intuition to be wrong. I knew in my gut Q was cheating; I just didn't want to believe it. I was blinded by love and purposely looked away from all the evidence. Now, it was impossible not to see what was right in front of me. I had the opportunity to find out for sure.

When I got home, to my rented room, I immediately called the number I was given. No answer. I was left with thoughts that kept me up all night. Thoughts of Q being there with her. Thoughts of him sleeping with her. I slept in the next morning, too afraid to face the day. I felt something coming. It felt like those days when I knew I was going to get in trouble for something when Marie got home. Those nights I didn't want to fall asleep because I would be awakened by the sting of a belt across my back. It felt like fear—my stomach in knots. I knew this feeling well. I tried to keep my head under the covers. No place was dark enough for me to disappear. Hours passed with me lying in bed, and just when I finally was about to fall asleep, my phone rang. I prayed that it was Q. It wasn't.

"Hello, is this Felicia?"

"Yea… Who dis?"

"It's Danni. I saw your number on my caller ID. So you ready to hear the truth?"

Danni went on to tell me all the times she had been with Q, including the night before. She described the house just as I left it as proof. She told me all the jokes he repeats, the same ones he told me to make me laugh. I learned that the song he sang to me to make me feel special—"Fortunate" by Maxwell—was the same song he sang to her, and probably plenty of others. Q was a real Don Juan.

I had heard enough. I believed every word. But I had no idea what to do with it. I felt this pain coming but I couldn't imagine in a million years it would hurt like this. Deon was my first heartbreak, but Q was the first person to actually break me. I was completely broken. Shattered into a million pieces. I wailed on my knees by my bedside that night, for hours. I couldn't compose myself. I screamed, I threw things and I pleaded with God to take the pain away. I loved him. He was my world. He was all I had. I had no mother, no father, and a sister I thought resented me. No future, no education, and no money. All I had in that moment was God. So I begged God to fix it. I asked God to help me.

God did help me and gave me the strength to leave Q. After days of crying, I quickly recovered by turning my pain to anger. I convinced myself that I hated Q. I promised myself that I would never let him back in. I told myself that things had to change. This broken-hearted mess was not a good look, and I had to pull myself together. I started picking up more hours at Express. I even started going back to class at Germantown High. I enjoyed not being consumed with the worries of a boy, a boy I couldn't trust anymore anyway.

Bianca made a decision that she really wanted to graduate the next year and was attending all her classes. I still cut the boring ones where half the kids couldn't read, but I did attend my mass media classes and any class that seemed halfway challenging. I started to feel like a teen again. And then the best news of all came. Debora had finally saved up enough money to get us the hell out of Germantown. She wasn't going to have to work both jobs anymore either. I might actually get my sister back. The entire time we lived in those rented rooms, Debora had tunnel vision to get us exactly where we were going—to a nice, clean two-bedroom apartment in Northeast Philly. She wasn't tired of taking care of me; she was just plain ole tired.

Moving to Northeast Philly meant my ninth transfer to a new school. I was so behind that the only way for me to graduate on time was Twilight School. That meant in addition to regular classes during the day, I would attend a special class three nights a week that prepared me for a high school equivalency test to prove I was on a 12th-grade academic level. It also meant I couldn't fail a single class that year. And so I worked, went to school, and shared an apartment with my 20-year-old sister. This was my new normal. I liked normal.

Chapter 25

Normal Love

Our new normal included having my sister's boyfriend over all the time. His name was David. Debora described him as nerdy, but I thought he was cool. He wore glasses, was about 6'2", thin and very handsome. He could have very well been a model for some very popular, very male, very American magazine, because he was also very white. With blond hair, blue eyes, a pointed nose, and chiseled chin, her boyfriend came from a family whose American roots went back generations; a far cry from his first generation Haitian-American girlfriend. But they worked. And they worked differently than any other couple I had seen.

    I never witnessed a normal relationship before being around my sister and her boyfriend. I didn't know what love was if it wasn't drama. I thought being in love meant you had to cry. If you didn't cry, it wasn't real. When my sister was with her boyfriend, she only laughed. They hung out with their friends a lot and ate at restaurants all the time. They cuddled on the couch and watched movies. I didn't hear them talk a lot, but I did see a smile in my sister's eyes whenever she looked at him. They were very normal. So, I thought it would never last.

    They say women are hardwired to fall for men that are like their fathers because dads are their first experiences with love. In my case, that is spot on. I was always attracted to guys that were narcissistic charmers, like my father. Debora, on the other hand, was able to fall for someone so different from her father. Maybe because her father just wasn't around. Or maybe because when he was around, Debora, with all her self-preservation and instinctual superpowers, picked up on exactly what she didn't want.

    I only met Debora's father two or three times during the few visits he made from Haiti. And at first glance, you would think Debora was attracted to someone just like him. Like David, he was tall. Like David, he was handsome. Like David, he had light eyes, and I personally believe, like David, he loved my sister. But the way he treated my mother made him exactly what my sister knew to avoid.

Chapter 26
My Sister's Father

When Marie hopped on a plane to America, she was running away from a life she didn't sign up for. When my mother's mother died, she left all that was hers to a trusted friend, local Police Chief, Henry Alexander.

Henry Alexander was a very tall, caramel complexioned, handsome man. An alpha male to say the least, he was driven by power and his governmental ranking. He carried himself in a way that told others that to be in his company was not just a pleasure, but an honor. Right before she died, Marie's mother, Lucienne, put all the proof of her assets and important documents in a box and instructed her only child to give that box to Henry. She told 20-year-old Marie that Henry would take care of everything. Not once did Marie ask how much her inheritance was. She never asked to see the will. She never even asked how she would gain access to what was now hers.

The day Lucienne died, she held Marie's hand and told her she was leaving. "I know you will be okay," she said, almost trying to convince herself. "Now go get Henry so I can say goodbye to him too." With tears in her eyes, Marie did as she always did, never questioning her mother and always obeying. She ran off, weeping, looking for Henry. She finally caught up with him at the police station. It took her so long to get to him that she was panicked.

"Henry, hurry! She doesn't have much time left," she pleaded, out of breath. "She says it's time. She wants to say goodbye. I'm scared." The two ran off and into his car. They were too late. When they walked through the door, they could see it on all of the faces that surrounded Lucienne's bed. She was gone. Marie fell to the ground and wept until she was carried away. She cried until her tear ducts swelled and dried up. *What is this pain?* She had experienced losing her grandmother only a few years earlier. It didn't feel like this. *What is this emptiness, this fear, these emotions I've never experienced?* For the first time, Marie felt alone.

After the funeral, Marie found herself dazed and depressed. She didn't know what to do next. Moving forward with everyday life just didn't seem right with Lucienne gone. *Am I to take over her business now?* Before Lucienne died, Marie started sewing, but she didn't sell anything, just made her own clothes. She spent most of her days hanging out with her friends in town, visiting shops, taking in the cinema, and just enjoying a carefree life. *Now what?*

She went to Henry and asked him what he thought. He was 20 years her senior. She knew her mother entrusted her care to him, and he was to be some sort of protector: a mentor and father figure. But Marie was young, beautiful, and gullible. Henry had other ideas for their relationship.

"Marie, let me take care of you," he tried to convince her. "You don't have to worry about the business, or what to do. You are young and beautiful. You should be someone's wife, a mother." Henry convinced Marie she needed him. It was only a matter of time before Marie had her first experiences of intimacy with a man, the man she saw as a father.

UNRAVEL

Marie called Henry "Poppy." All of his women did.

Before she realized what was happening, Marie had become Poppy's youngest mistress. Time after time, Poppy would have his way with Marie and then go home to his wife. Marie began to resent Poppy's apparent disregard for what she wanted and his overt disrespect by assuming she was okay being someone's mistress. By the time she opened her eyes to what she had become, she was bringing a new life into the world. It had only been a year since her mother died when Marie had a daughter of her own. "Lucienne. I will name her Lucienne," she asserted.

Marie felt less alone with a new baby. But she certainly did not want to take care of a child by herself. She had very little choice in the matter. Her baby's daddy felt more like her daddy, and she listened to him because that's who was taking care of her. He also continued to take advantage of her. Poppy visited Marie on a regular basis in the home Lucienne raised her in. He would drop off her weekly allowance, tell her the bills were paid, and tell her to lie down so she could thank him. Marie did what she was told and, as she describes it, "Let him do his business." That eventually led to a second pregnancy.

Marie says she never wanted or planned to have children that early in life. Perhaps at all. Growing up in a life of luxury and freedom from responsibility, she certainly never planned to be tied down as a mistress and mother of two baby girls. In a matter of two years, Marie's life had become something she did not recognize. She was confused and enraged with the injustice of it all; these were not her choices. The fire that had been laying in the pit of her belly since her mother died began to swell and surface.

Before her youngest baby was two years old, Marie obtained her passport. She did so during a time when migrating to America for Haitians was somewhat of a free-for-all. All you needed was a passport and money for a ticket. That she had. Marie told everyone that she was going to the United States to visit friends and would only be staying a short time. The truth of the matter was that Marie did not know when she would return. What Marie also didn't know is that she had enough money from her inheritance to run away anywhere she wanted and start her whole life over with her two children. If she wanted to, she had enough to buy a house in America and did not need to work when she got there. What she didn't realize is that she didn't have to run away from the life she hated so much. She didn't know that she had enough money to have power over her own life, the life Poppy had come to take over. But how could she have known? All Marie thought she actually had was her desperation to leave.

Marie sat her staff down and explained the situation. "I have to leave. But I will come back for my girls. Promise me while I'm gone you will take good care of them and protect them. Only their father can visit with them." Marie's staff was like her family. They would do anything for her, even without the promise of a reward. With total confidence that her children were safe and happy, she went to the airport with just a suitcase, headed for an unfamiliar land. She fully intended on seeing her children again soon. Either she would make a life for herself in America and send for them, or she would simply come home if things didn't work out.

UNRAVEL

Marie didn't know she was pregnant with my sister when she boarded that plane in Haiti. And there was no way to even imagine a man like my father would take advantage of her, weighing her down with a fourth unwanted child. That's what Marie had now, four daughters. Four daughters she never intended on having. Four daughters she never wanted. Four daughters, separated by sea, fathers, and hardship.

Marie's two daughters in Haiti were raised with about a dozen of Poppy's other children by him and his wife. Much of what they possessed were thanks to what Marie left behind, her inheritance. They were well loved and cared for, but I imagine they felt abandoned by their mother. I'm sure Marie had the best intentions for all her children once she had us. But the truth is, Debora and I got the short end of the stick when it came to quality of life as kids. In comparison, our brutal childhood in America couldn't hold a match to the safe childhood my other sisters had in Haiti. My only consolation is that I got the best sister. I hit the jackpot when I got stuck with Debora.

Chapter 27

A Shift

I was finding the rhythm to my new normal. Most days I just hung out at home in the new apartment with Debora and David. When I wasn't studying, I watched TV or talked on the phone with Bianca. No more hanging out. After I left Q, it felt like my entire life changed. I never officially broke up with him, but things were definitely over. Once I heard the truth from that phone call with Danni, it became easy to ignore his calls and stop visiting him. I was hurt and I knew there was nothing he could say to change that. The weeks I managed to stay away from Q felt like a lifetime, but I knew my future would look bright if I could just stay the course. The plan was to finally finish high school and start thinking about college. My sister made it clear she would support me all the way through. The tides were changing, and I could see a new horizon, full of promise. Looking out at that horizon, I was blinded by the sun and totally missed the moment I was hit by a wave.

That wave was Q.

There he was, sitting at the back of the bus after work. I hadn't run into him lately, but he apparently was still working at the food joint in the mall. I acted like I didn't see him. He took his chances moving up and sitting right next to me. "What's up, Felicia? Can't speak?" I kept silent, staring out the window. "Oh, okay. It's like that? Cool… Fuck it then." He got off the bus before it pulled out of the mall depot. He sat out there to wait for the next bus. I couldn't help but feel sorry for him; he looked so sad as we pulled off. I told myself to be strong.

When the weekend came, I worked an earlier shift just so I wouldn't run into him again. Bianca and I took the early buses together. Q managed to find us; he changed shifts too. The first day we were all on the bus together, we all randomly started to talk as if nothing ever happened. We laughed and reminisced about crazy times we had together. We all got off the bus and onto The El. Things were getting awkward as we got closer to 56th Street. I knew Bianca was getting off to go see Jason. *Am I going to let both of them get off and leave me, or is this really going to be like old times?* The 56th Street stop approached, and Bianca got up and gave us the "come on" head gesture. "Let's go."

Q looked inquisitively at me and agreed, "Yea, let's go." I hesitated for a second, then Q grabbed my hand. "C'mon. Hang out for a little, for old time's sake."

I followed.

The four of us hung out for about an hour on the same corner we did when we first met, feet from Q's house. Looking at his stoop made me cringe. I was so mixed up inside. So many memories. So many amazing times, the best of my life. It was also the reminder of some of the worse pain of my life.

After a while, Jason and Bianca made it painfully clear they were only standing out there for us. "So like, we ain't gotta be out here. I got granny's house to myself, and we about to go chill. Y'all welcome to come over but…we out!" Jason advised. I laughed and told Bianca to go ahead. I would be getting back on

UNRAVEL

The El soon to head home. We hugged and off they went. Q and I stood in awkward silence.

"So you really not fuckin with me like that no more?" he finally asked.

"Q, are you serious? I saw what you did that night. You lied to me. Your mother was not coming home that night. And God always showing me what I don't want to see… He always looking out for me! Because your little play thang rolled up just as I was leaving, and she told me all your dirt. And I know she came over that night and…" My rant went on for 20 minutes.

"Okay, but I didn't fuck her," was Q's response.

"I don't believe you," was mine.

"You don't have to, but I'm telling you, I didn't. Her and her friends wanted to come over to drink and smoke. I said it was cool, but I knew if you were around, she would try and start some stuff, so I told her to come the next night after you left. I had a feeling she was going to try some slick shit and come when she knew you were there. I just ain't want y'all to run into each other because I knew she always trying to break us up. And I'm mad because you let her win. Like, you didn't even fight for us." Q's rant was shorter. He shook his head and became quiet.

"What is there to fight for, Q? Your baby-mom and Danni both made it clear I don't have a chance with you and all your girls." I sounded defeated. "I'm too good to you to put up with all that."

"You right. You are too good. That's why I'm not letting you go."

"What you mean not letting me go? I'm already gone!"

"If you was gone, you wouldn't be standing here in front of me, looking at me with those beautiful eyes, making me want to kiss you."

"Boy, please," I said, pushing him away as he got closer. "Q, how am I supposed to trust you?"

"It's up to you." His tone turned serious. "You gotta make a choice. I'm telling you right now that I haven't always been the best dude but I'm willing to be totally straight with you. If you make the choice tonight to forgive me, then we can move forward. If you choose me, I'm choosing you, simple as that."

I made a decision that night that changed the course of the rest of my life. I felt it in that moment. I heard my higher self say to me in my spirit that there was no going back with this decision. It scared me, but I decided that this was the choice I would risk for the sake of love. It ended up being the choice that saved my life.

Chapter 28
Bitch

Q and I were back to us. Hanging out, on the phone until the sun came up, and overnight stays when we had the place to ourselves. Debora barely paid us any mind. She was fine with him coming over whenever. He would spend the night, and she had no objections. She was in her world, and I was in mine. She worked all day, and her boyfriend came over on the weekends.

Debora and I had survived hell. We survived The Grownups, The Monsters, Marie, and The Dark. I believed we would survive adulthood too, but I wondered how. I was trying to figure out what it meant to have freedom *and* be responsible for myself. I wasn't good at the responsibility part. After a few months of being back with Q, I stopped showing up to twilight school and cut my hours back at work again. The freedom became addictive. I didn't feel anyone could say anything to me. I went to school when I wanted and even though I didn't pay a cent in rent or bills, I had my friends over as I pleased. The nights Q stayed over, I couldn't get out of bed early enough to get to school. By the time I did wake up, I couldn't convince myself to do the responsible thing, go to school, even if I was late. Debora would already be out to work, and Q and I just wanted to stay in bed all day. He was 19, dropped out of West Philly High and planned on getting his GED.

When Q's birthday rolled around, I made grown-up plans that would lead to the most grown-up test of all. Debora was spending the weekend at her boyfriend's, and we had the place to ourselves. Bianca and I spent the day getting the apartment ready for Jason and Q. We bought lingerie, candles, fruit, and chocolate. We giggled at each other when the cashier smirked at us at the register. We knew what it took to keep our men. We had a CD made of all slow jams and love songs. She would take my room, and I would take my sister's. The four of us had dinner, and I had a surprise for Q; I handed him a box. Both guys seemed overly excited when he opened it. A spare key to my apartment, or what I felt like was my apartment. In all actuality, I had no right giving a key to my boyfriend because I contributed nothing to the household. My level of entitlement was impressive.

The night continued with over-the-top passion and heat. So much so that Q's hair caught on fire from one of the candles on the headboard. We all had a good laugh about it when we reconvened in the living room while we smoked and drank until the morning.

For the next month Q and I continued the way we always had. He was there for me when I started to get sick. It got to the point where we stayed in bed almost every day because I was so nauseas and tired. Another month passed, and I noticed I didn't get a period. I thought my period was off because I was on the pill.

When Q and I got back together after the breakup, I was smart enough to go to Planned Parenthood. I made sure to make regular trips, especially with thoughts of him sleeping around always circling in the back of my mind. The staff there were great at educating me on birth control, and I opted for the pill. I

UNRAVEL

convinced myself that the pill had to be the reason I was getting so sick every day and all of a sudden extremely exhausted. I constantly had to leave work early because of the symptoms. I told my boss it was the flu, then food poisoning, then stomach ulcers. After a couple of weeks passed with no improvement, she wasn't convinced. "Maybe you're pregnant," she suggested. I rolled my eyes at her and tried to finish my shift. *Am I?*

The next day I told Bianca I needed to get a pregnancy test. She couldn't believe what I was saying. We had recently made a pact that we would be careful and absolutely not get pregnant. Imagine her disappointment when I told her my symptoms. She agreed that I should get the test. But I had no money, and it would be a week before I got paid again. "Meet me at the Acme around the corner from your house after school today, okay?" I ordered Bianca.

We met up at the Acme and without a word, I grabbed Bianca's hand and went right for the women's care section. I wanted to be sure so I grabbed the box that had two tests inside—and the one that said it was most accurate, the most expensive. "That's 20 dollars! You don't have that kinda money for a tes—" I covered Bianca's mouth and put the test in my book bag. We power walked out of there and ran all the way to her house. We quickly waved at Bianca's mother when we walked in and ran up the stairs. We both went into the bathroom, and Bianca read the box while I peed on the stick. We went into her room and sat on her bed while we watched the stick go from nothing to two purple lines. Bianca told me what that meant but I didn't believe her. So I grabbed the box from her and read what it said for myself. I still couldn't believe it, so I peed on the second stick. Two lines.

I burst into a gleeful laughter. "I can't believe it," I said in shock. With wide eyes and my mouth to the floor, I smiled ear to ear, laughing and crying for 10 minutes straight; repeating "I can't believe it." I couldn't catch my breath. I was overjoyed; it was an unexpected reaction, a feeling I had never felt before.

I called Q and told him I needed to see him. He told me he was busy, but I urged him to meet me on the block for a few minutes. "It's important" I explained.

"Aight, aight" he grudgingly agreed.

When I got off the train, Q was already on the corner. He was guarding his block for dear life. "Why you out here?" I asked.

"Because Dukes got company," he snapped.

"Well, what's wrong with you?" My interrogation continued. "I don't want to have this conversation with you if you gonna have an attitude, Q."

"I'm here, ain't I? You said it's important. What's up?"

At that point I was getting angry. "Did I do something wrong?" I asked.

"Naw… but I told you this was a bad time, and you still got me out here, so what's up?"

I handed him the positive test. He looked at it for two seconds, then threw it across the street into an abandoned parking lot.

"I'm guessing you're not happy?" I fired.

"I already got a seed," he fired back.

"Okay, well, that's not what I asked you."

UNRAVEL

"I don't know how I feel. And foreal, it's not a good time to talk about it."

"Well, I want to talk about it now, Q. I'm pregnant, and you acting like you can't even look at me right now."

Q was eyeing every person that walked within three feet of us. A homeless person walked up and asked for some change. Q started punching him in the head. "Q, stop!" I shouted. After a few more two pieces, he let the poor bastard run off. He grabbed me and forcefully pulled me towards The El steps. "So this what you gonna do? Just act out and not say anything?" I demanded. Q grew more and more silent and started looking more and more insane, searching for an outlet. An Asian delivery man was his next victim.

I ran to Q's house to let his mother know he had finally lost his shit. The door was always unlocked, and I'd let myself in enough times to know that Q beating people up on the block was ample reason to come in without knocking. I rushed in ready to call for help when I saw none other than the beautiful girl, Q's baby-mom. There she was, sitting on the couch with their two-year-old daughter. I didn't know what to say. Then there wasn't much to say because Q ran in after me. She didn't look phased. She turned back to looking through a family photo album with Laci, repeating names of the people they recognized, and paid me no mind. Q walked to the kitchen to grab something to drink and back to me as if we weren't all in the same room. "Yo, you ready to go?" Q summoned to me.

I knew I had no place here. The mother of Q's only child made it clear I was no competition. But wait, maybe now I did have a place. I had new leverage and I refused to be dismissed without using it. Q's mother came down the stairs. "Hello," she said as if I was a stranger. I spoke back and stood at the bottom of the stairwell, contemplating my next move. *Do I tell his mother he was just losing his shit on the block and why? Do I start a fight between him and his baby mom? Do I spill the tea?*

Q and I still hadn't had a chance to really talk about me being pregnant, but there was too much rejection being fired at me for me to just turn around and walk away. I thought about the day I walked in the rain after Deon used me. I thought about the day Q lied to me to make me leave his house. There was new life growing inside me now, and I refused to be dismissed. "Q, I left my jeans upstairs the last time I stayed over, can you go get them for me please? And then I will leave." I started my strategy. Without a word, Q ran upstairs to get the clothes I kept there. At that moment, Q's mom yelled out the kitchen to his baby-mom to get ready because she was about to take her home. They really were a family. Q's baby-mom seemed agitated. She didn't want to leave before me, and she really wanted to see if I had clothes there. Maybe she was feeling a bit less sure of herself. Q jumped down the stairs and handed me my clothes. I smirked at her.

"Ho ho ho… what the hell is going on here?" she demanded.

Q flagged her, still enraged. "Don't worry about it. Ain't you going home?" he snapped.

"Yea, but before I leave, I want to know what the hell is going on!"

"C'mon, y'all," his mother walked in and interjected, "not in front of the baby." Q's mother always knew of Q's many relationships and basically helped him keep them up.

UNRAVEL

"You right, Mom," Q's baby mom said. I stood staring and thought, *She calls her "mom"?* "Don't nobody got time for this home-wrecker," she continued, looking me up and down.

"Home wrecker?" I yelled in fury.

Q's mom interjected, "Well, yea, you kinda are. You see this boy has a whole family here. Why are you here? What are you trying to do?" With that question, Q's mother opened a door I am sure she wished she could have locked forever. I saw the opening and walked right on through. I was finally going to have my moment.

"Well, I'm here because me and Q got some things to talk about." Q's mother and the mother of his child both started throwing insults and assuring me that I had nothing to talk about when it came to Q. I interjected. "Well, maybe me having his baby is something we should probably talk about!" They both stood stunned, mouths hanging open. Q's baby-mom's toned changed.

"You got her pregnant, Q?" she asked, hurt in her voice.

Q plopped down on the couch and threw his hands up. "Yea, I guess. I'm a fuck up. Everybody in this room knows it."

The room was silent for an entire minute. Then, in what I am guessing was an attempt to comfort Q and justify her own parenting, Q's mother went on and on about how he shouldn't beat himself up and that it's the girl that has to make sure no babies are produced. "It's their bodies, so they gotta make sure they are careful. Ain't nothing you can do, Q."

I couldn't believe my ears.

"Q can't take care of no kids y'all. This is on y'all. Now c'mon, Sasha. I'm taking you home. You can leave the baby here cuz she done fell asleep on the couch."

That's her name? Sasha?

With pain and disgust in her eyes, Sasha finally stopped staring at Q and moved to gather her things. She rolled her eyes as she passed me with no words, just a huff. Q and I were left standing in silence. I thought my announcement would have a bigger reaction from them and a better reaction from him. I was confused. I looked over at his daughter sleeping on the couch and I wondered if I could handle all of it. *Who do I think I am?* Q took a deep breath and grabbed my hand and led me to the kitchen. He sat me down at the kitchen table and pulled up a chair to sit close to me. He held my hand as we sat in silence for a good while. Then, he asked me what I wanted. "What do you mean what do I want?" I asked back.

"I mean… do you want to keep the baby?" he replied. I couldn't answer. I started to cry. The idea that I had an option never even crossed my mind. But now the question sunk in.

"What do you mean 'keep the baby'?" I asked with tears. "You mean an abortion? Why are you asking me that? You don't want me to have your baby?" Q started rubbing his head and then his eyes. I had never seen him cry before.

"I don't know… I mean, of course, but is this really the right time?" He stuttered. "We're both still young. I'm trying to get my GED and figure out what I'm going to do with my life and you…"

Q's mom interrupted by swinging open the front door. She poked her head in and saw that I was still there. She mumbled

UNRAVEL

something, huffed and puffed, and stomped up the stairs, slamming her bedroom door.

"I'm what, Q? Go head and say it… I'm what?" I started projecting. Although Q knew about the abuse from my dad, he never knew about the others, and I never told him the effects of it. I never told him about The Dark and my desires to leave this planet. But all of a sudden, I thought he could see right through me. It was Deon all over again. *He thinks I'm unstable, crazy, and too much.* We sat quiet for what seemed like eternity, neither of us able to grasp words. Finally, I came to terms with the fact that he wanted me to get an abortion.

"Just say it, Q." Tears came steadily.

"I love you so much." He grabbed both my hands and held them to his face. "I just don't know." We both started to weep as we silently made a decision. Before we could get to the actual words to have "that" conversation, there was a knock at the door. He wiped my tears. "Don't move. I'll be right back."

I heard some commotion and a girl yelling. Then a door slammed, and he was back. He stood me up and started hugging me. We stood that way for a few minutes when we heard a loud noise coming from the indoor porch. "Hold up," Q said as he let me go and hastily walked to the first doorway. Two girls emerged. "What the fuck, yo?" he yelled.

It was Danni.

Danni had climbed through the porch's open window. "You gonna talk to me today, nigga," she said, squeezing past him and into the living room. Q seemed lost. "Oh, hey, Felicia!" She smiled as I came closer.

"Umm can you please leave? Me and Q have something important we need to talk about." I said this so seriously I almost scared myself.

"Oh, go head. Me and my cousin just visiting. She actually here to see one of Q's homies. Where Nate at, Q?" Danni said this as her cousin walked in after Q let her in the front door.

Q's only response was to tell Danni to tone it down. "Yo...why is you being hype? My mom is upstairs sleep, and my daughter is right here. You gotta chill." Danni chuckled as she took a seat. "If I get Nate over here, y'all gonna leave?" Q asked in desperation. They agreed. Q grabbed me and walked me back into the kitchen.

"Why didn't you just tell them to leave?" I asked.

"Because I know them; they always looking for drama. They not just gonna leave. Imma just call Nate and tell him to come. Her cousin like him. He can get they drunk asses to go without all the extra drama." Q explained all this as he was dialing and waiting for Nate to answer. Nate agreed to come.

When we walked back in from the kitchen, I looked the way I felt: emotionally drained from what had to be the most intense day I had had in a long time. I just found out the biggest news of my life, and the reactions and emotions that roller-coastered throughout the day was becoming too much. I could hear The Dark calling. I sat on the arm of the couch across from where the girls were sitting. Q was pacing back and forth in front of the window, anxiously looking for Nate to walk up. "So what y'all was talking bout?" Danni asked with a ratchet tone.

"None of your business," I responded. I had had it. I felt entitled, emboldened, and fed up.

UNRAVEL

Danni sucked her teeth. "Girl, I don't know why you mad. I told you the truth about ole boi. I tried to put you on. But you prolly still falling for the okie doke. I mean the dick good and all, but damn girl…you in love?" She and her cousin started to laugh.

Her cousin jumped in. "This bitch act like she got a problem wit us being here."

"Excuse me?" I said as Nate walked through the door.

"Hey…wassup y'all. What's going on?" he asked in a chipper tone, unaware of all the tension in the room.

"This bitch acting like she got a problem with us being here," Danni's cousin replied.

"Yoooo…" Nate chuckled nervously, ready to interject, "No need for all that."

"Naw, Nate, it's cool," I said while staring at her like prey. "Let her call me a bitch one more time."

"Bitch."

This was the first time I went into The Dark and knew where I went. I went right in that girl's mouth. After that, I was gone. I went into The Dark and when I was back, I was being pulled off of Danni and her cousin. I was on top of them on the same couch where Q's daughter lay. His mother's screams from the staircase snapped me out of it. "What is going on? Stop! Oh my God! Stop!"

When Danni's cousin called me a bitch, I jumped up, charged at her, and punched her in the mouth. They both started swinging at me, and so I went batshit crazy on both of them. I had them pinned down on the couch, choked out. Q's mother kicked everyone out, including Q and me. Q walked me to the train to protect me from Danni and her cousin, who were circling the block in a car, waiting for me to be alone so they could attack. Q got me safely on the train, and I went home. I realized as I lay in bed that night that Q and I never finished our conversation. *Did we make the decision to get an abortion?* I wished we could have talked about it some more. I felt so confused and distraught. I didn't know what to do and so I started to pray. "Lord, please tell me what to do."

Chapter 29
The Choice

Christmas was coming, and I couldn't keep one meal down. As my sister tried to make our apartment a home by getting a tree and decorations, I laid on the couch, sick as a dog. I threw up. All. The. Time. Debora may have suspected something but she never asked. She told everyone I had the flu. And just when I thought my stomach couldn't get more upset, Debora told me something that made it flip upside down.

"I talked to Mom," she informed me as she kneeled down beside me, wrapping the tree skirt around the bottom of our four-foot artificial tree.

"Foreal?" I asked with my eyes closed, buried under covers. I did not have the strength for this conversation.

"Yea. She asked if she could come over. She said she has been back staying with a friend and working at some home health agency. I told her I guess she could come by."

"You did?" I asked, shocked. Debora had not said much to Marie since she found out the way she left me at Nedro Ave. We stayed focused on surviving while Marie stayed focused on what she always did, surviving too.

"Yea," Debora responded. "I guess I'm in the Christmas spirit."

A few days later, Marie came to visit, and I couldn't move. I was mixed up about seeing my mother but I was also throwing up at the slightest head movements. The resentment I had for Marie was at the bottom of the list of things I had to manage at the time: I was so sick, I thought I was going to die; I still hadn't finished my conversation with Q about getting an abortion. *If I was going to get an abortion, how was I going to pay for it?* The list just went on and on. But something in me felt comfort when Marie walked through our door. The moment I laid eyes on her was the moment I knew that I would be okay. I don't know why seeing her represented that. Perhaps she was just a reminder that what didn't kill me would only make me stronger. I had grown so strong since the last time I saw her. In any case, when I saw my mother this time, my natural instinct was to embrace her.

"Hi Mom!" I said as if the last two years didn't happen. Debora, Marie, and I picked up from where we left off. Things were different now, but our interactions were the same: awkward and tense. Marie seemed more comfortable whenever Debora left the room. Sitting next to just me, she warmed in conversation. "So, how's my baby?" She sounded like she needed something. All I wanted was to tell her right then was that I couldn't help her with whatever she needed because I had my own problems to deal with. I wanted to tell her that her baby was having a baby. Or maybe even having an abortion. I wanted to tell her that I needed a mother. I wanted her to just be my damn mom. But instead I told her what I had always told her: "I'm fine." The visit ended with that.

A few days passed, and I started to settle into the idea of being pregnant, having a baby, and being a mother. I knew I had no way of taking care of a kid. But the thought of a baby excited me while getting rid of it just made me sad. I decided it was time to test the waters.

It took a few more days, but one morning I mustered up the courage to finally do it. Or better yet, I was finally given the opportunity to do it. The jig was up. Debora came into my room and sat by my bed. "Why have you been so sick, Felicia?" she asked directly. "Are you pregnant?"

"If I tell you I am, you promise not to get mad?" I said, hiding under the covers.

"Ugh… Felicia!"

I emerged to look at her. "Well, what if I told you I was careful and I don't know how I got pregnant. I was on the pill!"

"Well, obviously you weren't careful enough." She had a point. "It doesn't matter anyway; there's no way you can have a baby."

Here was my chance to test those waters. "Well, I decided to keep it."

"Umm, no. You can't," Debora said as if it wasn't a conversation.

"Why not?"

"Felicia…you cannot take care of a baby."

"Okay," were my last words before she walked out. These waters were choppy.

Later, before she left for the day, Debora poked her head in my room and made it clear. "If you have this baby, you can't stay here."

That night, Q called me to ask me how much the abortion would cost. I guess the decision was made. The next morning, I went to Planned Parenthood to schedule the appointment to terminate my pregnancy. The girls at the clinic were all so very supportive and kind. They made me feel like I had all the choices in the world, but not that much time. The pressure consumed me. I set the appointment for the evaluation and counseling that was policy for anyone scheduling an abortion. And I found out the cost.

I called Q right after the appointment and I told him it would be $350. $475 if I wanted to be asleep. "Damn." He paused. "Aight, I gotchu." Q had never given me money before. I guess he really wanted this. "I will have it by the weekend."

I responded, "Okay," because I had no other words.

"I love you," he said, sounding desperate. I just hung up.

The next day I spent the entire day on The El, riding from one end of the line to the other, over and over. From seven o'clock in the morning to seven o'clock at night. I wanted to avoid everyone I knew, anyone who had an opinion about my body, my baby, my life. I had to search my own soul and try my hardest to hear from God. I knew what I felt inside. I just wanted some sort of backup because it seemed that I was all alone when it came to a final decision.

For hours I watched an endless flow of people get on and off the train. I watched mothers with their babies in admiration—flustered and rushing, holding them tight, smiling at their little faces despite the hustle and bustle. I watched people give up their seats to elderly people, respect in their eyes. I wondered how old the elderly people were, what their lives had been like. I watched young girls like me with their friends, laughing loud and free, looking like they didn't have a care in the world. Then, as the sun went down, I saw me; my reflection in the window staring back at me. I wondered what my life would look like if I had this baby. *What the hell will it look like if I don't?*

In that very moment, I knew. I knew with everything in me that the life that was growing inside me was meant to be. I knew that life was hard and it was not kind to me, but this life inside me would make all of the hardship finally worth it. I knew my baby had to live. If I did nothing else in this life, if I died giving birth, at least my life would have produced one good thing, at least my life would have had one good purpose.

After 12 hours of riding The El from one end of Philadelphia to the other, I made a choice. *I'm keeping my baby.*

Chapter 30

First Step

The weekend came, and I went to see Q to get the money for the abortion. I hadn't told him I decided to keep the baby. My mind was set, but I knew I was in a heap of trouble. The only reason I still had a place to live was because Debora knew I had scheduled the abortion. I believed that once she found out the truth, I would be back out on the streets, again. I had to bide my time.

With the choice to keep my baby, I found new strength. I felt confidence, knowing my baby wasn't a mistake. My baby was a choice. A hard choice. My choice. I didn't have a lot of choices growing up. But I felt power in this one. I was all alone in my choice, but I was strong in it. This strength reminded me of what it felt like when Marie left me alone at Nedro Ave. I felt strength in knowing no one had my back but me. Everyone could write me off as a failure; it didn't matter to me because the only person I had to answer to now was my child. I felt free.

I knew I would be a high-school dropout. That was okay. I knew that I would be shunned by the church; so be it. I knew I was a disappointment to Marie, but I always was, so that was okay too. It was all okay with me. I hummed "It Is Well with My Soul" to myself for days, quietly searching my heart for what I would do next. I felt a yearning in my soul. It was a fresh and original thought that rang true in my spirit. *If I am going to be a good mom, I need to get better.*

This thought made me take a look at my past as a whole. For the first time in my life, I sat back and thought about how I may have been affected by all the things that happened to me growing up. I knew I needed to get better because something deep inside of me was telling me I wasn't okay. Becoming pregnant started a chain of events that confused me, but I felt like I was called to some sort of action. This little life in me was pressuring me to face all the things I went into The Dark to avoid all these years. This little life in me was forcing me to cope so that I could survive, so that I could live in order for it to live.

A few days after deciding to keep my baby, I realized I didn't even know who I was. *How can I be a mom if I am so disconnected from myself?* It was time to take the first step to find myself. I had to take the first step towards healing. I could never go back to The Dark again.

Feeling anxious about the journey to find myself and begin healing, I took the money Q gave me for the abortion and booked a one-way train to Florida. I didn't know what I was going to do when I got there, but running away from all of the pain, disappointment, lies, and confusion that lived in Philly felt right. I needed to get far from The Dark. I needed to get as far away from it as possible so that I wouldn't always be so tempted to go back to it.

I sat on the train and settled in for the 24-hour ride. I exhaled and I watched the sky. I looked at every cloud and wondered about life. I admired the grandeur; beautiful landscapes of farms and acres of crops. I gazed at endless green of grass and trees. I remembered the feeling of admiration I had for trees; it filled me with gratefulness for how they sustained life, with air they supplied, the way they endured. I, too, was now sustaining life, providing what it needed, and enduring. My body was being used for something amazing. For the first time, I admired my body; I appreciated it. I relaxed into my seat, placed my hands on my belly, and smiled. Gazing out the window, I watched sun beams spray across land and I thought about how big the world was. I imagined endless possibilities and I knew that's what I wanted to give my baby, a world with no limits. I was filled with so much love in that moment that for the first time; I didn't feel the emptiness I felt every other moment of my life. Just for that moment, I didn't fear life. Just in that small moment I was given the gift of hope. So I decided right there, on that train, in that moment, to write a letter:

To: My sweet, sweet baby,

Hi, I'm your mommy. I haven't met you yet, but I know I love you already. I'm so scared to bring you into this life because I haven't been the best person. I've been such a mess. I've been lost and confused and I don't even have a place for you to live yet. But I promise you, I will soon. I just want you to know that I will do anything for you.

I promise to get better. I promise to work on myself so that you will have a much better life than mine. I promise to protect you so you won't have to go through what I have been through. I'm going to do everything I can to be okay by the time you get here. I'm working on it even in this very moment.

I love you...now and always,

Love, Your Mommy

FELICIA P. ROCHE

I folded my letter and held it tighter than I held anything. I felt a sigh of relief, and tears began to fall as I stared out the window. I felt so confident that I would do anything to make my baby happy. At the same time, I wondered what it would take and how hard it was actually going to be. My stomach was in knots as I thought about how long the journey to self-healing might be. I worried that I wouldn't complete it in time for my baby. It started to sink in that it was going to be a long, hard road. I felt like I couldn't breathe and stopped myself from wanting to just turn back, to go into The Dark. Reality was setting in, and I knew the first stop would be the scariest place in the world. My first step to healing was to find my father. I was on my way to see Lorenzo.

Part 2
UnRavel

Chapter 31
Triggered

Ten years after I visited Lorenzo in Florida, I got checked into a mental health facility—the result of being 302ed. 302 is an institutional code used for involuntary commitment. It's applied when a person who may have a mental illness is a danger to themselves or others and needs to be committed to a facility and monitored closely, often times held against their will. I met the criteria. I have no recollection of the events. The moments I am about to describe are all simply blacked out. But I have been told that when I was "302ed" and strapped into a stretcher, I became irate and attacked the paramedics. I slurred incoherent words, and nothing I was saying made sense. I had, in fact, in that moment, lost my mind.

When I was young, I went into The Dark whenever things became too much, too painful to deal with. As an adult, there was no escaping. Now, I had psychotic breaks, what some call a mental breakdown. Some of these episodes, like this one, led to suicide attempts. This particular episode started with disturbing text messages I sent to my best friend, who I was in love with at the time.

"when I'm gone ur gonna wish u treated me better. what's abt to happen is ur fault"

My best friend was a guy I knew from church. I was 27 at the time, and he was four years younger. We talked every single day;

his family had become my family, and he was "my person." He had been by my side through so many ups and downs for the last decade, and I just couldn't imagine my life without him. He was there through every mental breakdown and every suicide attempt. He knew I was fragile but he stayed by me anyway. He knew I could break, and I expected him to be careful with me.

After years of love and dedication between us, my feelings for him had turned romantic. But the feelings weren't mutual. I was in love; he was not. A few days before this episode, I professed my love to him, and he told me he simply didn't feel the same. I was devastated. I felt embarrassed, rejected, and alone. I asked him to come over so we could talk; he thought it was best that he didn't. So then I begged. His consistent "no" led to more shame, embarrassment, and feelings of desperation, and so I lost it. I broke.

I told my best friend I was going to kill myself. He knew my history and he knew to take my threat seriously. He also knew exactly what to do. He called my nearest relative, notified her that I wasn't safe, and insisted someone get over to me ASAP.

Debora panicked. She'd seen me lose my shit before, so she knew that if my best friend was concerned that I might hurt myself, then there was a strong possibility I would. My sister immediately rushed over, calling the ambulance and beating them to the small one-bedroom apartment I was renting, a block from our old house on Nedro Ave. While they all rushed to me, more text messages were sent, to her and my best friend. The messages were filled with goodbyes and apologies. I was ready to die.

UNRAVEL

Time lapsed and I was gone, escaping to The Dark. But this time I realized that The Dark was something bad, not an escape. It was a place I hid from the scary things. It was place I didn't want to have to go to anymore. The Dark evolved into a mental disturbance. The truth is—it was always a mental disturbance. It was only now that I was recognizing it.

I don't know where I went, but when I got back, I was sitting calmly in a hospital bed in a mental institution. My other best friend, and twin sister of the man I was in love with, was sitting by my side. "When did you get here?" I asked her as if we were casually meeting up at a café.

"Um, well, they called me and told me to meet them here." She seemed uncomfortable.

"You mean my sister?" I knew "them" meant my sister and my best friend but I wasn't ready to face the truth.

"Yea, your sister is in the waiting area, but you said you didn't want to see her." She explained.

"I did?" I couldn't remember.

"Yea. Do you want to see her? She's waiting to see you; I can go get her," she pushed.

"No, I don't want to see her," I pushed back. As confused as I was, I knew seeing my sister would be too painful. Seeing my sister meant seeing the past, a past filled with torture and shame. It meant facing what I had done.

The facility I was admitted to was filled with adults of all ages, genders, races, and backgrounds. We were all there because we posed a threat to ourselves and others. We were all a code 302.

Do I belong here? I wondered some days during my three-week stay. *Well...I did try to kill myself before. I did have thoughts of it regularly, desires and fantasies of what it would be like to end it all. So maybe I do belong here.*

The facility looked like a regular hospital. The rooms were clean, and everything smelled like Pine-Sol. There were two beds, covered in all white linen, in every room, usually two patients to a room. I did not have a roommate. I only interacted with others during group therapy and once in a while I did a puzzle with someone in the activity room. This wasn't my first stay at a mental facility, and so I knew it wasn't worth it to make friends. Those relationships never lasted. I ate my dinners alone in the cafeteria and I wrote A LOT. One afternoon, I sat in the lounge area with my journal, watching other residents. Some were talking to themselves; some looked catatonic like me. This is what I wrote in my journal that day:

> *"This is what happened to all those people who you see in the streets, wandering around in the dark, alone and detached from who they are. The ones you see smelly and incoherent; the ones who scare people as they walk by, babbling nonsensical babbles. They all were once people; people who were sane; people who had dreams, aspirations and goals. They were all children once, let down and failed by their own families and by society—just like you. They were all people that hurt and hid from their pain. They couldn't face it so they checked out. They disconnected, pulled the plug, and are no longer here with us in the present. Felicia, this is you. But it's not too late; you still have a choice. But you won't always, not once you are too far gone to come back. It's only a matter of time before that*

UNRAVEL

happens. Unless you decide today that you will fight to stay here. This is it. Make your choice."

I decided that day to do the work. Going that dark, to the place where my actions were no longer something I was conscious of, was the scariest thing I had ever experienced. I decided that this time, I would face my pain for me, no one else. I decided to do the work because I actually wanted to live. I knew it was going to be the most difficult thing I would do. I knew it would be scary and messy and exhausting. I knew it would take courage and strength I didn't have. What I didn't understand at the time, though, is that there were people and things I kept exposing myself to that kept me in a constant state of being triggered.

Ten years before I made this decision to do the work, I sat on a train and wrote a letter to my unborn child. In the years that followed, I would have multiple episodes like this. I said and did terrible things to the people I loved most. And it all started with that first trip I took to Florida after I met up with my biggest trigger, my father. Here is where I really began to unravel.

Chapter 32

Second Step

The day I arrived in Florida, pregnant, looking for my father, I stepped off the train full of optimism. I believed this was going to be a start to a new life. I was going to have a baby soon and I was going to fix my relationship with my father, and maybe with everyone from my past. I was going to work on myself and be an amazing mom. And it was all going to start as I got picked up from the train station by Freddie.

My big cousin Freddie, the one who was riding the bike during the accident that almost killed me when I was four, was now picking me up in a better mode of transportation, and this time I was more careful about taking a ride from him.

"Hey, little Felicia." I heard a voice come from an SUV. I smiled at the familiar face.

"Hey, Freddie! It's been too long!" We made a few jokes about how he was a safe driver now, embraced, and then loaded my bags into his car. It felt like centuries since Freddie and I played on Bayton Street. I felt a sense of safety with him because, even though I had that terrible bike accident with him, and he teased me all the time, he never really hurt me. Not like the rest of the people that lived on Bayton Street and Rittenhouse Street. The people I was about to see for the first time in 12 years.

After Marie, Gustave, Debora, and I moved out of Rittenhouse, all of The Grownups made the big move to Florida, together. The only one left behind was Joe, the dog. Freddie told me some childhood friends told him that Joe remained the neighborhood dog in Germantown and died of old age several years after the Delairs had left. We both gave a sigh when he told me. "Good ole Joe," we agreed.

Marie and Mrs. Delair had never lost contact, so through the years, I was periodically updated on the latest news from the south. Mr. and Mrs. Delair had divorced a few years after the big move and now lived in separate houses. Freddie stayed with his mom. She was still renting rooms to most of the same people while living in Florida, The Monsters included. Lorenzo had still been working for her on and off through the years but now, he had made a whole new life for himself. He had his own house, a wife, and kids. Lorenzo now had stepdaughters.

As Freddie drove, I took in the sights of Miami. I thought it was beautiful. I felt warmed by the sun and renewed by its light. As we got closer to his house, I also started to feel sick with nerves. I knew the point of being here was to get to know my dad better, to find some sort of closure or healing so I wouldn't pass on my trauma to my baby. I was also here to tell him that he was going to be a grandad. I had come to make an announcement to him and to the folks I considered distant relatives that a new baby was coming to the family.

Freddie had a bunk bed and generously offered to share his room with me for my visit. As soon as I put my bags down and settled in, I told him I was pregnant. That helped break me in. He was happy for me. Then I told his mom. She was weird about it.

"Marie know?" she asked with a squinched face.

UNRAVEL

"Yes, my mom knows," I lied.

"Okay, good." she said in her heavy Haitian accent, "Loco will be happy."

The truth was, very few people back home knew I was having a baby. Before I left, I told Debora I was keeping the baby and would figure things out on my own. I told Q that I wasn't getting the abortion and that he still had a choice. I told him he was welcome to sign over his rights, that I would raise the baby on my own if I had to. He said he would never do that. He asked for the abortion money back, and I told him I had used it for the train tickets and was leaving the following week. He stopped taking my calls. By the time I had arrived in Florida, I was more uncertain about my life in Philadelphia than I had ever been. Everything was left in the air: where I was going to live; whether I going to stay in a relationship with Q; what my mom was going to say about my pregnancy. It's strange to me now, but it seemed perfectly natural to me back then, that with my life in shambles, seeing my father was my priority.

I was filled with anticipation and anxiety to see my dad for the first time in so many years. I couldn't tell if my nausea was from my nerves or morning sickness. Mrs. Delair called my dad to tell him I had come to visit him. I froze as I observed her reaction to whatever he said on the other end of the phone. She said he couldn't wait to see me and would come over the next day. Hearing that allowed me to breathe again. I smiled a smile of relief and eased into what would soon be the moment of truth. The moment I would see the man who violated me more than anyone else ever did or ever could. I may have been harmed by plenty of others, but his violation was the ultimate, because my blood was his. My baby, growing inside me, was his blood too. I had to make everything right, for this new life.

The next day I got up early and did my hair. I changed my clothes about three times. I stared at myself in the bathroom mirror, sucking in my stomach. I couldn't help but wonder what was happening inside me. I wondered the same thing about the outside of me too. I thought I looked hideous. I had terrible acne and I had been wearing braces for three years. My life was so chaotic that I hadn't been to an orthodontist appointment in over two years. The braces were just on me, never getting tightened, so my teeth were still crooked. I was extremely thin, lanky, and hunched over with low self-esteem. I looked like a goof, always looking at the ground when I walked or encountered people. I didn't have money to take care of my hair, and it was stringy, oily, and dead at the ends. I hated what I looked like. I wondered why Q even still liked me. I wondered if my dad would be ashamed. I should have been wondering if he would have been ashamed of himself for not taking care of me, for leaving me when I was five and never coming back, and for molesting me. But those thoughts never entered my mind. In that moment, I just wondered if he would be ashamed of how I looked; that I was a pregnant teen.

I gathered my thoughts and my things and headed out of the bathroom. "Felicia, your dad is here," I heard Mrs. Delair call out from the living room. I couldn't breathe. I walked slowly from the bathroom to the front door with my toiletries in a plastic bag in my hand. *Where can I lay down my bag?* was the only thought I had. I started to panic.

UNRAVEL

"Felicia!!!" Lorenzo shouted in a strong Cuban accent. "Ahloooo…my beautiful daughtaaaaa!" I looked up to look into eyes as black as I remembered them. His hair was as curly and full as I remembered it; it just had way more gray now. His nose was just as big as I remembered it. His voice just as uplifting. He looked so happy to see me. He looked so proud.

"Hi, Dad," I said nonchalantly. I laid my bag on the floor. We embraced.

For the next few hours, we barely spoke. He rambled nonstop to everyone in the house about all of the carpentry and mechanical work he was doing and how crazy everyone he worked for was. I listened intently. I couldn't get a word out. He barely looked at me, but when he did, I just smiled and nodded. Finally, he talked about his wife and stepdaughters. Then he turned to me and said I was about to meet them. "Get your stuff. We are going to go now."

My emotions were going haywire. I was so scared to be alone with this man but I was so excited to be with my dad. I was anxious to tell him he was about to be a grandad but I never wanted him to come close to my child. I wanted to ask him why he was so horrible to me but I also wanted to tell him I loved him and I missed him growing up; that I needed a dad. I thought I was brave enough to handle it all. I thought my baby was giving me the courage to face my past. But alas, this moment was too much, and I went into The Dark. I was gone.

When I got back, I was in a room with two girls close to my age, maybe a little younger. I was laying on the bottom bunk of their bunk beds, and they were speaking Spanish among themselves. I sat up. "Oh, hi," one of them said. I nodded. I had no idea who they were or where I was. I assumed these were the girls that my dad said where his stepdaughters. They said more words, and I found none. After I got dressed and had breakfast, I asked Lorenzo if we could go somewhere alone. He took me to a fishing beach, and we took a walk. His wife and daughters came along but walked far enough behind so we could have some privacy. The words came out pretty easily. There was no emotion, no feeling connected to them. I came here to do a job and I just did it. I told him I was pregnant and that I wanted to work on having a father-daughter relationship. His response was that he was not happy to hear this news. He said he was happy for the baby but I was too young. There were no more words.

Later that night, I asked him if I could go back to Mrs. Delair's house because I was not comfortable at his house. His daughters were mean to me, and I did not know why. I was not very self-aware and totally missed how off-putting my demeanor was, especially when I went into The Dark. It would have made anyone uncomfortable to be around me. I get why they were standoffish and mean.

He agreed that it would be best for me to stay at Mrs. Delair's the rest of my trip and that he would come and pick me up each day so we could have time together before I left. He dropped me off there, and two days later, he called and said he was on his way over so we could hang out. It was the last time I heard his voice before I jumped back on the bus to Philly. He never showed up and never called again. And he also never picked up the phone when I called to tell him I was still waiting for him. After two weeks of waiting, I knew it was time to move on.

Chapter 33

Conversations

I cried most of the two weeks I waited around in Florida for my dad to show up. I cried on the bus ride home. But then, as I stared at the scenery up and down the east coast, I remembered how big the world was. I remembered how unlimited life was. I remembered how powerful God was and that my kid was going to be okay. So when the most beautiful skyline began to appear in my view, the city I loved, I began to cry tears of joy. So much misery happened here in Philadelphia, but it was also filled with so much life, and hope. I was learning that the world could be a monstrous place. Philly was the monster I knew. Philly was home. I never wanted to leave again.

Coming back home meant searching for strength to face what was next. Getting ready for baby. I put on my big girl pants and decided to have all the hard conversations I was putting off: telling my mother she was going to be a grandmother, asking my sister not to kick me out, asking Q to forgive me for taking the abortion money, and the conversation I was most nervous about—telling my pastor of my sins.

It was time to face the music. The man who had preached hell or holiness had also been someone I respected and admired. The guilt of becoming a teen mom was eating me inside, and I knew the church would judge me. But for many reasons, it was different when it came to my pastor. I wasn't afraid he would judge me; I was just afraid I had disappointed him. I made an appointment to see him my first day back.

Leonard T. Harris. He was the pastor and founder of Spirit & Truth, and I thought he was one of the greatest men I had ever met. We were close. Our relationship went beyond pastor and member, and it developed through circumstance—God's timing, my home address as a child, and his caring ways. Once Debora and I had become full-fledged members, he learned that our house was on the way to church from his house, and ensured we would not have to take the bus back and forth. Faithfully, he picked us up and dropped us off for every service. Over the years, my sister and I got to see what a lot of other church members did not. They only got to see Pastor Harris in the pulpit. I got to see how he reacted when someone cut him off in traffic. I saw how tired he was after service. I saw how human he was. And I appreciated it.

During the first year that Pastor Harris picked us up and dropped us off, I remember being in awe of his sermons and the reaction he got from the crowd when he preached. Here was this man that had ushers bring him water and people fighting for a chance to be able to have a word with him after service, giving little ole me door-to-door car rides.

I watched in amazement as this man preached hard and loud, the organ blasting and thunderous drums creating background noise to the powerful words he yelled from the Bible. But most times, on the car ride home, he was quiet as a mouse. The contrast intrigued me. During this first year of our car rides, I also watched him take care of his ailing wife of 43 years. I saw him pull over and hold her head as she threw up on the side of the road. We waited quietly while he made sure she was comfortable before he pulled off again. He was so rough in the pulpit, yet incredibly gentle with her. This contrast intrigued me too. His wife died the next year, and I can remember after he picked me up for church one day, sitting at a traffic light watching it turn green, then red, and then green again without him moving. He was turned towards his window, unwilling to let me see his tears. It was her birthday. He eventually wiped his tears and drove on so we could get to prayer. That left an impression on me, and I think about it every time I want to give up.

I knew the church as a whole was going to judge me, but meeting up with Pastor Harris that afternoon, I no longer cared. We met at the church, just the two of us. I sat at the edge of a pew on the choir stand, and he sat on the pulpit next to me.

"What's up, little girl?" he asked, using his usual term of endearment. "What was so important you had me rushing over here in the middle of the day? You know I'm usually napping right now."

Pastor Harris was in his 70s at the time, but he looked like he was in his 50s. He was the epitome of tall, dark, and handsome. He wore the sharpest suits and walked with a strut that made people call him the smoothest pastor this side of the planet. He wore big rings and drove a Lincoln. He fit all the clichés for pastors of black churches across America. But he was the real deal—no scandals, no hustles, no hiding. Just a man who really loved God and God's people. As best he could anyway.

"I messed up," I responded, looking down at the nails I was picking at.

"What do you mean?" he inquired. I started to cry, uncontrollably. He wrapped his arms around me and said it was okay. We sat quietly for a minute, then he guessed at what it was I had to say. "Is there a baby involved?" *Is this his way of asking if I'm pregnant?* I nodded as I wiped my tears and lifted off his shoulder. He grabbed my hand, looked at me straight in the eye, and said, "It's alright."

Pastor Harris told me that God loved me no matter what. I told him everyone wanted me to get an abortion. He smiled and said he was happy I decided against that. I told him for the first time, I felt real support. I told him my sister had kicked me out (she hadn't officially, but in my mind keeping the baby meant she would). He told me I could stay at the church for a few days, handed me some cash, and made arrangements for me to stay with one of the church elders.

Two weeks later, I finally mustered up the strength to face my next conversation. I had to tell my sister I was back and shed light on the fact that I was 17, pregnant, and homeless. I called her on the phone, and she told me to come home. Little was said when I walked through the door. Without skipping a beat, she hugged me and told me to stay home. "We will figure it out. We always do." It would be years before it dawned on me that my sister never really intended on kicking me out if I kept the baby. She was just using a scare tactic to protect me from something that she thought was going to make life much harder than it already was; something she knew I wasn't ready for. I ended up appreciating her for that, but even more, I appreciated her providing a home for me. I told her I would work hard to make her proud, that I would get my GED and a job and I wouldn't be a burden. I don't know if she believed me or not, but she became even more than supportive from that point on.

My next talk was with my mother. I invited her over to the apartment and just said it. Telling everyone else was plenty of practice, and it flowed right out. She told me she was happy she was going to be a nana and that she would help as much as she could. The conversation was short and so was her visit. Marie had her own life to worry about. At this point she was staying with a new boyfriend and trying to manage working and still living with her chronic pain. She made it clear before she left that day that she wanted more for herself, more for us. She seemed defeated as she walked out. I had no more contact with her throughout my pregnancy.

Finally, it was time to face the music with Q. I invited him over to the apartment, and when he walked in, much to my surprise and relief, he acted as if nothing ever happened. He embraced me, said he missed me and was just happy I was back. He got on his knees to kiss my belly, which was starting to bulge. He asked when we would find out what it was. I told him I wasn't sure, I didn't know how these things went, but that my first ultrasound was in a week. He kissed me and he spent the night. We stayed up all night talking about what we thought he or she would look like. We both wanted a boy and only discussed boy names.

Once Q fell asleep while the sun was coming up, I stared out the window from my bed and wondered how everything turned around so quickly. *How did I go from being so alone and scared to feeling so loved and supported?* I thought maybe the whole point of my trip to Florida was so that I could appreciate what I had at home. I didn't need the type of man my father was in my life or my baby's life. I needed the type of man my Pastor was, that David was, that Q was. I didn't need those people that hurt me over a decade ago and then disappeared. I had always had my sister, and now, my baby was going to have the best aunty ever. I realized all I needed to take care of my baby was inside of me and in the people that I belonged to. All I needed for my baby was right here, at home.

Q never brought up the abortion money, and the conversation about signing over his rights never resurfaced either. We were going to be a family. My excitement about how good things were going made me very optimistic, and I became reenergized. I immediately started job hunting, and within a week I got a job working full time at a telemarketing joint. Just as we did with Express, Bianca and I applied and interviewed and got hired together. I took a 2:00 p.m. to 9:00 p.m. shift, and she worked 5:00 p.m. to 9:00 p.m. because she was still in school.

My days became more and more pleasant as my tummy became more and more big and round. My heart grew more and more too. The day of my second ultrasound, when I would find out what I was having, I went alone. Q couldn't make it, and I didn't ask anyone else. There was something about that moment that was intimate enough for me to want it to be just mine. The moment had come; I was having a girl. The ultrasound tech handed me my sonogram, and I smiled ear to ear. With my eyes filling up, I held the image close to my heart and thanked God. It felt like I was granted some sort of assignment, an honor of some kind, charged with taking care of another life, my sweet, sweet baby girl. I felt like I knew who she was already and instantly knew her name. I didn't say it out loud, but it was there. I held my sonogram and felt my baby fluttering around. My baby girl growing inside of me felt like the most incredible love that existed; she felt like home.

I got on the train from my appointment and headed straight to Q. He was taking GED classes at the local community college, and we had made arrangements to meet in the cafeteria there. We giggled for a half hour over how much the baby's profile looked like his. We headed back to my apartment, all smiles. Q ended up spending most nights and weekends at my place, going back and forth to classes and work from there. I asked that he stop drinking and smoking, at least until after the baby was born. He agreed. We both worked and prepared for my baby's arrival. My entire pregnancy, I was happy and filled with anticipation. It was the happiest time of my life.

Surprisingly enough, Sasha seemed to embrace the new baby too. She was on board and excited that her daughter was going to have a little sister. She was embracing the fact that we were becoming a family. So much so that she asked if I would watch over Laci from time to time. Sasha was in a housing crisis and needed support while she tried to find a permanent place to live. I knew what that life was like, and my heart went out to her. I told her I would support her in any way I could. So, towards the end of my pregnancy, Laci stayed with us a lot of the time.

But when Laci was with her mom, it was just us: me, Q, and my bump. We ordered pizza, watched *Saturday Night Live*, and cuddled close, every chance we got. Sometimes we went to see a movie or we went to the mall. I felt like we were a real couple, a real family. It felt like keeping my baby was the right decision because all my dreams seemed to be coming true.

Watching me work hard to prepare for the baby, Debora started to believe that I was becoming a responsible adult. She made the decision to move out of our two-bedroom apartment and into her own. She transferred the lease into my name, thinking Q and I could handle the cost, and everything else, together.

I was now 18 years old with real adult responsibilities and I believed I could handle it all. The apartment was affordable, and my bills were paid. Q got a better gig with UPS and paid half of everything. I may have been a pregnant high school dropout but I had a beautiful man, people who loved me, and my own apartment. I felt safe and I was at peace. For a little while.

Chapter 34

My Joy

For the rest of my pregnancy, I had productive days and quiet nights. I loved reading articles, pamphlets, and brochures on becoming a mother. I followed the pregnancy calendar to a T. I never missed a doctor's appointment and I read how much my baby developed week by week. She already had all her toes and all her fingers. She could hear my voice and she reacted to my moods. She slept all day and moved all night. The bigger I got, the more I fell in love. I told her to stay still whenever I was trying to sleep. I think she listened. I asked her what she wanted to eat, and she answered. She hated Pepsi; the sight and smell of it made me vomit. She hated the smell of baby powder too. She loved music. Soft music calmed her and the "Thong Song" made her jump around in my belly. She made me laugh every day, and I didn't even know what she looked like.

My productivity and upbeat energy started making things happen a little too quickly though. At around seven months, my doctors shut it all down. I was put on bedrest. I had to stop working. I got a cat because I was getting lonely spending so much time home alone, in bed. Because I had to stop working, Q had to work even more, and I only saw him some weekends. But it didn't bother me. I was on cloud nine.

My baby brought me so much contentment, I thought I was somewhere else living someone else's life. I drew my curtains back and allowed the sun to shine through my windows. Once I was put on bedrest, I had to get on welfare and WIC. I was approved for cash and food stamps. My bills were paid, and I ate well. I started buying baby furniture and clothes. The weekends Q did come over, we assembled the furniture together and decorated the baby room. My sister stopped by for visits and always had some new baby items in tow. She bought baby clothes, blankets, bottles, and toys. Before I knew it, my apartment was filled with everything baby needed. She also brought me any food I was craving. I was being spoiled. Life was good as I continued to nest.

The last month of my pregnancy, I watched *A Baby Story* on the TLC network every day. Q massaged my feet and showed up whenever I called, with whatever I asked for. Marie even called a few times to give me her version of maternal wisdom. I didn't really see Bianca that often anymore, but we talked on the phone all the time. Nothing anyone did bothered me, and all was right in the world. My baby made everything perfect.

There was a time in my life where I believed that there was no amount of love that could heal my dark past and bring me light. I believed that there was no amount of joy worth the horrors and pains I had suffered. That was, until I met Kayla. With no hesitation, I'd go through it all again, a million times over, if it meant I got to be with her.

On August 7, 2000, Kayla Quinae made her way into this world and made mine whole.

Chapter 35
The Great Depression

Kayla's entrance into this world was pretty painless and as easy as she was perfect. She was 6lbs 7oz of pure dream. Her head was covered with the softest and blackest hair I had ever seen. Her skin was a tone I couldn't fathom, a beaming autumn auburn. And she was quiet. She latched on to my breast immediately and she was the gentlest soul I had ever encountered. Everything about her was just easy. That may be why everything about me was easy during my pregnancy, because her spirit and soul lived within mine.

Once the umbilical cord was cut though, I was cut from my joy, and my broken spirit resurfaced. I was back to just me—dark, confused, and scared. Kayla and I were now two different people, our internal bond severed, never to connect on that level again. I felt uneasy and distorted. There was a piece of me missing now, and I didn't know how to get it back. I went from feeling the purest of joy for what seemed like an endless amount of time to now feeling all the pain I forgot existed in me, and it all seemed to happen in one day. I was in hell. The doctors would later call it postpartum psychosis.

The first few days in the hospital, I just couldn't let her go. I didn't want anyone to touch her, and everyone who came to visit felt unwanted. I hated how Q rocked her. I yelled at him. Marie came for only a few hours and only after the day I delivered. I didn't even think about why she didn't fulfill what was arguably one of a mother's most important roles. My resentment towards her boiled over. She told me to go shower while she watched the baby. *I'd rather stink.* I didn't want her to come close to my baby. She held her once, then I made her leave with my nasty attitude. She had no patience for it.

Bianca visited—*no touching*.

Debora came—*you can leave*.

It was no wonder I was completely alone the day I came home from the hospital. I took a cab and I was so scared. I was confused about how to dress a newborn in 90-degree weather. My instincts told me to keep her cool, just a onesie, but keep her covered, a light receiving blanket to protect her from the sun. I was so scared that I would put her in the car seat wrong. I was sacred she wouldn't be getting enough air and stop breathing. I was scared that once we got home, something, anything could happen that would make her make a weird sound, or look weird, and I wouldn't have nurses and doctors around to ease my confusion and worry.

I put her in her car seat as best I could and watched her every second of the ride home. I carried her up the stairs to my apartment and placed her car seat on the floor while I settled in. I walked into my bedroom and saw balloons and cards. Q had cleaned the apartment and left me the surprise. I smiled, picked Kayla up, and sat in a chair, gazing down at my precious new baby, only three days old. Tears began to fall as I thought about how much I loved her already. I thought about the letter I wrote to her that day on the train to Florida. More tears. I tried to wipe my eyes with my shoulders, too afraid to move her head too much. In that moment, I realized I only had two hands, and I wondered if that was enough. *How will I take care of her and myself?* Suddenly, I wasn't sure about the promises I made to her in that letter I wrote when I was pregnant. In an instant that felt like looking at the rest of my entire life, I was scared shitless. I was in way over my head. With that thought, I rocked my baby, and I cried until we were both asleep.

I was awakened by her little wiggles and moans. I knew my baby was hungry. I fed her from my bosom. She ate, I changed her, and we slept. This happened every hour on the hour. And, as exhausted as I was, there was nothing else to do. Not eating, bathing, watching TV, nothing. Just nourishing my baby so she could grow and making sure she was safe. My very existence depended on her survival, and vice versa.

After the initial visits to come see the new baby, it was weeks before anyone visited us again. That's because I hated everyone who was not my child. I started to go deeper into darkness. I cried every single day. I cried profusely, loudly. All. The. Time. I could explode in a rage at any given moment, weeping and cursing my existence. Q would take Kayla and Laci and go into whatever room I wasn't in to protect them from my crazy. He thought I had finally lost it. My mother could only stomach it for minutes. She would come for a visit and act like she was there to help with Kayla. But when I screamed and cried, she made no effort to see if she could calm me or comfort me. In typical Marie fashion, she just walked out the door.

My sister tried the hardest, and the most. Looking back, I wonder what manner of depression this was that even her love couldn't pierce through. My hero couldn't save me this time. She tried, though, by offering me some space and time to breathe. "You need to get out, Felicia. Why don't you take a few hours to go for a walk or something? I'll watch Kayla."

"I WILL NEVER LEAVE MY BABY WITH YOU OR ANYONE... NEVER!!!!" was how I responded to the nice gesture. It was as if I was told Nazis had come to take my baby.

It was only a matter of time before everyone left me to myself. Q stayed at his mother's with Laci, and I was alone. There was no helping me; there was no getting through to me. So I went into the deepest depression I'd ever had. I laid in my bed for weeks. I didn't eat, I didn't shower, I didn't move. All I did was stare at Kayla, almost catatonic. I fed her from bed, I bathed her from bed, and I changed every diaper while I laid in bed. She was safe and happy, and that's all I could make happen. There was nothing left to even address myself—how I smelled, how I looked, how I was slowly dying.

Kayla was the perfect baby. She never cried. She stared back at me as if to say, "I know this is hard for you." She slept most of the time. She wished me peace before she could even hold her own head up.

The days pushed forward, and she started to sit up. She began making baby noises and grabbed my lips. She started to laugh when I made certain faces, and I laughed back at her. I felt an emotion besides sadness and started to feel life coming back to me. The time had come for me to face myself. But I didn't know how. And I had no one around me to tell me how. But I knew Kayla would soon need to go to her missed doctor's appointments to get her shots and to make sure she was healthy.

UNRAVEL

So eventually, I shuffled myself into the bathroom to see if I could clean myself up. Kayla was in her basinet only a room away, and I couldn't stomach it. I cried at the thought of leaving her and ran back into my room. I crumbled to the floor and cried until I fell asleep.

The sound of Kayla's hungry whine woke me up. I felt the dry tears and snot on my face and in an instant realized that Kayla would soon be old enough to watch how I was behaving. I stood up, grabbed some baby wipes, and wiped my face. I walked over to her basinet, and she looked up at me and smiled. I smiled back and I told her we would be okay. I promised. I changed and fed her and put her in her car seat so I could bring her with me into the bathroom. Now, I could shower without worrying if she needed me. I peeked out the shower curtain every minute to check on her. My shower started to take some of the fog away. Coming out of the daze of a very heavy depression, my brain had a thought. *I could use this same car seat method to get dressed, and maybe even clean up around the apartment, and maybe even eat!* I strapped Kayla in and walked us into the kitchen. When I saw the mess that I had created in my weeks of depression, my mouth dropped. It was like I was waking up for the first time in a long time, and my eyes were very open. "Kayla…what happened? When did Mommy make this mess?" I said in a baby-talk voice.

While I had no memory of it, I must have ordered in any time I did have a desire to eat because there were piles of take-out trash, maggots, and flies all over. I grabbed a trash bag and started cleaning. One room led to another, and by the end of the day, I had turned on music and cleaned the whole apartment. It felt so good to have accomplished something for the first time in so long. I thanked God for using my precious baby girl to remind me how to live. I looked around and took a deep breath. "I can do this."

Chapter 36

I'm Fine, Officer

Something happens when you wake up out of a depression. Everything looks new. It's so new, you forget how nasty you had been to everyone when you were depressed. Q was the only one who answered when I made calls back out to the world. He agreed to go with me to Kayla's doctor's appointment the following day.

The whole of Kayla's checkup, my stomach was in knots because I didn't know if Q would be coming back to the apartment with me. We had met at the doctor's office and barely spoke about anything besides how big Kayla was getting. I smiled and gazed into his eyes after the doctor gave a healthy report. I had forgotten just how pleasing to my eyes he was. I had forgotten why I loved him so much. I just wanted to be in his arms again. I got butterflies and couldn't hide my excitement when he didn't mention where he was going after the appointment. He just asked which bus route we were going to take. I grinned from ear to ear, and we went home. When we got there, he used his key. He reminded me that he paid half the bills and lived there too. I explained to him that I thought my out-of-whack hormones were the reason I had been acting so crazy before. He kissed me on the forehead and said all was forgiven. We ordered in and watched TV for the rest of the day, taking turns holding Kayla. I felt complete again. My family was whole again.

"So, you all healed up now right?" he asked when we finally turned in.

"Umm...yea." I giggled. "It has been over six weeks. Why?"

"Because I have missed you so much. And I can't wait another second," he said as he pulled me in closer.

"You really haven't done anything with anyone this whole time, Q?"

"Is that what you think?" He backed up as if he was offended.

"Well, I did tell you I was done with you the last time I kicked you out, so I guess I couldn't really be mad if you did. So...did you?"

"C'mon, now. You know what it is," he said as he came close again and started kissing my neck.

I had no idea what it was I was supposed to know, but I didn't stop him from kissing me. I really wanted to know what he had been up to for the last three months, who he'd been hanging out with, how was he fulfilling his sexual desires. But instead of asking for clarity, I simply did what I always did. The more he kissed me, the more I forgot about everything I was unsure about when it came to being with him. My gut told me I wasn't the only one he was kissing these days, but he was back in my arms, and I felt warm again. I needed someone else there with me. Taking care of Kayla filled my heart, but I still felt a sense of loneliness. I embraced the moment and let Q back in. We made love, and he slept in our bed. He didn't leave for days.

When it was finally time for him to leave, I asked him when he would be back. He said next weekend. I asked why so long.

"It's always been the weekends. What you mean?" he said, instantly irritated.

"I know, but I thought things would be different now, since we have Kayla here. I thought you would live here full time."

"Well, I can't do that. Work is too far from here, and since I work overnight, it only makes sense to go back to my mom's to sleep afterwards."

"Why can't you just come here and sleep?"

"Ugh…. C'mon, don't start your shit." He grunted.

"Well, what's going to happen when I go back to work? I have to go back soon," I probed.

"Okay, well, when you go back to work, I won't have a choice now, will I? Imma have to come straight here in the mornings. But that's not the case now, so I will see you on Friday night, okay?"

"With Laci?" I interrogated some more.

"What you mean? Why you ask that? Is there a problem with me bringing my daughter to my spot when I have her?"

His words were delivered with an intensity that scared me a little, and I responded in a shaken voice. "No, no…of course not. I was just asking."

But really, I wasn't just asking. I started to resent the commitment he had towards his first daughter. I didn't see it when it came to Kayla. Sure, he loved her. He fed her and sang her to sleep every chance he got. But there was something missing. My instinct was telling me something was off, but I had no choice in the moment but to let it go; otherwise, I might lose time with him again.

And so he left, and my weekdays became empty. I felt lonely and anxious for the weekends. I couldn't handle Kayla needing me. I needed people too, and they weren't there. I began to lose my temper when she wasn't the perfect baby she normally was. "Stop crying!" I yelled at her once. I got so afraid of the anger I felt rising up that I threw her on the bed and stormed out of the room and slammed the door. She screamed.

I sat on the couch, arms crossed, and frowned like a two year old. Tears fell, and I buried my face in my hands. "God, I can't do this!" I pleaded. I cried like I had cried when I was in my depression. *I thought I was better. Why is this happening?* I let Kayla cry for hours. I was too afraid of what I might do to her if I went back in that room and couldn't quiet her down. Then, when there was silence, I became afraid that she may have cried herself to death. I jumped up and ran into the room. She was sound asleep. She cried herself to sleep, and I believed I had failed as a mother.

The weeks were slowly passing, and after a while, all I cared about was making sure Q spent as much time with us as possible. I didn't want to be alone with Kayla anymore. Sasha had found a place to stay, and the schedule had changed. Laci came to our house every other weekend. Those seemed to be the only weekends Q came home. I started to become obsessed with why he wasn't coming home on the weekends he didn't have Laci. I started packing Kayla up and showing up at his mother's house just to see when he would show up there. I would pop up on him whenever I could and ask around about him. I finally started taking my sister up on her offers to watch Kayla just so I could stalk Q. I wasn't ashamed. I was out of control.

UNRAVEL

Every time I did see Q, it turned into an argument. "Where you been?" and "Who you been with?" was the totality of my communication with him. "Fuck you" was a regular statement, and an occasional "You ain't shit" would resound as well. Insults were thrown, and eventually objects were too. Every argument ended with my declaration that I was done with him and to never come around again. But somehow, every other weekend, with no resolve, Q would end up back in my bed.

As tensions were building, I became less amused with his visits and with Laci being at our place. One particular afternoon, the four of us had just walked from the shopping plaza about a block from the apartment. Kayla was in a carrier, which was still strapped on to me as we were putting away groceries. I was slamming everything down and clearly pissed about something, per usual.

"What the fuck now?" Q sighed.

"I know you fucking her," I said, almost out of nowhere.

"Who?" He was beyond annoyed.

"Her mother." You could tell by the way I said it that I resented Laci for who her mother was. "I'm sitting up here, helping take care of her daughter, while y'all having a grand ole fucking time huh? She got a new place, and that's where you been at. Cause you damn sure don't be where you say you be!"

"No, you just need to stop trying to figure out where I'm at all the time. I'm a grown-ass man and I can do what the fuck I want to do and go where the fuck I want to go."

"Well, you can get the fuck from me then because I don't have time for that. I'm going back to work next week, and your ass needs to be here every morning."

"If I said Imma do that shit, then Imma do it. But as soon as you get home, and on the weekends, Imma do what the fuck I want to do. Period."

"So that means not being with me?" I sounded desperate.

"Did I say that? If I want to be with you, Imma be with you. If I want to go see my daughter and her mother, that's what Imma do."

"Are you fucking her, Q?! Just say it. Because if you are, we can be done and you can just do what you need to do for Kayla," I demanded.

"So what if I was fucking her? How does that change anything? So what if I am?" he yelled.

Hearing that last sentence took me over the edge. The rage and frustration of not being able to make our situation work took over. Kayla was still strapped to me. She was asleep, and I didn't want her to wake up. Without thinking, I threw a glass at the wall. It was a wall Q was standing next to, but the glass didn't hit him, because I wasn't aiming at him. As much as he frustrated me, I would never intentionally cause him physical harm; I loved him too much. But throwing that glass felt liberating. I was letting out a lot of pent up frustration.

I screamed, and I cried, and I threw another one. He was startled and covered himself. Once he realized I wasn't aiming at him, he yelled at me. "What the fuck you doing, yo!" I felt empowered and threw another. "Yo, my fucking daughter is right there!" Laci was feet away in the room next to the kitchen.

I screamed again, "Fuck you!" Q charged towards me. Before I could pick up another glass, he punched me right in the mouth. Then in the eye. Then across the face. I ran into the bedroom, bloodied, Kayla still strapped on. He charged after me, cursing and asking what was wrong with me. I had seen this Q before. When he beat the crap out of that homeless guy, and the delivery man, the day I told him I was pregnant. He was relentless with his beatings. He beat his victims until he got out his frustrations. I knew he wasn't satisfied with the three punches to my face. He wanted more.

As he tried to push through, I stood against the bedroom door, screaming for mercy. "Nooooo... Noooo... Please... Please... Stop!" I screamed and I screamed at the top of lungs. Then I realized that, as I was holding the door shut, screaming with blood pouring down my face, Kayla wasn't moving. I had been squeezing her the entire time. "Oh my God! Q stop! Kayla isn't breathing. Please stop!"

That got through to him. "Let me in so you can put her down. I'm not going to hit you!" We both instantly forgot about our fight and turned our attention to Kayla. He helped me unstrap the carrier. Kayla looked lifeless. We laid her on the bed. He yelled, "Why the fuck she not breathing?"

We were both too afraid to check. Just then there was a knock at the door. We ignored it because we could not move without knowing if Kayla was alive. Finally, she moved her head and did a little baby stretch. She was just sleeping as hard and as peacefully as she always had. No noise or disturbance could ever interrupt that, not even this fight.

With the relief that Kayla was okay, our fight was over. I washed the blood from my mouth, and he gave me ice for my eye. We continued to put the groceries away when another knock came at the door. It was the police. My landlord lived downstairs and called the cops when he heard all the commotion. He stood behind the officer when I answered.

"Yes, can I help you?"

"Good evening Miss. Uh, we got a call about a disturbance in your apartment. Someone was screaming for help?" the officer replied. My landlord looked away as if it wasn't clear that he was the one that called.

"No, everything is fine," I responded.

"Are you sure? Because if you're not safe, we can take whoever did that to your lip to jail tonight."

I was sure. I was still in shock and pretty upset by what Q did to my face, but I was sure I didn't want him to have to go to jail for it. I was sure that it was all my fault because I started it when I threw that glass. I was sure that I didn't want to be alone that night. I couldn't face all this alone.

"No, sir. It was just a misunderstanding. Everything is fine now." My landlord put his hand through his hair and shook his head.

"Okay, well, there really isn't much we can do if you don't report anything," the officer said to me while looking back at my landlord.

"Okay, well, thank you," I said with a smile as I shut the door.

Q was at the top of the stairwell, where he had listened to the whole thing while holding his breath. He wasn't cut out for jail. His relief looked like admiration for me. We hugged tighter than ever when I got to the top of the stairs.

Q bathed and put Laci to bed while I cleaned up the kitchen. Kayla stayed asleep. I cooked us a nice steak dinner, and we sat at the table and ate, and talked, and laughed as if nothing ever happened. Q avoided my swollen lip and black eye as we made love that night.

The next few weeks went the way we expected them to. Debora got me a job at a litigation company she worked at. She was a case manager and had some pull. My job was simply filing and copying, but it paid well. It was refreshing to go into work each day to a fancy office, a far cry from the broken-down warehouse-looking building the telemarketing place was in. I got to wear slacks and I started putting on makeup. I wanted to fit in with these people who seemed to have their whole lives together. I sat at a small desk by the copier, and every person who walked by smiled and said good morning, hello, and good night, like clockwork, every day. It was hard to smile back every time.

My soul died a little each day I had to leave my precious baby. Q showed up in the mornings after his shift at UPS, and I dreaded the moment I had to say goodbye. Nothing in me wanted to leave them, but welfare and Q's part-time checks just weren't cutting it anymore. Besides, welfare required you to find a job six months after you had a baby.

Some days, I left work early because I was worried about Kayla. I knew that Q worked all night and would sleep all day. I knew Kayla was not getting the best care. Not like the care I gave her when I was home. I made sure to feed her every morning before I left because some days she wouldn't eat again until Q woke up around 1:00 or 2:00 p.m. The days I left work early I would come home to find her still in her crib, diaper filled and stomach empty. She was such a good baby that she just played in her crib like that for hours, alone. I felt shame for leaving her like this; she deserved better. After catching her this way more than a few times, I knew I couldn't do it anymore. I may as well have been leaving her by herself.

The quality of care, or the lack thereof, that Q had for Kayla was the biggest turn off for me and before long, I just didn't find him attractive anymore. I began seeing him as a loser, a man who couldn't even wake up early enough to feed and change his baby. I wondered why I kept him around anymore. I wondered why I was in this dangerous cycle.

And then I remembered that it was because I was determined to make this family work. I wanted Kayla to have a mommy and a daddy in the same house. I wanted her to be safe and cared for. I knew Q would never hurt her and I knew he would, at the very least, protect her. I knew he would harm anyone who even thought about harming her. I didn't have that kind of protector when I was small. My child would. So I kept trying to make it work.

I had a serious talk with Q and asked him what he wanted. I asked him to be honest but I had no idea what being honest would mean. He told me that Sasha was his girlfriend. That she always was. That she knew about us and she was okay with it. He told me he didn't want to lose me and that sometimes people just love two people at the same time. I had no words. Feeling defeated, I told Q that I gave up. I told him that he and I would always be friends but that Sasha could have him. I told him I wasn't going to be in competition with her anymore; that I couldn't be. He said he didn't accept that and that he wasn't going to let me go. I didn't know what that meant but I didn't have any strength in me left to try and figure it out. So I focused on myself instead. The small window of time in which I found the strength to leave Q was overtaken by the sudden familiar feeling of constant nausea. I couldn't believe it.

I was pregnant again.

I wanted this pregnancy to end for no better reason than to stop the unbearable daily nausea and vomiting. I just wanted to get back to my life of caring for my baby. This constant state of being sick made that impossible. The day I got the positive results from Planned Parenthood was the same day I made the appointment for the abortion. The co-pay was $360, $450 if I wanted to be put to sleep. Q was there with me when I scheduled the appointment. We didn't talk about it. I didn't think about it. I couldn't allow myself to feel anything. I had to just survive. I had to just get past it. We decided to skip rent that month so we could afford the abortion. Rent remained a month behind from that point on.

The day of the procedure I was alone. I took the bus to the clinic and got an ultrasound so they could confirm how far along I was. Only a few weeks. I remembered from my pregnancy books that meant it was tiny and alien-looking, no longer just an egg. I closed my eyes and tried not to think about it. I was here and now I didn't have a choice. I started to wonder why I wasn't as sure about this life as I was about Kayla's. I got so sad and so confused. I convinced myself I was doing this for Kayla. *I can barely take care of her; if I have another one, what kind of life would she have? Would her childhood be taken away, like my big sister's was?*

I felt like I needed more time to think. *What if I could give this baby AND Kayla all the love they need to be happy? But, I am already here.* As I laid on the procedure table and put my legs up, I became consumed with grief. I wished now with everything in me that we had spent the extra hundred dollars to put me to sleep. But we just couldn't afford it. It hurt like hell, worse than labor. The life being ripped from my body crushed my soul. Into The Dark I looked and soon disappeared. I was gone. I don't know where I went, but when I got back, I wasn't pregnant anymore. I was back home laying on my side with a heating pad against my uterus. I cried for days.

Despite this firsthand experience, I don't hold strong views on abortion. I am grateful my mother was not successful in aborting me. And while I am happy I decided to keep Kayla, I chose otherwise for this pregnancy. I don't consider these "good" or "bad" choices, but I am grateful that I had the freedom to choose.

At the time, Q also seemed to have no real opinion. He didn't say a word about the abortion to me nor I a word to him. He simply came to check in on me and cared for Kayla. I stared at him a lot, quietly watching his interactions with his baby and wondered if he could have really taken care of another. I wondered how we got to this point. I looked at him playing with Kayla, singing to her. "Nothing but a little pumpkin, nothing but a little pumpkin," his song to her that made her giggle little baby giggles. His song to her to calm her when she was fussy. His song to her to put her to sleep. He was so good with her; he made her happy. Kayla had a daddy who loved her. She was safe and she was whole. I wondered what it would have been like to have a father that could make me feel that way, someone I could depend on my whole life. Then I remembered, I did have someone. I always did.

Chapter 37
Never Alone

During my postpartum depression, I was blind to all the love I had around me. I believed I was totally alone. And it wasn't a pity party; it was a true and real belief system. I felt alone and I truly believed I was. The truth though, was that I was never actually alone. My sister never once stopped supporting me. I don't have a lot of memory of it, because of the depression, but my sister was there. I was able to experience moments of peace and joy while I was pregnant with Kayla, mostly because my sister was loving me, caring for me. Debora threw me a baby shower when I was about seven months pregnant, but I barely remember it. And on the Fourth of July, a month before going into labor, Debora invited me out with her, David, and their friends to see fireworks. This night I do remember. Although to the average person it might seem like just a regular night out, it meant the world to me.

Debora and her friends were young, free, and full of life, all in their early 20s. My sister didn't seem annoyed that she had her little sister tagging along like she was when we lived on Bayton Street. She patiently waited for me to catch up as I waddled toward the large crowd at Penn's Landing, about to join in on all the Independence Day festivities. We rested often by the waterfront, trying to make out the lights from the buildings across the river in New Jersey. The Benjamin Franklin Bridge was lit up in red, white, and blue. I felt like a kid again, remembering the feeling of anticipation of the fireworks. The Delairs brought us to this same spot once or twice as kids to see fireworks. Whenever we stopped so I could rest, we'd stare out into the water past the crowd and Debora would bring up a good memory like that, many of which I had forgotten.

Everyone around us, including David and all their friends, were drinking that night, but not my sister. She normally would, but that night, she made sure to stay sober to watch after me. She kept checking in, asking if I was having fun. She stayed with me, present and engaged. She was actively loving me.

Love means being present, and my sister was always present, right there with me when I didn't even know it, when I couldn't see it. She was right there in front of me. She paid the bills and rent when I first got home from the hospital. She dropped in from time to time when I was mean and nasty, just to make sure I knew she was present. It's a lie that Q was the only person who answered the phone when I came out of my depression. Because no matter how ugly I got towards her, my sister never stopped answering the phone. She did create boundaries; she certainly was never going to be anyone's punching bag. But the truth is, she was always just a phone call away.

Had I seen any of this for what it truly was, maybe I would have stopped running.

Chapter 38
Welfare to Work

After the abortion, Q stopped showing up to watch Kayla, and I lost my job. The less he came around, the less money he gave me. With no childcare in place, I couldn't even go job searching, let alone go to work. The welfare checks weren't enough to make ends meet, and there was no additional income in sight. The first to go was my phone; it got cut off. My heart broke every time I had to run out to the corner to use a pay phone. Next came the shut off notices for the utilities. Debora, of course, would always "lend" me the money to pay them. "I don't want my niece in the dark," she would say as she paid a bill, knowing full well I would never be able to pay her back. I could tell she was disappointed in me so I avoided her as much as I could. I thought she was growing weary of my inability to care for myself, and now my kid.

Some days I used all my resources to better my life, try to find a job, or figure out a way to make money. But most days, I just hid from all of those pressures. I drew my curtains and laid in the dark. I pulled the covers over my head while Kayla watched *Sesame Street* reruns all day from her walker. I was depressed again. A relapse. I couldn't move from off the couch. I cried and prayed something would happen, that anything to distract me from the pain would happen. And it did. An eviction notice. I knew I had no way to pay my rent. I started to believe I had no way of going to work. I started to believe that all I knew how to do is show up to the welfare office for my appointments. I told myself I was good for nothing.

Every Sunday when the paper came, I looked at the classifieds. I thought maybe if I found a night job that someone—Q's mother, my mother, or even Debora—could at least keep Kayla overnight. All she did overnight was sleep. Surely, they wouldn't say no to that if it meant I could work. I searched and searched and saw no overnight jobs I was qualified for, except for one: "Wanted: Dancers at XXX Club. Must be 18 and willing to work every weekend. Make as much as $500 a night."

With that kind of money, I could pay my rent after just one weekend! I was almost 19 and I knew I had the body for it. *This is the answer to all my problems*, I thought.

One night, I asked Debora to watch Kayla so I could go on my interview. She had no clue what her baby sister was about to get herself into. The guy I spoke to on the phone, the owner of the place, told me to be there by 8:00 p.m. so I could meet the other girls. They usually got there around that time to get ready.

When I walked through the doors of the club, I was greeted by a harsh-looking woman. She had dark brown skin, broad shoulders, and a matted wig on. She wore a sequined bra, and her stomach was hanging over the shiny black tights she seemed to have squeezed into. She greeted me, and I hesitated to speak back, distracted by her front gold tooth, next to a chipped one. I told her why I was there. She looked me up and down and told me to wait there. In that moment, I realized I probably wasn't dressed right for the interview. I had on jeans and a jacket; I wasn't

UNRAVEL

showing any skin. I wondered if I would have to show more to get the job.

"Oh, yes, yes, yes, you will surely do," a dark skinned, bald man said as he walked up, rubbing his hands together, looking at me as if I was a T-bone steak. I was used to being cat called on the streets in the same manner, almost daily since I was a kid. I was used to being stared at by creeps. But it was something about being in that place at that time, for work, with a baby at home, that made his mannerisms piss me off. I thought that somehow, I deserved more respect than that from a potential employer. I felt something I wasn't used to. *Is this pride?*

I put my hand out for him to shake, as if I wanted him to be clear that I was there for business. He grabbed my hand and kissed it. I wiped it off. "Follow me. I'll introduce you to the other girls," he said. He walked me past the bar and the stage where one girl was already dancing. The place was still pretty empty with one or two men lazily drinking beer at the bar. The place was filled with smoke, and the smell of weed, which was all too fitting for a gritty strip joint in the middle of Kensington, a neighborhood in Philly that was overrun by drugs. Hardcore rap played in the background. When we got to the back, I was introduced to a young girl, maybe a few years older than me. She looked just as rough as the girl up front, but younger. She was nicer too. She smiled and introduced herself by her stage name, Diamond.

Diamond told me I was pretty and that I would do well. She introduced me to the rest of the girls. They all said hi, one by one. Some were naked, shaving their lady parts, and others were putting make up on, also naked. I felt uneasy. I wondered why these girls had chosen this profession. They all told me how much money they were making, and I realized that the choice wasn't that hard.

For some reason, though, the choice was hard for me. I didn't judge any of the ladies who were there. I didn't know where I was going to live if I didn't come up with rent money. I understood being in a position of just having to do what you needed to do. I also understood that for some ladies, they simply enjoyed the job. But I wasn't sure if I was really in that place just yet. I wasn't sure if I was ready to give up on the hard work I had done to value my body, a body I now believed was meant to bring beautiful life, not be used and abused. For me, it would have meant going back to not caring about what I was doing with my body, again. And I wasn't sure if I could handle that.

So, I walked out, unsure.

The next day I lay in bed thinking about how much money I could make if I would at least give it a try. I had about two weeks before I had to pay rent or leave. I could still make enough money to stay. I thought about my options. Q had stopped paying half of the rent months ago. I never asked why he had all of a sudden stopped giving me any money, afraid to bring it up. I couldn't bring myself to tell him that I was now actually considering becoming a stripper. But one night when he was over, I asked him what he thought was going to happen if I (not we) didn't come up with the money. He shrugged and answered, "I don't understand why we gotta pay so much anyway. Like why? Why do we have to pay rent? I can't be giving that man half my check every month no more, so do what you gotta do."

UNRAVEL

"So you rather me and Kayla have nowhere to live?" I asked, frustrated. He told me to shut the fuck up, and I told him he was an idiot and a deadbeat. He punched me in the mouth, again. I knew I wasn't going to do anything about it and so did he. I ran out the house so we could both cool off.

As I walked up the street, I made a decision. I felt completely alone and on my own in every sense of the word. I felt like I was the only somebody Kayla was ever going to have. I was convinced that if I didn't go out and make money, we would be living on the streets. With the pain of how Q—a man that once adored me—was treating me, I felt an overwhelming feeling of abandonment. I started to believe that everyone who ever loved me would get tired of me at some point, even my sister. I and I alone was responsible for Kayla now. I knew what I had to do.

I walked up the block to go get the paper from the market. I knew that even if I didn't want to go back to that last club, because of how gritty it was, that there were plenty of other ads for exotic dancers and I would just pick one and start that night. My mind was made up. When I got closer to the market, a blue pickup truck slowly drove past me. The man driving the truck was a broad-shouldered, bald, white man. He reminded me of Mr. Clean. As he drove past, our eyes locked. It was if he stayed while the truck drove off. Once the truck turned the corner, I came back to myself and shook off the feeling I got from locking eyes with that guy. Weird.

I turned the corner and cut through a parking lot towards the market entrance where all the newspapers were. I got close to the entrance when I saw the blue pickup truck pull up and park. The man got out and called for my attention. "Hey, Miss! Yea, you.

Can I have a moment of your time? It's okay… I'm not gonna bite."

I giggled uncomfortably. "Yea…sure. What's up?"

"I have a message for you."

"A message for me?"

"Yea, for you. It's a message from God. He wanted me to tell you that you aren't alone. You think you are but you're not. He wanted me to tell you that He sees all the hard work you are doing, and you're headed in the right direction, so just keep going. Don't turn back. He said, anything you need, just ask Him for it, and He will give it to you. Oh, and one more thing, He said He wants you to smile."

I stood there frozen. It felt like I was staring at myself from that man's body. I could see how shocked I was. I could see I was stunned that God had actually spoken directly to my situation. I could tell how much I needed to hear that and I could also see in me how much I believed every word to be true. With that, the bald man winked at me, jumped back in his truck, and drove off. I was still standing in the same spot, wondering what to do now. I ran to a pay phone and called Pastor Harris. I wanted someone to tell me that what just happened could actually happen. No answer; just the machine.

I walked home with a smile on my face and tears in my eyes. I knew God was with me. I also knew I was being evicted and I had no clue where I was going. But God just told me I would be okay, and for some reason, I believed it.

After my miraculous encounter, I didn't become a stripper, but I also didn't find other work. I stayed in the apartment another month past my eviction date. I was officially a squatter, scrounging and begging for money so I could save up enough to possibly stay, hoping to bide time to find other work. I continued my participation in a welfare-to-work program, and that made me think about going back to school. The program required we report to a resource center located in center city, across the street from The Gallery. We were expected to show up every day from 9:00 a.m. to 3:00 p.m., with our kids, and social workers would help us find jobs, childcare, and other resources to help us become gainfully employed. I spent each day there doing online job searches on the computer and attending resume-building and other self-development workshops. I became committed to making this program work for me because I still needed to get a GED and no one would hire me without one. I knew I needed to secure some sort of childcare. More than anything, I knew things desperately needed to change.

The eye-opening moment that something drastically needed to change came when I got punched again in said eye. My last beating from Q. I realized he would probably never stop hitting me. It became his go-to to get me to stop asking him for anything; to get me to stop complaining about how he wasn't pulling his weight. At some point I knew that was never going to change and even more, I knew I never wanted Kayla to see me get hit by her father, or anyone for that matter. I wanted more for her. I would be damned if I ever allowed anyone to hit my baby, and I realized I had to set the example. Wanting better for Kayla is what always led to the most pivotal moments of my life.

After another abortion, many beatings, and all his sleeping around, I had finally had enough of Q. I was leaving him, and it was for good this time. I decided I needed to start over. In my subconscious, I knew the root of all my emptiness and all my issues with men came from Lorenzo. Leaving Q instantly and instinctually made me want to try to fix things with my dad again. Beneath all I was dealing with, at the very core, was my hope for a father. The little girl inside me resurfaced again, and I fantasied, even believed, that if I reconnected with my father this time, he would be ready to be there for me.

I took all the money I was saving to pay rent and bought bus tickets to Miami. I just up and left. I didn't pack anything besides a duffle bag worth of clothes for Kayla and me and abandoned all our belongings. My impulsive decision to just up and go cost me all I owned, all I accumulated over the last two years I lived in that apartment. All our furniture, walkers, baby seats, pictures, accessories, everything. I thought I didn't care because I desperately wanted to be free from all the responsibility that came with that apartment. I never wanted to look back.

Chapter 39
Starting Over

When I got to Florida this time, everyone was excited to see the latest addition to the family. "Little Felicia" is what they called her. They couldn't get over how cute she was. Freddie planned out our activities for the entire trip. He always made me feel welcome. He worked at the Greyhound Race Tracks, so we hung out with him there a few days, watching the dogs race. Over the weekend, on his days off, he took us to Sea World and then to Monkey Jungle. At two years old, Kayla's eyes lit up with every adventure. Freddie's second job was at the mall, running the kids' train. Kayla got on as many free rides as she could stomach. Then, at night, we went to the outdoor mall. Freddie drove us anywhere we needed to go. We had sunny beach days and ate Caribbean food. It was the vacation I longed for. Me and my baby, having as much fun as I believed she deserved. Not one moment was wasted with me stressing or worrying. I was doing a great job at mentally escaping everything I had just physically run away from in Philly.

After long, fulfilling, hot days, we would return to Mrs. Delair's house in the evenings where Freddie was still living, and where I still shared his bunk bed, this time with Kayla. I'd give her a bath and sing her lullabies until we fell asleep, knowing a pleasant carefree day was to follow. Florida seemed to be the place where I could feel what it felt like to not just exist or survive; I felt like I was living. I never wanted to leave. I wondered now if I could just stay. *Maybe I could start a new life here.*

When we weren't on some fun adventure, Freddie took us to visit everyone we mutually knew who now lived in Florida. This included Doris and the little brother I hadn't seen since I was small. Doris moved to Florida around the same time Lorenzo did, leaving Amber behind to stay with her biological father. During our visit, Doris was quiet, shy and meek. She smiled politely but didn't say more than a few words. My brother had more to say. He asked me tons of questions about Philly. He left when he was just a baby and he had only taken a few trips back. He was big for 17, and we looked alike; he was a more masculine version of me. He told me he rarely ever spoke to our dad but was very happy to meet his new niece. The meeting was awkward for me; I didn't really know what to say. But we decided that we would stay in touch.

After two weeks of just hanging out, I had to decide if I was going to face the real reason I had come. *Am I going to ask my father for support so I can make a life here? Am I going to ask him to love me and help me get on my feet? Am I ready for him to meet the purest and truest thing in my life, my sweet, sweet Kayla?* Looking back, I cannot for the life of me understand why my deep-seeded need for my father overrode my protection for my child. Desperation is a dangerous thing.

The day had come for Kayla to meet her grandfather. Freddie said Lorenzo knew we were in town and had been calling, wondering when I was coming to visit him. He lived in a town

UNRAVEL

over from Little Haiti—what they called the section of Miami that Mrs. Delair lived in. Right away, I thought of how Lorenzo disappointed me before. I remembered how he said he was coming to pick me up the last time I was there and never showed up. I remembered the feeling of abandonment. *How can I trust him now to show up to meet his granddaughter?* Before I could decide on these questions stirring my mind, and before I was ready to visit him, Lorenzo showed up at Mrs. Delair's house with his new "wife."

Lorenzo's current live-in girlfriend was a tiny Venezuelan lady with a high, nasally voice. She was cuter than the last "wife." And she was especially happy to meet Kayla and me. "Ohhhh muy bonita" were the words she sang when my father introduced us. Kayla was taking a nap when they stopped in. They waited around and we chatted. I didn't have the words, but Lorenzo's words were never ending. He never mentioned how he blew me off the last time. He only spoke with glee about how happy he was I came for another visit.

Kayla waddled into the living room from Freddie's room where she was napping, calling for her mommy, or "Monnie" as she adorably called me. Lorenzo took one look at Kayla, and I could see in his eyes that everything had changed.

I could see in his eyes that everything would be different now. I could see that he saw in Kayla what I had felt from the beginning of her existence, that our purpose in life was more than us. That we had a responsibility and duty to be better, because whatever we would leave behind would carry it forever. I could see in his eyes that he was sorry.

Chapter 40
Confronting Chaos

As we caught up, I was surprised to learn that Lorenzo and his new girlfriend Yadi had a baby boy. I had a baby brother who apparently looked just like me. It was mind blowing to hear and it confused my spirit. I immediately thought of my new baby brother's safety. Lorenzo convinced me to come stay with him and Yadi for a little while. This was an open-ended trip, and I really didn't have a game plan for if and when I was going back to Philly, so I decided that maybe it wasn't a bad idea to stay with my dad. He had a stable construction job that afforded him a cute little three-bedroom house, with a pool. So, I packed some things, and Kayla and I stayed with my dad and his—my—new family. In addition to my baby brother, Yadi had four other sons who I was now related to via our shared brother.

As the days passed, I felt love for my dad and for this new family. And yet, somehow at the same time, I could feel my anger and rage about the past begin to consume me. I was having flashbacks and nightmares constantly and gradually started having flashes of what my dad had done to me as a kid. I felt like I was actually four years old again, powerless and being used. I could smell him. I could hear his voice and feel his hard breath in my ear. I became dizzy and nauseous. I had no idea why these flashes were suddenly coming to me; I didn't have the language.

I didn't know I was triggered. And I didn't know my father was my trigger. Being exposed to my abuser put me in a constant triggered state. Without the ability to recognize this and with no therapeutic intervention, all of it only intensified, day after day. Soon all of my flashes would be followed by a vision, a fantasy out of my control. It was always of me stabbing Lorenzo to death, at my current age and in my current state of mind, always stabbing him in the chest. It took everything in me, all my strength and energy, to keep me from acting out what was happening inside my mind. It would only be a matter of time before my behaviors would mimic what was happening inside.

I began a plan in my head. *What would it look like to kill Loco?*

My anger kept me present. I didn't hide it anymore. I was vigilant over Kayla, protecting her at every moment, never letting her leave my side. Never. This annoyed Lorenzo and his new baby-mom. I dared them to challenge me on it with my dirty looks. I was going mad.

One evening, while we were preparing to sit around the kitchen table for dinner, Yadi questioned me. "Why are you acting like you can't be away from Kayla for even a second?" I told her she didn't want to know. This sparked some tension, tension that rose higher and became stronger. Then, Lorenzo, in all his frustration, gathered the nerve to actually question me.

"You said you moved here to start over. You have to eventually let us watch Kayla if you are going to find a job, Felicia."

"No, no, I don't. I will find a job when I know Kayla is safe," I snapped.

"What do you mean? She is safe with us," Lorenzo protested.

UNRAVEL

"Are you serious?" I shot back at him. "I would never leave my child with you!" Twenty years of pain, resentment, confusion and feeling like a victim started to unravel.

"What?" Lorenzo yelled. "How is she not safe?" His accent was stronger than usual. He went off on a rant, yelling and cursing. Whatever he was spurting was not comprehensible to me, but I knew he was questioning my parenting.

"I will always be a better parent to Kayla than you ever were to me! 100 times better!" I shouted in his face.

Lorenzo took a step back. "Why, because I wasn't there?" he had the gall to ask. "Your mother kept you from me. I told you this before. It's not my fault I didn't see you growing up. You can't hold that against me forever. I'm here now."

Everything he was saying felt like hot burning slaps to my face. The fact that he thought I was angry because he just wasn't there while I was growing up made me realize that he didn't think I knew. It was the first time it ever even crossed my mind, the idea that he thought I was too young to remember. He thought I forgot. He had no clue what I was referring to. This made me question myself. *Did what I think happened to me as a kid really happen? Did my sister and I really experience something so horrible?* The question took me back to the times it did happen and what it felt like. And then I was present again, more present than I had ever been.

"You really want me to tell you why I would never leave Kayla with you? You want me to say it right here, out loud, in front of Yadi? Because I could."

Lorenzo's eyes widened; he looked like a deer in headlights. His face was flushed.

"I can line up Amber and all the other kids you did that to, right here, and we can go down the line, one by one, and tell exactly what you did!"

I blurted out the accusations with a different voice, a deep grunge that was so serious and rough, I thought my chest was going to collapse. I found my courage, mixed up in rage. I was simply too emotionally exhausted to hold on to any of it any longer. I felt fire inside. And so did Lorenzo. His entire body was red now. He wasn't breathing and he grabbed his chest. The truth about his past was in front of him, and he could not face it. He tried to leave his body.

Lorenzo couldn't respond to my allegations. He knew the next thing I was going to say was that he molested me and other kids. He knew I was going to tell him he belonged in jail. He knew that I was ready to kill him or send him there before I would let him hurt Kayla, or any other child for that matter. He would face death before he would face that truth. Lorenzo suffered a heart attack right there in the living room after I uttered those words.

Yadi called 911 while I stood there looking down at him on the floor, ready to watch him die. An ambulance was there within minutes, and I stood my ground. I told him I wasn't done with him, grabbed Kayla, and went into our bedroom. I felt powerful and unafraid. It was a feeling I was unfamiliar with, but I knew I wanted more of it. The time Lorenzo spent in the hospital calmed me. I had time to think and process and understand the power I held. I asked myself what I would do with it. I had no idea because I never felt like I had power over someone before. I decided to save it for when I would really need it. I knew the day

UNRAVEL

would come when I would. My gut told me there was more to learn about Lorenzo. And while my pride wanted to destroy him, my love for him wanted to show grace. Which I would do, I hadn't decided yet.

I waited with grace for Lorenzo to get home from the hospital. He rested for a day, and we avoided each other. Then, after a day of silence, he asked that I come sit with him outside.

"Your daddy is loco." These were the words that started a very long conversation, mostly of Lorenzo telling me everything that had happened to him from his earliest memories; from his father attempting to murder him to the trauma he suffered coming to America. I listened and I was fascinated.

Chapter 41

Lorenzo

As a child, Lorenzo adored his mother and clung to her like a lifejacket. He was the youngest of five kids, and for some reason his mother saw him as special. Lorenzo was the only one of his mother's children that she breastfed. He was the only one allowed to sleep in his parents' bed. She loved all her children, but Lorenzo was to be kept close to her.

By the time Lorenzo started primary school, Cuba was going through its own transition. Many Cubans—those who had the means—were leaving the island as the new government started implementing new ideologies that would control their everyday lives. The persistent dictatorships halted the modernization and development of the country, and its citizens felt powerless to rise up against them. This led to the country cutting itself off from other governments, which meant fewer and fewer resources for its people. In the 1960s, Cubans were forced to scramble for food and a means to survive. Lorenzo was lucky that his father was able to consistently secure work. Lorenzo's father did everything in his power to keep a roof over his family's head, including building said roof. He performed back-breaking jobs, from building houses to loading ships day in and day out while Lorenzo's mother tended a vegetable garden in their small backyard so they were never short of food.

The troubles in Cuba were no match for the happiness inside the bubble Lorenzo's mother created for her children. She made sure her children were safe, clean, and fed. She would talk to them from sunup to sundown, keeping them distracted from the violence and hardships on the periphery. It seemed nothing could penetrate that safe and happy bubble for Lorenzo. Until, one day, suddenly, it popped.

The love Lorenzo had for his mother was only challenged by the complicated relationship he had with his father. Every year, before he became Loco, as Lorenzo grew bigger, his father's jealousy grew stronger, gaining mass and muscle in the same way. While his mother protected and spoiled him, his father treated him less like a son and more like a threat. Maybe he *was* a threat.

Before Lorenzo was born, his parents were in love. His father was never a gentle man, but he provided for Ma-ma and vowed to always protect her. That was enough for Ma-ma. But when Lorenzo came along, Ma-ma learned what companionship felt like. Lorenzo's charm and sense of humor sparked a desire for freedom and laughter in Ma-ma, something she had never known before. Before she married, Ma-ma only knew a life of control and solitude. That's what Cuba meant for women in the early 1900s. To find a man to marry and to serve; to bear his children and keep his home, that was all life had to offer. Charm, romance, and feeling good was never taken into consideration when Ma-ma found a man, or rather when a man found her. She felt honored and lucky that a man who could provide wanted to marry her. What more could she ask for? Strangely, it was her son who would teach her that as a woman—as a human being—there was more to experience.

UNRAVEL

In the small town of Guantánamo, Cuba, Lorenzo shared his Ma-ma with his siblings and his father as best as he could, considering Ma-ma did little to be shared. But by the time Lorenzo had turned 10, his father's jealousy could no longer be contained. One afternoon, the air was thick, and Lorenzo's father could smell his son's stench before he arrived at their front gate. He had just gotten home from a long day of work only to find no greeting at the door. The house they lived in had a small backyard with a water well big enough for people to cool off in on hot days. Lorenzo and Ma-ma spent most evenings together sitting out there while everyone else bigger than him and livelier than her were out, living bigger lives. Ma-ma sat on an old stool, snapping peas while Lorenzo began his chore of cutting down weeds. Ma-ma watched him closely and with enough admiration to fill her heart and distract her from her worries. That day was quiet, until The Beast arrived.

Lorenzo's father was loud and violent. He couldn't help but stir up trouble whenever he walked in the door. If anyone was home when he arrived from work, their heart would pound at the sound of his footsteps, mostly from fear of his yelling and complaining. Lorenzo's heart pounded with rage. When Lorenzo saw his father, he saw red. After years of watching him hit his mother, yelling and controlling her, he came to know his father as The Beast. Lorenzo was the one to comfort his mother whenever she cried from being hurt by The Beast, and The Beast challenged him for it. He would ask Lorenzo if he thought he was better than he was. He told him he would never know what it was like to come in after a hard day of work and have to discipline his wife for her laziness. He said Lorenzo was a pussy, weak, and would never be a man.

As soon as The Beast walked through the back door into the backyard, he screamed at Ma-ma. "Where the hell is everybody? Why is there no food ready for me at the table when I come home from working all day!? Why are you wasting time back here making this boy weak!?"

The Beast resented the quality time he noticed his wife spending with their son every day. He didn't think it was natural and made it clear he wanted it to stop. But Ma-ma and Lorenzo never obliged. Their bond was no match for the threats of The Beast, until this day. Usually, Ma-ma was good at ignoring her disgruntled husband and could humor him enough until he was too tired to be angry, avoiding a fight or being snapped at. A meal and giving in to his every command was usually enough. But this afternoon, hearing the way her husband spoke about her precious son, calling him weak, something in her snapped.

"Don't talk about my son! He's a good boy!"

Ma-ma had known he was special from the day he was born. She couldn't quite put her finger on it, but it was something different from her first four kids. No, not different—special. Perhaps it was her motherly intuition that made her know her time with him would be short. She wanted to hold on to him for all eternity, and Lorenzo could feel it. His father could feel that too, and this evening he finally found an excuse to allow his jealously to manifest. "Don't talk back to me, woman!" He screamed while striking her down, a backhand smack straight across her face. She fell to the ground and stayed there.

UNRAVEL

Everything happened so fast, but to Lorenzo, each second lasted for an eternity: the moment Ma-ma's eyes looked up in fear, shocked at The Beast's huge, rough hand cocked back, coming straight for her face; the wincing sound she made in fear; the sound of her cheek cracking under the force; seeing her tumble to the ground—all in slow motion, each moment slower than the one before, quickly turning rage into fire.

With all that rage and fire in tow, Lorenzo took the machete he had been using to cut down the weeds and went right for The Beast. "AAAAAHHHHHHHH" he screamed. His small frame was no match for his innate reaction to protect and avenge his beloved Ma-ma. Small as he was, he could only get a good angle of The Beast if he swung hard and low. So, swing hard and low he did—cutting right into The Beast's leg, almost severing it. The Beast was down! But not out. After realizing how injured he was, The Beast grew angrier and stronger. Down on one knee and with his injured leg barely hanging on, he hopped right for Lorenzo.

Lorenzo should have swung again, but his mother's screams in the background for both of them to stop was distracting and he froze. He stood confused. Before he could have a thought, The Beast grabbed Lorenzo by the shirt with one hand, carried him over to the well, and dunked him in. The Beast fully intended on drowning young Lorenzo and kept him under; his wife in the background screaming and pleading for mercy. With blood pouring down both her face and his leg, she pulled at him, trying to get him to turn the boy loose. But a mother's love was not strong enough to stop a father's hate. He kept Lorenzo under until he stopped moving. Once he thought he was dead, he dropped him to the ground. Lorenzo was gone.

The agony from the screams of his beloved Ma-ma must have reached Lorenzo on the other side because moments later, with his mother pounding on his chest, trying to revive him, Lorenzo opened his eyes. The Beast had disappeared, most likely trying to save his leg. Ma-ma stayed right there in that backyard, holding her baby and thanking Jesus over and over and over—just rocking and thanking Jesus. She had never been more grateful for anything in her entire life. Lorenzo did not want to move. He wanted his mother to hold him for eternity.

My dad was physically saved that day, but who knows what happened to his spirit, or his brain. From that day on, he was never the same. The mental trauma and/or brain damage from what he experienced would manifest itself into what some would call "batshit crazy." Science calls it post-traumatic stress disorder and traumatic brain injury.

Lorenzo was no longer welcome in The Beast's home. He came and went to see Ma-ma but was sure never to cross paths with his father again. From this point on, home was the streets. And so began his life of crime. Lorenzo turned to the streets and found a new family; he joined a gang—fighting, robbing people, and selling drugs to survive. He became addicted to the lifestyle, and before he knew it, hurting others had no emotional effect on him. With no feelings or sense of regard for others, Lorenzo had turned into what he wanted to be that day in the backyard with The Beast, a killer. He was 13 years old when he and his gang came up with a plan to attack the local police. "They have to go!" said one of Lorenzo's closest friends. Lorenzo's gang were known for terrorizing their neighborhoods, but the real terrorists were corrupt cops who were stealing drugs and money from the gangs, killing anyone who fought against them. Lorenzo and his crew robbed a place for explosives one night, with the intent to send a message to the cops that repeatedly harassed and stole from them. They wanted to show them who was in charge. Not realizing how powerful the explosives they had stolen were, Lorenzo and his friends threw them at a police car that two officers sat in while on a night watch. Both men were killed instantly.

With other cops on a mission to find out who had committed the crime, they terrorized gang members, torturing them to give them a lead. Word got out that it was Lorenzo and his crew that killed the officers. There was so much heat on them to be captured that they were forced to run and hide up in the mountains. There, they tried to survive in caves. In one attempt to find food, Lorenzo and his closest friend ventured into town where they were met with gunfire. "We want them dead or alive!" was the cops' rallying cry.

Lorenzo ran as bullets flew past him, shots ringing out. Too small and fast for the police, he again escaped into the mountains. But his best friend wasn't with him. Lorenzo never did find out if that was because he was captured or because he was dead. Lorenzo ran until the gunfire sounds and screams to catch him had faded. His adrenaline came down as he sat in a cave, trying to catch his breath. He felt something warm running down his leg. "I've been shot," he whispered to himself. Finding the wound and seeing that the bullet went straight through, Lorenzo began to chuckle. He had been shot in the same place he had cut his father. He smiled and fell asleep.

Days had passed, and it wasn't much longer before Lorenzo had come to terms with the fact that he would either have to turn himself in or die from the gunshot wound in his leg. The wound had become infected, and he was in a bad way. After surviving his father's attempt to kill him and surviving life on the streets, he wasn't prepared to die for the life on the run. So Lorenzo turned himself into the authorities. He was 14 years old when he became an inmate in one of the harshest prisons systems in the world.

Even with all the crimes he committed, in Lorenzo's mind, his defining story would be that he was the victim of an attempted murder at the hands of his own father. This was no different in prison. Lorenzo shared his story, day after day, with his fellow prisoners. This gained him sympathy and admiration. As a self-proclaimed survivor and hero, he elevated himself as stronger and wiser than the rest. Lorenzo's street rep also preceded him. Some feared him, while others respected him. His brilliant mind for survival, intertwined with his demented outlook on life, created a deeply effective sociopathic personality that amplified both an irresistible charm and a presence that subdued even the craziest of them. To be caught up with Lorenzo was both scary and mesmerizing to say the least.

It only took a few months for unlivable prison conditions to become livable for a young man with such abilities to captivate and manipulate. Lorenzo had somehow managed to have the warden agree to allow him to have visits with a girl who his mother fancied for him. For the next few years, he had the pleasures of intimacy with a girl and, as a bonus, family dinners with his mother and siblings on special occasions. His beloved Ma-ma visited him on a regular basis. And his "wife" did too. By the time Lorenzo was 17, he had a son and a baby on the way. Having kids opened Lorenzo's eyes, and he was reminded of what life on the outside was like—what freedom felt like. Even with the family visits and the prison guards eating from the palm of his hand, Lorenzo was living the worst life he imagined. Prison life was harder than any of his trials before. He would go days without eating. He never slept, for fear of being taken out or robbed. He fought daily to maintain his status as the crazy kid you didn't want to fuck with. The years were becoming too much.

At the same time, tensions were building daily between prison guards and inmates. So many had been injured and killed on both sides that everyone knew that more days of unrest would eventually lead to a massacre. On what side, no one could tell. Rumors spread that the inmates were planning to overtake the prison and it could happen at any moment. Over the years, Cuban leader Fidel Castro knew the conditions of the prisons in his country were less than deplorable. He insisted on making sure they stayed that way. He also insisted on making things even worse for troublemakers. The troublemakers were identified. My father was on "the list," which included the crazies, the sociopaths, the murders, the rapists. The political prisoners.

Yes, indeed, if there was anything Castro wouldn't tolerate, it was a traitor. Anyone who had risen up against his dictatorship, protested the government, or had a hand in harming any government official as my father had, they were traitors. With so many Cubans desperately trying to leave Cuba and gain asylum, Castro had recently announced that anyone who wanted to go was free to leave. He insisted that Cuba's traitors go with them.

On Mother's Day 1980, Fidel Castro announced "the list." Visiting mothers at the prison were present to hear the names of their sons read off as traitors. Once the list was read, the guards instructed, "Say your goodbyes. You will never see your sons again." In that moment, Lorenzo saw pure shock on his beloved mother's face. "Ma-ma… don't worry," he begged. What Lorenzo had just said to his beloved mother didn't register with her; she was in a complete state of shock. She stood to try and leave but fainted right there in the visiting room at the prison. Alas, the news that she would never see her son again devastated her to the extent that her last visit with him was cut short. The last time Lorenzo saw his beloved mother was that day, being carried away by guards attempting to revive her.

Lorenzo was officially banned from Cuba. If he ever returned, he would be killed. He could not live with the thought of never seeing his mother again, never seeing his children grow up, and never breathing the air of his homeland. He knew he had to escape, to stay. And escape he would. Lorenzo's escape from prison that day would set the stage for his part in the ongoing Cuban Revolution, the last leg of the historic Cuban Migration.

Lorenzo, along with his prison buddies, carried out their plan. During transportation to join the thousands already waiting asylum, they overtook the guards on the bus and retrieved their firearms, killing one of the guards in the process.

UNRAVEL

Lorenzo attempted to separate himself from the group so he could hide and stay. But, the group was cornered. More officers eventually caught up with the group as they tried to get away on the bus they hijacked. With gunfire heavy on their trail, they were surrounded and driven right into the gates of the Peruvian Embassy where they crashed their bus. Gunshots ringing behind them, they ran into the embassy building for safety. Lorenzo knew as he ran that it would be his last run in Cuba. Towards what, he had no idea.

Once inside, my father gained refuge. The Peruvian government not only agreed to provide asylum for my father and his prison mates, but also to the 10,000 people who would no longer live under the dictatorship of Fidel Castro. The Mariel boat rides of 1980 would follow.

One of the first two boats to leave Cuba with inmates as well as anti-Fidel Cubans seeking asylum was filled with over 250 people. Off the coast of Havana, the inmates in the Peruvian Embassy were told to board as fast as they could and to get off the land quickly. Just as quickly, a terrible storm came crashing down on the two boats in the middle of the ocean between Cuba and Peru.

Lorenzo went right into survival mode. He was now a strong, athletic 19-year-old man who had survived all but a sinking ship. He and other men like him went into high gear as the ships rocked back and forth, tossing everyone, including women and children, to and fro. In an attempt to keep the boats afloat, they tied them together. As the storm violently pushed the boats along, they had no choice but to leave those that fell overboard to drown.

Lorenzo saved a few women and children but by his third trip into the water, he was being pulled down by desperate hands. He swam away from the doomed and made it back to the boats with all he had left in him.

Being lost at sea for days, he and the survivors like him became ill, some falling into the troubled waters again as they fought for the strength to stay alive. Finally, darkness had come over Lorenzo. It was a good fight for freedom, but he knew there was only a slice of hope that the powers-that-be would let a beast like him survive while children died beneath him. With this thought he closed his eyes and drifted away.

If our souls decide who we will be conceived by—what route we will take into the universe—then perhaps my soul is what breathed life into Lorenzo when his father killed him, and then again that day on the boat. Because right as Lorenzo found himself back at that place he once visited on the other side, right as he was crossing into death, he opened his eyes, and suddenly, he was back again. Although he was prepared to die this time, salvation came yet again and now in the form of a lifesaver falling on top of him. This got Lorenzo out of his daze as he saw Navy Seals in helicopters above him.

They're here to take me back, he thought. At that moment, he heard voices in a language familiar to him. His rescuers grabbed him and plopped him on the floor of a rescue jet, right as everything went black again. He drifted off, and peace came over him as he thought he was going back home, back to Cuba.

But peace would never find Lorenzo again. He woke up in Peru. Here he would learn about the agreement the Peruvian Embassy had made with the American government to give

UNRAVEL

Cubans safe passage. He was safe and on his way to America. But safe did not mean free. He heard shouts of "Viva America! Viva America!" all around him. His hope began to dwindle. *Is freedom anywhere? Even in the America?* His heart was heavy—the weight of it multiplied by panic. Braving the waters and once again almost dying from drowning, Lorenzo's PTSD was triggered. His time in Peru was fogged by nightmares, dissociation, and shock. Lorenzo boarded a plane in Peru headed for America. Like a zombie, dazed and confused, he got off the plane in Wisconsin.

Some historians relish in the details of the Cuban Migration by painting a scene of hundreds of thousands of Cuban immigrants landing by boat on the cost of Florida, overjoyed by their newfound freedom. What many seem to leave out are the rescue missions for sinking boats that carried thousands of Cubans by air into Midwest America where they lived in refugee camps. On Lorenzo's first night in the United States, he would make his bed at the worst refugee camp in the history of modern America.

Fort McCoy in Wisconsin is notoriously known as the place Fidel Castro dumped all of his undesirables. Escaped convicts and patients from mental institutions filled acres. Among them, my murderous father. Lorenzo had to scrounge for food, fight to keep from being sodomized, and watch newfound friends being stabbed, cut, and killed with machetes. Lorenzo became quiet. What soul he had left was black, and his desire for freedom had now become his desire to feel something, anything other than despair. What was that feeling of love he faintly remembered from his beloved Ma-ma? Sprinkles of it may still save him.

Lorenzo was saved. It took a few months, but the Lutheran Church sponsored my father and rescued him from the hell he lived in, eventually landing him in a gritty section of Philadelphia called Germantown. Germantown represented new life for Lorenzo, and he hadn't yet realized the monster he had become. He never realized how damaged he was from all of his trauma, not until that day I confronted him about the monstrous things he had done to me.

Chapter 42
Freedom

My parents came to America in search of freedom, and while I have no strong opinions or stance on immigration, I am grateful that they did. I have been afforded opportunities that are a direct result, including being conceived. A few years before I first reconnected with Lorenzo in Miami, Marie completed all legal obligations to become an American Citizen, and I am proud of her for doing so.

I am a product of the human desire, and the human need to be free. Marie couldn't live in the bondage of the life her mother left for her, being tied down to one place, or tied down to responsibility. She fled a life that would have held her captive as a mistress and mother. A heart of a woman whose spirit is as free as the black bird cannot and will never be captive. There is such a thing as living a life not meant for you.

My father, on the other hand, was the product of a wild beast. The child he was before his trauma deserved the love and protection of his father. Perhaps The Beast that created him had his own dark past, never healed and never afforded the opportunity to be free. Maybe if he was loved and protected, he would not have created the monster that would become Loco. Lorenzo became so that he needed to be tamed, all his innocence gone at the age of 10.

Eventually, innocence would come again, and it would come in the form of a baby. That baby was me, unaware of the shackles that had to be broken to bring forth the events that led to my conception. But the cycle continued, and my innocence was gone before my first memory of it. I may have been born free, but the sins of my father carried their weight until they broke me. Was I the result of my mother and father's freedom or the price they paid for it? Was my life and all its darkness the cost? Would I, could I, break the cycle so my child could truly be free?

Chapter 43

Home

I was so fascinated with my father's story, I almost forgot the whole reason I was sitting there listening to him in the first place. My father and I sat for hours on his porch, reliving his dark life in an attempt to explain why he molested me. For the first time, he faced the hell he left behind so that we could attempt to face our past together. But this was all he could offer. The most he could muster up in terms of an apology was that he was genuinely sorry he was so messed up. But honestly, how does a father apologize for molesting his daughter? There are no words for that. And no words would suffice.

The events that happened from this point on would be the unraveling of my relationship with my father. Because facing what happened to me, what he did, would be his greatest pain. Lorenzo had been through unbelievable hardships in his life. Starting from the time his father attempted to murder him, leading all the way up to the life he experienced when he escaped prison and was banned from Cuba, he endured hell. And it all boiled down to this moment, the moment he had to face the truth of what he had become. Being present for this moment made me feel sorry for him. I felt compassion and somehow, I found grace.

Every time I had to go into The Dark, every whooping, every time I got punched in the mouth, every time I went into a deep depression, none of that hurt like the pain I felt from facing the fact that my father molested me. I was older now and I wasn't confused anymore. I knew what he did and I knew how disgusting and wrong it was. As a child, I knew no better than what I was taught. My father taught me everything that was wrong about love, sex, and human connection. But now I had my own child, and it was up to me to fix all of that. I looked at my father with pity and I decided to forgive him, to love him. Or at least, to try.

His explanation and half-assed apology wasn't enough to repair the past, but it was enough for me to move forward, just a little. It had to be enough because I did not have much more strength to process much more. It would have to do. Because I was tired.

After our conversation, we spent the next few days just greeting each other pleasantly. Not much was said, but it felt like we now shared some new inside secret, a new bond built from shared pain. I felt a sense of peace. It wasn't enough peace to leave Kayla alone with him or say all was forgiven. It was just enough peace to make me miss home. I wanted to go home.

During the few months I lived in Florida, David had proposed to Debora, and she was about to become someone's wife. I couldn't believe it and I couldn't contain myself. I made plans to go home temporarily, just for a visit because: one, I still had no place to permanently live in Philly; and two, there was no way I wouldn't be by sister's side when she walked down the aisle. Her getting married meant more to us than anyone could ever know. The idea that either of us could have a healthy and happy relationship was nothing short of a miracle. Her strength was unmatched. She continued to be my hero.

Although I made plans to go to my hometown for the wedding, I also made plans to come back afterward to what I believed would be my new home. As much as I missed Philly, I had to make things work in Florida because I did not have a lot of options. I was going to stay with Lorenzo and his new family to make a new life. I started looking for work online and I tried to enjoy the company of my new brothers. I even tested what it would be like to let Kayla out of my sight.

One afternoon, when Lorenzo was at work, Yadi, Kayla, and I spent the day running errands. When we got back to the house, Kayla was napping. She had fallen asleep during the car ride. I laid her on the couch and went for a walk. I wanted to walk and pray to clear my mind, alone. On my walk I thought about all that had happened in the last two years since I had Kayla. I thought about how proud I was for leaving an abusive relationship but prayed Kayla would have a better relationship with her dad than I did with mine. I thought about how much I missed my sister but how happy I was that she was safe and happy. I felt envy for how healthy she was and how fucked up I was, but nonetheless, I was overjoyed for her. I prayed that someday I too would be healthy and happy, and even in love. I was praying through all my conflicting feelings, daydreaming of peace.

I was walking back to the house when the sight of Yadi and her son walking in my direction snapped me out of my daydreams. I instantly worried. "Where's Kayla?" I yelled as they got closer.

"She was still asleep on the couch. We didn't want to wake her," Yadi responded. "It's okay. Your dad came home early. She's not alone."

With that, I took off running. I ran faster than I had ever run. I was only about two blocks away, but it felt like the longest two blocks of my existence. I just couldn't move fast enough. Tears started to well as I ran because I realized I was running because my father was a monster. He was a monster that I had to protect my daughter from. I was sickened with the idea and ready to kill him if I had to. But killing him would never help Kayla if it was too late. Once a child is violated, there is nothing anyone can do to fix it. People can help that child to heal, justice can be served, and time will stitch up wounds, but nothing can ever fix it. If that happened to Kayla, I would be dead inside twice over. I mourned the child in me, forever damaged and never safe. I could not withstand mourning the same for my child. I could not fathom the same fate for my baby. I ran until my legs were red, tears and sweat covered me, and the scent of fear exuded from my pores.

I ran so fast past the open front door that I ran past Kayla still sleeping peacefully on the couch, in the same exact position I left her in. Lorenzo was in the backyard. I turned to look at her innocence and straight away scooped her up, walked into our bedroom, and wept. I laid next to her and although it was still early afternoon, I slept next to her the rest of the day. She felt my spirit and stayed asleep, never waking up for food or to use the bathroom. For 16 hours, I wept and we slept.

This was the moment I knew I couldn't stay. I knew that when I left to go to my sister's wedding, I would have to stay in Philly. I knew there was never going to be a way to know Kayla was safe. Just because my father realized he was sick didn't mean he wasn't still sick.

And so it was time to say goodbye to Lorenzo and his family—my new family that included my new baby brother. I left Florida with more than I had come with. I left with a feeling of closure. I knew my father was sick and while that didn't take away the pain that his actions caused, I now understood that trauma was real. I now had firsthand knowledge that if you don't deal with your demons, they will take control of your mind and make you sick, causing you to hurt people. I realized that the gut feeling I had always had about how I could pass down my trauma to my kid was valid. If we don't heal, the trauma and its effects simply get passed down from generation to generation.

I would leave knowing I didn't want to be sick like my father but I wondered how much of that I could control. *Was his illness all trauma induced? Or was some of his evil genetically inherited from his evil father? Was his evil, his sickness, passed to me through his blood?* I worried about this incessantly. I had no answers. All I knew was that my sister was getting married and it was time to go home.

Chapter 44
Higher Learning

"Just because Fate doesn't deal you the right cards, it doesn't mean you should give up. It just means you have to play the cards you get to their maximum potential."
~ Les Brown

When I made arrangements to come back to Philadelphia, I knew I had no home to come back to. My sister and her now-fiancé rented a house together and they had a roommate, his childhood friend. My sister and I wondered if me and Kayla staying with Marie would be a feasible temporary plan. My mother was more stable these days; she found a new boyfriend, and she moved into his house. They had the space, and frankly, Marie owed me.

Against our better judgment, we decided Marie should offer some support. I swallowed my resentment for her abandonment and for the sake of stability, I decided to move in with Marie and her boyfriend. The truth of the matter, though, is that I had run out of options. Where else would I have stayed?

At the time, Marie was working as a home health aide. She was doing her best to live a normal life. She just wanted to work and come home, as always, free from any real responsibility. So she wasn't exactly thrilled when I told her I had no other place to go. Marie came up with a lot of rules and guidelines for me to stay with her and she made it painfully clear I was only to stay for a short period of time; just enough time to save up and get my own place or find someone else to stay with. Because I was considered homeless and in desperate need of work, I reentered a welfare-to-work program. It was the same center-based program that I could bring Kayla to. The staff sat with me to fill out job applications and work on resumes. I wondered how this would ever help me find a job that paid enough to get my own place and pay for childcare. I wondered if I actually would ever leave Kayla at a childcare center. I hadn't thought much about it because wherever I went, Kayla went. I never let her out my sight. It never even crossed my mind that she would ever be in the care of strangers. If she wasn't with my sister or Marie or Q, she was with me. That was it and that was all.

While I was in the welfare-to-work program, I didn't even think I was good enough to get a GED, let alone a college degree. My goal was simply to maintain a job, and even that seemed impossible at the time. I thought welfare was going to be my forever. In my eyes, my future was bleak at best. But then, during a "Setting Goals" workshop the program was offering, we had to watch a video, and I heard my first motivational speech.

That's when everything changed.

The video was a speech by none other than Mr. Les Brown. He spoke directly to my soul, to the spirit in me that was searching for an answer. I never thought about my future before. I didn't think I had one. I spent so long trying to survive, I never figured out a plan for if I did.

UNRAVEL

But Mr. Les Brown made me believe I could have a future, and that future was up to me. I had little to no control in my past. Abuse makes you always feel like the victim you are, powerless, having no say in your own fate. But maybe I didn't have to be a victim anymore. Les Brown made me believe that was possible. I smiled awkwardly at his words and I felt like I was glowing. The activity we had to do after watching the video was to write down a dream or two, things we wanted but believed were impossible to obtain. For each dream, we were to write down the steps or goals that we would have to achieve in order to reach those dreams. Then, we were asked to think about the limits set on us because of our circumstances. We were to write down barriers to those goals, and then write down how we would get around them. I wrote:

<u>Dreams:</u>
1. *Become a doctor or psychologist w/my own practice.*
2. *Become a motivational speaker like Les Brown.*

<u>Steps:</u>
1. *Find a babysitter.*
2. *Get a job.*
3. *Get my own place.*
4. *Go to community college and get my high school diploma/associate degree.*
5. *Keep going to school.*
6. *Start doing speeches.*

FELICIA P. ROCHE

Barriers:
1. *No babysitter or daycare – ask my mom and Q's mom if they can watch Kayla.*
2. *Can't find a job – apply to more places. Even McDonald's.*
3. *School – schedule GED test and go from there.*
4. *Nowhere to live – after I get the job, save up and get a small apartment for now.*

There it was: the road map to my bright, new future. "Shoot for the moon. Even if you miss, you'll land among the stars," Les Brown said. Eventually, I would live by these words. But for now, sitting in that training, I wondered how realistic my goals were. I wondered if I was smart enough, strong enough. When I went home that day, I stared at Kayla and for a moment thought that maybe I was. It was at that welfare-to-work program where I learned I could go to college. A staff member there asked me if I wanted to just get my GED or if I wanted to enroll into higher learning. Prior to being asked that, I didn't even know I had those options. I opted for higher education and was scheduled to take an "Ability to Benefit" test at Philadelphia Community College. It was an exam for bright young people who dropped out of high school because of tough circumstances. It tested how smart you were, not how much knowledge you gained. It measured your potential, not your education. If you scored high enough, you could enroll into college courses and achieve high school equivalency while earning an associate degree. I opted to schedule for that test instead of the GED.

With the impossible dream of being a doctor, and the encouragement of my mother who was already a nurse's aide, I decided the best route to take was in healthcare. So many of the girls from my program were becoming certified nurse's aides, and I thought to myself, *Why not?* It did not require a high school diploma or a GED to start. So I began a six-week certificate program before taking the "Ability to Benefit" test. The classes took place every weekday from 9:00 a.m. to 3:00 p.m. I managed to arrange babysitting for enough days to get all I needed to pass the test. I was now certified.

Chapter 45
Not Without My Sister

It only took a few days for me to begin using my nurse's aide certification. Marie put in a good word at the nursing home she had worked at for years and got me an overnight job right away. I worked 11:00 p.m. to 7:00 a.m. while Kayla slept at my mom's. And during the day I did my best to try and catch some sleep while Kayla watched *Elmo* and *Caillou* all day. Now that I could help out with bills, Marie practically stopped working and only took partial hours every once in a while. She watched Kayla overnight, as she slept, and even helped me some days while I slept by feeding her and taking her to run errands. When Marie didn't help out or just left for the day, I tried to get in some sleep between feeding Kayla, making sure she didn't get into anything dangerous, and keeping her clean. I was exhausted. But the more money I made, the more I wanted to make. I asked Marie to watch Kayla some days so I could work doubles. She resented it.

But now I was finding a rhythm and I didn't want to miss a beat. I was working and sleeping and missing my baby. I picked up even more doubles. The more money I made, the more realistic my goals seemed. I wanted to save up enough money to get my own place and maybe even a car. I was so tired of the hours—long bus rides to work and to drop Kayla off in West Philly, which was the other side of the city from my job. I had to endure the strenuous commute because I had enlisted Q and his mother for weekend and daytime childcare. I used a lot of guilt trips, deadbeat daddy talk, and heated debates to get them to help me out. It worked for the most part. Before I knew it, I was cutting out sleep all together. I tried to find as many ways as possible to snooze at work. I tried to catch 20-minute naps during my breaks. I really wanted to do a good job and I loved my patients. I cleaned and cared for them with gentleness and dignity. I was enraged when I saw mistreatment at the hands of my co-workers, but I never spoke up. I didn't know how. The stress of it all and the lack of sleep began to take its toll.

These days started getting darker than usual. Seemingly, out of nowhere, I found myself having more and more flashbacks of The Monsters. I wondered why I couldn't control my thoughts. I got scared all the time. I was always angry. I couldn't seem to get along with anyone. I was tired and irritated; I just wanted a break. I started to resent the love I was gifted. I wanted to be left alone by everyone, even Kayla. And then I realized people were finding me in a zoned-out state of mind from time to time.

Marie would come home from work or some outing in the evening and find me sitting on the steps with Kayla, in the dark and in the cold, not moving, just staring in a daze. Kayla, ever the quiet, happy child, played in some dirt nearby. Marie, afraid to trigger one of my regular temper tantrums, would only tell me to come in. She would feed Kayla, give her a warm bath, and put her to sleep. I would flip out, screaming about how I could take care of my baby myself, and storm off. If she could help it, Marie would make sure Kayla stayed asleep, inside the warm house. But there were days this part of me, the other me, would snatch my child and dare anyone to come near her, run back out in the cold, and walk for miles until I just couldn't anymore. I would wake up back at Marie's with no memory of how I got there, how long I had been gone, or what I did the night before. Kayla was always with Marie when I came to. These events happened while I was in The Dark, gone somewhere else, never present. I don't know where I went but when I got back, I was always in pain, hurting and ashamed that I was unable to take care of my baby.

Q started taking Kayla more often and for longer stretches while I was steadily losing my mind. He and Sasha made a nice little home for themselves, and Sasha loved having Kayla over. She and I had come to an understanding. She could have Q, because he was never going to choose between us, and she and I would co-mother our girls. Oddly, she and I grew closer, comparing notes on how Q hit us and how terrible of a boyfriend he was. She told me he was still cheating on her with other girls and how he didn't help out financially. I didn't have the mental capacity to understand why she was still with him despite all of this but remembered how I stayed with him through some of the same things. I decided it was best not to judge her and opted instead to just listen.

I did all I could to keep up with work in my dazed state of mind. The life I was living interfered with my ability to keep up with my hygiene. I woke up from where I caught a few minutes or hours of sleep and walked right out the door, not thinking to wash up before moving on to the next part of my day. My teeth started to rot. The pain I got from my toothaches would land me in the emergency room, and I was prescribed pain meds. I was now using the pain meds to disappear even more into The Dark.

I wandered aimlessly when I was supposed to be picking up Kayla or going to work. Hours were now missing from my existence, and I didn't know where they went. I had unraveled to the point that I didn't even recognize my own face.

When I came across my reflection, all I saw were The Monsters I had spent all this time running from staring back at me. When I had Kayla, I thought I had all the strength I needed to face my past, my childhood—The Monsters. I thought facing all of it would make me better, wiser—a good mommy. Instead, I was becoming a shell of a woman, hollow and dark inside, nothing good or warm to fill me up. I unraveled and I was gone. Healing seemed impossible and death, desirable.

All of this came to a head when Q kept Kayla an entire week because I had scheduled so many back-to-back shifts. Kayla had never been away from me that long, and I missed her with my entire soul. I had a shift that night but I wanted Kayla. Q always met me at the train station for drop offs and pick up. As exhausted as I was, I wanted to see Kayla before my shift and was willing to meet him so I could bring her back to my place and put her to sleep and have my mom keep an eye on her. I called Q to make the arrangements.

"She can just stay here another week," he decided without me.

"What, why?" Panic was in my voice.

"What's the point if you just gonna bring her back in a few days? She's having a good time with her sister. Just let her stay, Felicia." In that moment all I could hear was that I was an unfit mother and she was better off with them. I was projecting.

"Q, please don't do this."

UNRAVEL

"Do what? See now, don't start your crazy shit. Don't start your drama. It's not that serious. I don't feel like coming out, and the kids are chillin. She's fine. We'll just see you in a couple days."

I started to scream and cry. Nothing he was saying was unfair or unreasonable. But the words were translating to me that I was somehow losing control, maybe even losing my child.

"Q, bring me my child! Bring her now. I'm calling the police if you don't meet me at the train station in an hour!"

"Yo, you trippin. She's staying here a few more days. That's it. Period."

"Please, Q!!! NOOOOO..." I started screaming and crying even more. Exhaustion, my desire for my child, and the inability to regulate my emotions turned into an all-out meltdown. Q simply hung up.

I was powerless. In my mind, I had just lost my child. In my mind, I had just lost my world. In my mind, I had no control over my life. I couldn't bear it one more moment. I looked at the pills on the nightstand next to me and I grew silent. I looked at them with such desire, desire to rest, to escape, to finally be free from all the pain, the confusion, the lack of control, and the loss of dignity and power. I knew that enough of those pills could make it all go away. It was time.

After I took all the pills in the bottle, without a thought, I picked up the phone on the nightstand and dialed a number. Perhaps it was my spirit's last attempt to survive. Because the call I made was to the only person who would know what to do, the only person who ever gave a shit, the only person who never hurt me and always did what they could to protect me.

I called my sister.

Here is when feeling and knowing are different. I didn't feel love from my sister. I felt guilt and resentment. I felt like I was her burden. But something in my core, something that was buried so deep that only this moment could I get to it, something so true and clear inside of me KNEW my sister was the only somebody that I could call.

"Hello?"

"Debora… I'm sorry."

"What, Felicia? What's wrong?"

"I did it. I'm sorry… I just couldn't take it anymore."

"Did what, Felicia? What did you do?"

"I'm scared."

"What did you do, Felicia?"

"I took a bottle of pills."

My crying became less intense, and I couldn't breathe. *Are the pills kicking in?* I was exhausted and pretty much done by then. There was a sense of matter-of-factness that came over me. I regretted what I had done but I also thought there was nothing I could do about it now. It was over. Quietly I said, either to her or myself, I can't remember which, "I think I'm dying. I'm going to die. I'm sorry. I didn't mean to. I'm sorry." Suddenly, the line dropped. I thought this was it. The room started to fade. It was over. I hung up the phone and lay down. Silence consumed me, and darkness was taking over.

The phone rang, and I woke up. I heard Marie answer it in her room down the hall. A minute later, she came crashing through the door. The tone of her screams reminded me of the rage I endured from her as a child. She lost total control the way she did when she used to beat us until our skin broke. I wanted

UNRAVEL

her to beat me now, beat me until I was unconscious, anything to silence her. *For once, Marie, just shut up.* But instead she made my head hurt worse.

"What did you do, Felicia? What did you do!? Oh my god!" she screamed as she picked up the empty bottle. Before she had the chance to gather an idea for how to deal with the situation in front of her, there were sirens and a bang at the door. Debora must have called 911 before she called Marie to tell her to get to me. The ambulance had arrived, and I was 302ed for the first time. They explained what was about to happen to Marie as I drifted away. I was gone.

I remember sitting in an office, or conference room. I was about three years old. There was a woman sitting across from me on the other side of a large conference table, smiling at me with a glow. She looked just like me but bigger, older. She felt familiar. Even more familiar, was a song playing softly in the background.

"*I see your true colors, shining through, I see your true colors, and that's why I love you, so don't be afraid, to let them show. True colors, true colors.*"

I remembered hearing that song all the time when I was growing up and I hummed along while I was in that conference room with the beautiful woman smiling at me. I told her, in my sweet little three-year-old voice, gasping with glee, "I know that song! I love that song!" I said it smiling ear to ear. I closed my eyes and started singing along, mumbling the words the way three year olds do.

Then the woman across from me gently interrupted, "Little Felicia, I see your true colors too, and they are beautiful." I stopped singing and listened to the woman. "I know you don't let them shine anymore, but I promise it's okay to let them shine now. Remember your mood tree? With all your colors? Well, I remember those colors and I promise, they will come back someday. I couldn't protect you before, but someday you'll be safe. I'm going to make sure you shine bright someday, and then we'll be free." The woman looked over at a seat in the corner of the room. In it, my sister, as an adult. The lady who looked just like me turned back to me and said, "She's going to make sure too." I giggled and closed my eyes, Cyndi Lauper singing in the background. *True colors, True colors.* The woman told me to open my eyes. "I know you want to stay here, little Felicia, but you can't. Your sister is waiting for you. Open up your eyes."

I slowly came to, opening up my eyes. I was strapped into a hospital bed, wearing just a gown and in a hospital room, tubes attached to me everywhere. Debora was seated in the corner, alone, positioned exactly as she was in that conference room when I was little. *Did I die? Where am I? Was I dreaming?* So many thoughts wandered through my mind. I became more present and scanned the room. There was a cup of a thick black substance by my bed. *Is that charcoal?* I wondered. A nurse came in and checked my vitals. I could tell Debora had been crying, but she walked over to me and started talking as if nothing had happened. Debora's coping mechanism, come hell or high water, was avoid, push forward, and just… keep… swimming.

We talked about where Kayla would be while I was in the hospital, and how she thought it was best for me to come live with her and David when I got released. We cracked a few jokes about how their weird roommate would be freaked out with a crazy single mom living with them. I agreed that staying with them might be best. Without us ever mentioning that I had just survived a suicide attempt, we gave each other a sad smile and a soldier's nod.

We were survivors and we would keep on surviving. She left to prepare for whenever it was the hospital thought it might be safe to let me leave. I laid there alone, trying not to go into The Dark.

I stayed in the psych ward at the hospital for a week. I was given sleep medicine and group therapy. I connected with a few people who understood what it was like to almost die at your own hands. I was told to follow up with an outpatient psych therapist and discharged. I took a cab home, my new home.

When I arrived at my sister's house, Kayla was sitting on the front steps with Debora. They were certainly a sight for sore eyes. I could feel life coming back to me. The sun was shining bright. It was April, and my birthday was in a week. I felt a sense of hope that with a stable place to stay, and with the support of the person who I clearly, and literally, could not live without, I would be okay. I was overzealous in my hopes, but it was what I needed to get myself to the front door.

"Monnieeeee!!!!" was what I heard as soon as I stepped out of the cab. It was the sweetest sound my ears would ever hear. Kayla ran right up to me and into my arms. It had only been two weeks since I had seen her, but I was so afraid she had forgotten me. I picked her up and hugged her so tight. I made a promise in my heart right there and then that I would never do it again, I would never leave her. I never wanted to let her go.

I sat on the steps in front of my sister's cute three-bedroom house on South Street, one of the liveliest and hippest parts of the city. Grad students, the young working class, and new families just started filling the area with energized hope and newness—positive vibes filled the air. Debora's small row home on her quiet block had a navy-blue door. That blue door looked like a door to a new life. I hesitated to walk in. I stalled as we sat on the steps. Eventually, David came out to greet me and to take Kayla inside so Debora and I could be alone. Kayla seemed so comfortable with him. They seemed to have really bonded already. This made me feel levels better.

"So, what you thinking?" Debora asked.

We were never great at sharing, but I tried. "I am feeling anxious." I used one of the new words I learned at the hospital.

Debora already knew the word. "Anxious about what?" she asked.

"I don't know... I mean, I'm happy to be here. Thank you for letting us stay too. I'm going to make sure I get back to work and help out. Once I save up enough, I will find my own place and—"

Debora cut me off. "Just take it one day at a time, Felicia. We are here to help. We just want you to be okay." I smiled and looked at the ground, trying to be quiet for more than a few seconds. Just when my brain began to go another million miles a minute and I started to ramble again, everything went dark. But this time, I wasn't gone.

"Oh my God, look…" Debora pointed to the sky. We both looked up and gazed at the sun disappearing behind the moon. It was a total solar eclipse. It was the first time I saw that beyond darkness, there is light.

In that moment, sitting next to the one person who had been with me through it all, I was in the dark and I wasn't alone. I wished then that my sister could have always come to The Dark with me, to take me out—to rescue me. Someday, I would learn, however, that there was no rescuing me. There was only this: My sister had been, and always would be by my side.

Chapter 46
The Cycle Is Broken

It's been 18 years since that day I sat with my sister and watched the eclipse. In those years, I had two more suicide attempts, countless depressive and manic episodes, and plenty more stays in mental institutions. As of the time that I am writing this, my last stay was the one described in the prologue of this book. I word it this way because the truth is, I can never rule out a relapse. I consider myself a healed person, but I know that mental illness is just that, an illness. I have had a very long battle with that illness, and it is in remission. I pray every day that it never comes back. But all I can do is take it day by day, do the work, and stay positive.

My 20-year healing journey started with the conception of my child and it continues as I work every single day to win. I am intentional about not letting The Monsters, my past, and The Dark, beat me. These intentions include meditating daily, staying in therapy, and using my support system, which includes but is not limited to my therapist, my mentor, my closest friends, Kayla, and Debora.

Debora and David went on to have two children, who have become more than my support. Those two, along with Kayla, have become my driving force to *stay* healthy. I don't only survive; I strive. I strive for all I can get out of life, setting an example for them. I want them to associate me with the good things life has to offer.

I started mommy-daughter day with Kayla every other weekend when she was four years old and have continued the tradition for 16 years. It has evolved to mommy-daughter road trips, but hey, same idea—quality time. Our little family is my world. I have devoted so much time to Kayla and Debora's kids, determined to show them genuine fun, laughter, and sharing as often as possible.

I learned through therapy to do the real work—facing the truth about myself, how I acted and reacted, the way I thought, and who I was, all so that I could address any unhealthy patterns that were producing toxic relationships. I faced the pain of *why* I am wired the way I am wired. Early childhood development sets the stage for the rest of our existence, but we still have choices. We must do the work of self-discovery, self-awareness, and tracing the roots of our values. Knowledge of self produces love of self. I know who I am and now, and I can accept all that I am. I can rest in that acceptance; I have found peace. It was a lot of hard work, but it was more than worth it.

The more I helped myself, the more support I got. The more support I got, the more I helped myself. And the cycle continues. Before long, I needed less and less support. The more I learned, the less I needed. A lot of what I learned about my mental illnesses was through therapy, but most of it was through education.

I passed that "Ability to Benefit" test with flying colors and eventually enrolled in community college. From there, I continued my education, earning a number of degrees and certifications, a fate I never imagined for myself before that welfare-to-work program. It took 12 years for me to complete my undergrad, earning a psych degree from Drexel University. This led to a master's program at NYU for mental health and wellness. I am that much closer to reaching the dreams that I wrote down in that goal-setting workshop and becoming the success Les Brown told me I could be.

One of the reasons it took 12 years for me to get through undergrad was because my nightmares never stopped. I developed severe insomnia and had debilitating panic attacks in the middle of the night. There were a few years where, as a single mom, I tried to work full time and go to school, all while living with a panic disorder. I was living in hell. There was no escaping it. For years, Debora answered hundreds of calls in the middle of the night, just sitting on the phone with me while I got through an attack, talking me through it, until I fell asleep on the phone with her. She could miss hours of sleep on any given night because she believed in me; she saw me doing the work, and she helped me. No matter how long it took. Because that's what you do. You help the people you love. When you see them doing the work, you help them.

Through cognitive behavioral therapy I learned to train my brain in order to regulate my emotions and manage my intrusive thoughts and flashbacks. I kept flashcards by my beside so when I had panic attacks in the middle of the night, I grabbed them and calmed myself, training my brain to have a different thought process during those moments of terror. Eventually, after years of training, the terror has gone away. Today I am symptom free, free from panic attacks with a calm, healthy, and positive mind.

Getting to this point took more than hard work and support. It took love too. Some of my darkest nights, Debora couldn't calm me over the phone, so I ended up calling the paramedics, and they would rush me to the ER, telling me I would be fine. Every single one of those nights someone that loved me showed up. Some nights it was Debora; other nights it was one of my best friends, one of the twins. But most nights it was Pastor Harris. He would immediately get out of bed and rush to my side, often times picking me up from the ER once I realized I wasn't dying and taking me and Kayla to church so I could sleep on the alter.

Pastor Harris, over the past 20 years, had become the father figure I longed for in Lorenzo. Once I stopped searching, I could see what was right in front of me. Those rides he gave me to church all those years eventually turned into rides back and forth to therapy appointments and visits to see me every time I was in the hospital. Our rides became rides home from scheduled minor surgeries, where he sometimes was the only one in the waiting area. The thing about trauma and its effects is that it can lead to a lot of inflammation, chronic pain, and autoimmune disorders. My pastor not only prayed that my pain would end; he supported me in finding treatments too.

And he always had my back. A ride from Pastor Harris was sometimes a ride to get me out of trouble, like when I had to get my car out of impound when it was towed because of unpaid parking tickets. He showed up. Court hearings, fights with Q, sick nights. You name it, he was there. Pastor Harris before long became my ride or die, literally. A lot of our rides provided a safe space for intimate conversations. I had come to really know him, and he me. I had come to know Leonard Harris the man. The

UNRAVEL

closer I got to him, the less I cared to be close to Pastor Harris the preacher and eventually left Spirit & Truth. Debora left about a decade before me. I had come to resent my church with all their judgment and talking behind my back. After I had Kayla, I was labeled a "smut," which they referenced as dirtier than a slut. The young people even teased and called me "Little Ms. Smuttigins." I overheard people saying Kayla was going to be a slut, just like her mother.

I often wondered why no one at that church besides my pastor helped me when I was younger, only judged me. Why couldn't they see that I was a baby, crying out for help? I thought for a long time that my church family loved me. But now that I know what love is, I realize it wasn't my church family that loved me; it was my pastor.

I didn't realize it back then, but Leonard Harris had become the first, and a lot of times, the only man I could trust, the only man I felt safe with. My pastor was the one who comforted me and told me everything was going to be okay. He was the one who gave me a shoulder to cry on, made sure I had a place to rest my head when no one else could, and gave me money when I had nothing to eat. He offered me some sort of stability throughout an unstable life. He did this by being patient and consistent. In him, I was blessed to know a man that was able to see my potential. He recognized the innocence and the beauty of the little girl inside me that I thought had died a long time ago. With genuine concern, and simply by being whom he was, my pastor was able to show that little girl that she is valuable and deserved to be treated as such. He helped me believe I am worthy of love.

Leonard T. Harris took his final rest in May 2018. He now lives in my heart. I will forever miss him and I will always cherish the gift of our time together. The gift of a father.

As for my biological father, he will always have my forgiveness. He still lives in Florida and has reached out to me numerous times over the years. During my darkest days, when my mental illness was at its worse, I kept trying to have a relationship with him too. I think that some part of me believed that if I loved my dad hard enough, and truly forgave me him for everything he did, I could be the one to save him. Then, he wouldn't be a monster anymore. Which would mean I didn't come from a monster. I wanted so desperately to make things right. I learned over the years, though, that constantly exposing myself to him was always going to be triggering and that in the end, my mental health was more important than a relationship with him. I pray he finds healing before his time on Earth ends.

On May 12, 2015, I reported my father's sexual abuse to the special victims unit in Philadelphia. I tried to get my mother to report that he raped her, but she couldn't bring herself to do it. I did it for me, I did it to protect other children, I did it for my sister, and I did it for everyone who has ever been violated. I did it for Amber.

A few years ago, Amber reached out to me on Facebook to tell me her truth. She said she didn't know if I remembered what my dad had done to us, but she had heard over the years that I had a relationship with him. That was gut-wrenching to me. I hated that her trauma was from my dad. I knew it wasn't my fault but I also knew her pain, and I wanted her to know she wasn't alone. Amber, you are not alone.

UNRAVEL

It took a long time for me to understand this, but our duty, my duty, every citizen's duty, is to report all known child abusers and rapists. And I do mean all. Not only for justice, but to protect children everywhere. It is just one more reason I have written this book. While some names have been changed to protect identities, all of my abuser's names are real (except the ones who were minors at the time).

I forgive Lorenzo and I also forgive Marie for everything that has happened. Like me, they were both wounded by the people who were supposed to love and care for them the most. I have mourned the loss of the parents I deserved, and I can only be grateful that unlike them, my wounds have healed. The psychological effects of trauma are relentless, easily passed down from generation to generation, without intention. The effects exist because the trauma goes unresolved. My parents' trauma lived and died through me. Never to be passed down again. It's why I never went back to Q and Kayla has a loving yet distant relationship with him. The cycle ended with me.

The scars that were beaten into my mother were also beaten into Debora and me, where they ended. Our scars faded, and our children were never beaten. They were never hungry and they never go a day without hearing that they are loved. Not one day.

What most fascinates me about my healing journey is the way in which my sister saved me. Throughout the years, during my worst depressions, she knew to show up if Kayla called her and said I was having a "bad day." Her just showing up, sitting in a chair, taking no notice of me yet being totally present, was the difference between me swallowing a bottle of pills or just sleeping on the couch for hours. The sounds of Kayla's voice talking to her, being in their own conversation, just hearing them, is why I wouldn't give into the urge of putting a belt around my neck. When Debora didn't know how to help, she just sat beside me, just being there, waiting until I figured it out. And because she was there, Kayla doesn't carry the burden of having to take care of her mother, another cycle broken. Debora saved us in the most subtle ways, by just being.

When you truly love others and they love you, you save them by simply being. Just by existing, you change the world, their world. I did all the work. But the love of my family saved me. When we are wounded, we don't love ourselves and we push those who love us furthest away. We reject their love and we scream to the universe, "No one loves me." We believe we are unlovable and want to prove it. We test, most times subconsciously, and tell the ones that do love us that they shouldn't; that they can't. And the ones that love us for real don't listen... They simply, often times quietly, just do.

This kind of love is reminiscent of that small, still voice that's at the very core of all of us. Sometimes we hear it, sometimes we don't, but it's always there. It's that still voice that we trust; that we know won't guide us the wrong way. Some call it God, others call it intuition, but we all have it... that small, still voice. That's love.

My sister's love carried me until I could love myself. Self-love is why I am here today. Self-love is why I wrote this book. And self-love is why I will keep moving forward.

I know my own strength is why I am still alive today. But I have no doubt that God sent Kayla to teach me love because she is love. And I also don't think I would have survived mental illness without getting help or without Debora. Human connection is how we get through life on Earth.

I have found the answers to my questions: Are we more than beings floating through time and space, subject to the mercy of a random universe? *Yes, we are.* They say you can't choose your family. So I often wonder, if I had the opportunity, would I? *No I wouldn't.* I would not have wanted to take this journey and experience this beautiful thing called life any other way—not without the ones I love—and certainly not without my sister.

Acknowledgments

To the absolute best daughter anyone can imagine, Kayla. The rewards of this final product are as much yours as they are mine. With every turn of this process, you have been there. The late nights, the tears, the many, many, many moods, triggers, and emotions I went through while writing—you stayed positive and just kept encouraging me. No one believes in me like you do, and I am forever grateful. You push me to move past my doubts and my fears. You inspire me in ways I cannot put into words. Thank you.

I am grateful for my sister, Debora, who I owe so much to. This story tells of all you helped me with in the past, but I also want to thank you for helping with this book. I know it wasn't easy revisiting so many stories and helping me work things out from memory. Thank you for answering the phone, every day.

To my mentor, Andrea, thank you for seeing me through this process. You have been instrumental, not only in writing this book but also in helping me find my voice. I never understood the power of a positive role model, a nurturing mother figure, and a genuine spirit until I met you.

I am extremely fortunate to have an amazing circle of friends who believe in me. Your support, motivation, and encouraging words have carried me through so many times that I wanted to throw in the towel. I am eternally grateful for each of you—especially my girlfriends—never underestimate the power of a good cry, a good laugh or a good drink shared amongst people who wish you well.

I want to give a special acknowledgement to two friends that took the time to thoroughly read early versions of this book and supported me through the rollercoaster of my thought process, ideas, and details. To Sasha and Don, thank you for the dedication that is your friendship.

To early readers who gave such important and thoughtful feedback—Daniel, Joshua, and Jenny—thank you.

Anne Dubuisson, without your expertise, my manuscript would still be collecting dust. You are truly blessed with a gift. Thank you.

Thank you to my copy editor, Zora Knauf. Your kind words and professionalism mean so much to writers like me. It is such an important and fragile time, and we need more people like you in the business.

Finally, I'd like to thank my creator—to whom I owe my existence, my insight, and the light to the path of this incredible journey. I now understand my purpose and why I even came to be. And I owe it all to the love of God.

www.ingramcontent.com/pod-product-compliance
Lightning Source LLC
Chambersburg PA
CBHW030300010526
44108CB00038B/828